— Barbour's —

BIBLE TRIVIA

Encyclopedia

Nearly 3,000 Questions Arranged
Topically from A to Z!

BARBOUR BOOKS

An Imprint of Barbour Publishing, Inc.

Welcome to
BARBOUR'S BIBLE TRIVIA ENCYCLOPEDIA

Bible trivia is a fun and interesting way to learn more about God's Word. With almost 3,000 entries, this encyclopedia format allows you to look trivia up alphabetically, and many of the 230 categories are cross-referenced to provide you with more information on similar subjects. Answers are provided at the end of each subject. Surprise yourself with what you already know. Enjoy learning more about Bible characters and Bible stories that you thought you knew. Use this encyclopedia as a teaching tool to add fun facts to Sunday school lessons and family devotions. Amaze your friends with the new facts you learn. Above all, grow in the knowledge of our God and give Him the glory!

A

ALTARS

(see also Offerings, Priests, Sacrifices, Tabernacle, Temple)

And he cried against the altar in the word of the LORD, and said, O altar, altar, thus saith the LORD; Behold, a child shall be born unto the house of David, Josiah by name; and upon thee shall he offer the priests of the high places that burn incense upon thee, and men's bones shall be burnt upon thee. And he gave a sign the same day, saying, This is the sign which the LORD hath spoken; Behold, the altar shall be rent, and the ashes that are upon it shall be poured out.
1 KINGS 13:2–3

1. How often did the high priest burn incense on the golden altar?

...

2. How many altars did the tabernacle have?

3. Joshua 22:34 mentions an altar named Ed. According to the verse, what does Ed mean?

...

4. What did Noah offer on the altar he built when he came out of the ark?

...

5. What is the altar made out of in Exodus 20:24?

...

6. What did Elijah use to make his altar on Mount Carmel?

...

7. True or False: An altar made of stone was to be made of hewn stone.

...

8. What part of the altar was to be grasped by someone seeking sanctuary?

9. What was under the altar in heaven?

• • •

10. True or False: In John's vision of heaven, there was a golden altar before the throne of God.

• • •

11. Where did Paul find an altar "to the Unknown God"?

• • •

12. Who built seven altars three separate times?

• • •

13. Which did the Pharisees say was a more binding oath?
   a) to swear by the altar in the temple
   b) to swear by the gift that was on the altar

• • •

14. Which altar in the tabernacle was made "hollow with boards"?

15. Who consecrated the altar of burnt offering in the tabernacle?

• • •

16. True or False: A king of Judah saw a foreign altar and made one just like it because he liked the design.

Altars Answers

1. every day (Exodus 30:7–9)

2. two: bronze altar (Exodus 27:1–2), altar of incense (Exodus 30:1)

3. witness

4. one of every clean animal and bird (Genesis 8:20)

5. earth

6. twelve stones (1 Kings 18:31–32)

7. false (Exodus 20:25)

8. the horns (1 Kings 2:28)

9. souls of the slain (Revelation 6:9)

10. true (Revelation 9:13)

11. Athens (Acts 17:22–23)

the angel of the Lord?
  a) strength
  b) might
  c) wisdom
  d) love of God

•••

3. How many times did the angel of the Lord speak to Abraham during the attempted sacrifice of Isaac?

•••

4. What animal saw the angel of the Lord?

•••

5. In Isaiah 63:9, Isaiah calls the angel of the Lord "the Angel of His _____."

•••

6. What did an angel of the Lord tell Paul when the ship he was on was in a bad storm?
  a) you will all die
  b) you will all be saved
  c) you will run aground
  d) you will not be shipwrecked

---

12. Balaam (Numbers 23:1, 14, 29)

13. b) to swear by the gift that was on the altar (Matthew 23:18)

14. altar of burnt offerings (Exodus 38:1, 7)

15. God (Exodus 29:44)

16. true (2 Kings 16:10–11)

ANGEL OF THE LORD

(see also Angels)

When an angel of the Lord released Peter from prison, the people praying for Peter's release refused to believe it and thought Peter himself was an angel (see Acts 12:7, 15–16)

1. Whom does the angel of the Lord encamp around?

•••

2. According to 2 Samuel 14:20, which of the following is an attribute of

7. To whom did the angel of the Lord appear and then ascend to heaven in the flame from the altar?

    a) Samson's father

    b) Solomon

    c) Moses

    d) Elijah

Angel of the Lord Answers

1. those who fear the Lord (Psalm 34:7)

2. c) wisdom

3. twice (Genesis 22:10–18)

4. Balaam's donkey (Numbers 22:23)

5. Presence (Isaiah 63:9 nkjv)

6. c) you will run aground (Acts 27:26)

7. a) Samson's father (Judges 13:19–29)

ANGELS

(see also Angel of the Lord)

According to Hebrews 1:14, one of the chief jobs an angel has is to minister to those who will inherit salvation.

1. Who was called the "cherub in the garden of Eden"?

• • •

2. How many types of angels are mentioned in the Bible?

• • •

3. What type of angel was on top of the ark of the covenant?

• • •

4. What angel was associated with Passover?

• • •

5. In Hebrews 13:2, why are we told to practice hospitality?

• • •

6. What angel is described in the book of Daniel as "one of the chief princes"?

7. Who can appear as an angel of light?

• • •

8. What prophet referred to the cherubim as "living creatures"?

• • •

9. How many wings do cherubim have?

• • •

10. How many wings do seraphim have?

• • •

11. In Revelation 5:11 and 7:11, where were the angels in heaven standing?

• • •

12. The angels have charge over the righteous to do what?
   a) keep you in all your ways
   b) bear you up in their hands
   c) take you to heaven
   d) a & b

13. In David's time, God sent an angel to Jerusalem to do what?
   a) anoint Solomon to be the next king
   b) destroy the city
   c) save David from the Philistines
   d) give David a special message

• • •

14. Why did an angel appear to Zechariah the prophet?
   a) to answer his question
   b) to interpret Zechariah's visions
   c) to show Zechariah visions
   d) all of the above

• • •

15. What did the angels do when God created the world?

• • •

16. How many angels appeared to the women who came to Jesus' tomb?

17. How many angels told the disciples that Jesus would return in the same manner as He left?

...

18. How many angels appeared to the shepherds to announce Jesus' birth?

...

19. To whom was Jesus speaking when He said that children have angels?

...

20. According to 1 Peter 1:12, what is the angels' attitude toward God's plan of salvation for mankind?

...

21. What do the angels in heaven do?

...

22. What does Psalm 78:25 refer to as angels' food?

...

23. What devout Gentile saw an angel?

24. Who will judge the angels?

...

25. Who spoke of an angel who had redeemed him from evil?

...

26. Which of the following did NOT see a host of angels?
   a) Jacob
   b) Peter
   c) shepherds at Bethlehem
   d) John

...

27. In Revelation 10:6, an angel declared that
   a) the kingdom of God had come
   b) Jesus is King of Kings
   c) there should be time no longer
   d) all of the above

...

28. How many angels went to save Lot from the destruction of his city?

Angels Answers

1. Lucifer (Ezekiel 28:13–14)

2. three: cherubim (Genesis 3:24), seraphim (Isaiah 6:2), archangel (Jude 9)

3. cherubim (Exodus 25:18)

4. the destroyer (Exodus 12:23)

5. we might be entertaining angels unawares

6. Michael (Daniel 10:13)

7. Satan (2 Corinthians 11:14)

8. Ezekiel 10:20

9. four (Ezekiel 1:6)

10. six (Isaiah 6:2)

11. around the throne

12. d) a & b (Psalm 91:11–12)

13. b) destroy the city (1 Chronicles 21:15)

14. d) all of the above (Zechariah 4:4–7, 12–14; 5:1–3)

15. shouted for joy (Job 38:7 NIV)

16. two (Luke 24:4)

17. two (Acts 1:10–11)

18. one, followed by a multitude (Luke 2:9, 13)

19. His disciples (Matthew 18:10)

20. they desire to look into it

21. worship the Lamb who was slain (Revelation 5:11–12)

22. manna

23. Cornelius (Acts 10:3)

24. Christians (1 Corinthians 6:3)

25. Israel/Jacob (Genesis 48:14, 16)

26. b) Peter (Genesis 28:10–12; Luke 2:8–14; Revelation 7:11)

27. c) there should be time no longer

28. two (Genesis 19:1)

ANIMALS CLEAN/
UNCLEAN

(see also Animals, Misc.)

1. How many of each clean animal did Noah take on the ark?

• • •

2. What was the purpose of clean vs. unclean animals?

• • •

3. Which of the following describes an animal that was clean?
   a) chews the cud, does not have cloven hooves
   b) does not chew the cud, has cloven hooves
   c) chews the cud, has cloven hooves
   d) does not chew the cud, does not have cloven hooves

4. Which of the following is an unclean animal?
   a) cattle
   b) sheep
   c) grasshoppers
   d) camels

• • •

5. Which is longer: the list of clean animals or the list of unclean animals?

• • •

6. Is the following a description of a clean or an unclean animal? "...every flying insect that creeps on all fours, which have jointed legs upon their feet."

• • •

7. Is the following a description of a clean or an unclean animal? "...whatever in the water that has fins and scales."

Animals Clean/
Unclean Answers

1. seven pairs (Genesis 7:2)

2. clean animals could be eaten
(Leviticus 11:2)

3. c) chews the cud, has cloven
hooves (Leviticus 11:3)

4. d) camel (Leviticus 11:4)

5. unclean (Leviticus 11:1–47)

6. clean (Leviticus 11:21)

7. clean (Leviticus 11:9)

ANIMALS, MISC.

(see also Animals Clean/
Unclean, Donkeys, Lions)

*Unicorns are mentioned
in the Bible in Psalm 92:10.*

1. What kind of animals
helped Samson burn the
grain fields of his enemies?
   a) lightning bugs
   b) lions
   c) donkeys
   d) foxes

2. What kind of bird, released
from the ark, brought an olive
leaf back to Noah?

• • •

3. What do these three
things have in common?
   - Arcturus (the Bear)
   - Orion
   - Pleiades

• • •

4. What animal were the
Israelites not to muzzle as it
was treading grain (NIV) or
corn (KJV)?

• • •

5. What did Peter see inside
a sheet, coming down from
heaven by its four corners?
   a) animals, reptiles, and
      birds
   b) gold and silver
   c) people of many
      countries
   d) Christmas presents

• • •

6. After Adam and Eve
sinned, God provided
clothing for them made of

_____ _____.

7. What animal did God provide as a substitute burnt offering as Abraham prepared to offer Isaac?

• • •

8. What animal spoke to Balaam when it saw the angel of the Lord?

• • •

9. The psalmist said he longed for God even as a _____ panted for water brooks.

• • •

10. What animal did Jesus ride for His triumphal entry into Jerusalem?
   a) donkey
   b) warhorse
   c) camel

• • •

11. What is the strongest of beasts, according to Proverbs?

• • •

12. Whom was Paul referring to when he warned the Philippians to "beware of dogs"?

13. Peter likened Christ's atonement to a " _____ without _____ and without spot."

• • •

14. What animal did Goliath compare himself to when he saw David approaching him?

• • •

15. What creature of the wilderness does Malachi describe as laying waste to Esau's heritage?

• • •

16. What colors are the four horses mentioned in Revelation 6?

• • •

17. What type of animals did Jesus ask His disciples to ask a man for?

18. When some young people mocked Elisha by calling him "bald head," what animals did God send to punish them?
    a) lions
    b) bears
    c) wolves
    d) a & c

• • •

19. Jesus said it was easier for a _____ to go through the eye of a needle than for a rich man to enter heaven.

Animals, Misc. Answers

1. d) foxes (Judges 15:3–5)
2. dove (Genesis 8:11)
3. constellations (Job 9:9)
4. ox (Deuteronomy 25:4)
5. a) animals, reptiles, and birds (Acts 10:9–12)
6. animal skins (Genesis 3:21)
7. ram (Genesis 22:13)
8. ass/donkey (Numbers 22:27–28)
9. hart/deer (Psalm 42:1)
10. a) donkey (John 12:14–15)
11. lion (Proverbs 30:30)
12. evil workers who insisted on circumcision for Gentiles (Philippians 3:2)
13. lamb, blemish (1 Peter 1:19)
14. dog (1 Samuel 17:43)
15. dragons (Malachi 1:3)
16. white, red, black, pale
17. a donkey and a colt (Matthew 21:2)
18. b) bears (2 Kings 2:23–24)
19. camel (Matthew 19:24)

ANOINTING

(see also Kings, Priests)

Exodus 30:22–25 describes the spices used in anointing oil.

1. Which of the following were NOT anointed?
    a) prophets
    b) priests
    c) cleansed lepers
    d) brides and bridegrooms

. . .

2. Whom did Elijah anoint?

. . .

3. How many times was David anointed to be king?

. . .

4. Who anointed a pillar and made a vow to God at Bethel?

5. Who anointed Aaron and his sons to be priests?

6. Where, specifically, on his body was Aaron to be anointed?

. . .

7. What type of food in the tabernacle was anointed with oil?

. . .

8. When was the altar for burnt offerings to be anointed?

. . .

9. Which of the following items in the tabernacle were anointed?
    a) ark of the covenant
    b) table of showbread
    c) lampstand
    d) incense altar
    e) all of the above

Anointing Answers

1. d) brides and bridegrooms (1 Kings 19:16; Leviticus 8:30; 14:15–18)

2. Elisha (1 Kings 19:16)

3. three (1 Samuel 16:3; 2 Samuel 2:4; 5:3)

4. Jacob (Genesis 31:13)

5. Moses (Exodus 28:41)

6. his head (Exodus 29:7)

7. wafers (Exodus 29:2)

8. after atonement had been made for it (Exodus 29:36)

9. e) all of the above (Exodus 30:26–27)

APOSTLES

(see also Disciples of Jesus)

Apostle means "sent one."

1. Which of the following was not an apostle?
   a) Paul
   b) Peter
   c) Matthias
   d) John Mark

• • •

2. Which book of the Bible is specifically named for the apostles?

• • •

3. How were the apostles distinguished from other people?

• • •

4. In the future, what is to be the relationship of the apostles to the twelve tribes of Israel?

• • •

5. Who was the first apostle sent to a Gentile?

6. On the day of Pentecost, which apostle preached the sermon?

• • •

7. The apostle who spoke to the Ethiopian eunuch was
    a) Philip
    b) Peter
    c) Stephen
    d) Paul

• • •

8. Peter was sent to preach to Cornelius, who was a
    a) Gentile
    b) devout man
    c) centurion
    d) all of the above

• • •

9. True or False: The twelve apostles in Acts are the same twelve disciples whom Jesus picked.

• • •

10. What did Jesus say would be done to the apostles that had been done to the prophets?

11. What did the new members of the church continue in?
    a) the apostles' doctrine
    b) the apostles' fellowship
    c) the apostles' practices
    d) a & b

• • •

12. What did the early Christians lay at the apostles' feet?

• • •

13. True or False: When the church at Jerusalem was scattered because of persecution, the apostles were scattered also.

• • •

14. Who brought Paul to the apostles?

• • •

15. True or False: Barnabas was an apostle.

• • •

16. How did Paul become an apostle?

17. Paul said he was the chief of sinners (1 Timothy 1:15) and the _____ of the apostles.

• • •

18. True or False: Jesus is an apostle.

• • •

19. True or False: Peter and Paul had a confrontation.

Apostles Answers

1. d) John Mark (Romans 1:1; Matthew 10:2; Acts 1:26)

2. the Acts of the Apostles

3. they were endued with miraculous powers (Matthew 10:1)

4. the apostles will judge the tribes (Matthew 19:28)

5. Peter (Acts 10:19–22)

6. Peter (Acts 2:1, 14)

7. a) Philip (Acts 8:26–35)

8. d) all of the above (Acts 10:1–2)

9. false; only eleven—Judas wasn't an apostle (Acts 1:25)

10. some would be killed and persecuted (Luke 11:49)

11. d) a & b (Acts 2:42)

12. all the material things they wanted to share (Acts 4:34–35)

13. false (Acts 8:1)

14. Barnabas (Acts 9:27)

15. true (Acts 14:14)

16. he was called (1 Corinthians 1:1)

17. least (1 Corinthians 15:9)

18. true (Hebrews 3:1)

19. true (Galatians 2:11–14)

ARK OF THE COVENANT

(see also Tabernacle, Temple)

At Beth Shemesh, 50,070 men died because they looked into the ark of the covenant (1 Samuel 6:19).

1. What covered the poles used to carry the ark of the covenant?

• • •

2. Where were the rings for the poles attached to the ark?
   a) at its four top corners
   b) on its four feet

• • •

3. True or False: The ark of the covenant was made after the death of Moses.

• • •

4. Fill in the blank: "At that time the Lord set apart the tribe of _____ to carry the ark of the covenant of the Lord."

5. What was Eli's reaction when he learned his two sons had been killed and the ark captured by the enemy?

• • •

6. While the ark was being moved, what caused Uzzah to touch it in an attempt to right it, resulting in his death?
   a) a strong east wind blew and upset it
   b) the oxen pulling the cart carrying it stumbled
   c) the men holding it by poles through the rings stumbled
   d) Uzzah replaced the lid, which had slipped off

• • •

7. Fill in the blank: King David said, "Here I am, living in a _____ of cedar, while the ark of God remains in a tent."

• • •

8. Who built a temple for the ark?
   a) Absalom
   b) David
   c) Herod the Great
   d) Solomon

9. When in the tabernacle (tent), the ark was in an area called what?

•••

10. According to the book of Hebrews, the ark contained a gold jar of manna, the stone tablets of the covenant, and what third item?
   a) the bronze snake Moses had put on a pole that the people looked at and lived
   b) a tribute of gold given by the enemies of Israel when they returned the ark
   c) Aaron's staff that had budded
   d) the books of the law of Moses

•••

11. Where will the ark of the covenant ultimately be found?

•••

12. Who was the last person on earth to see the ark of the covenant?

13. On what mountain was the ark of the covenant built?

•••

14. Who was responsible for taking the ark of the covenant into battle and losing it to the Philistines?
   a) Eli's sons
   b) Samuel's sons
   c) the elders of Israel
   d) King Saul

•••

15. What did the Philistines return with the ark of the covenant when they returned it to Israel?

Ark of the Covenant Answers

1. gold (Exodus 25:13)

2. b) on its four feet (Exodus 25:12 NIV)

3. false; he inspected the work after it was built (Exodus 39:43)

4. Levi (Deuteronomy 10:8)

ARMIES AND SOLDIERS

(see also Enemies of Israel, Spiritual Warfare)

Gideon's original army had 32,000 men, but God told Gideon that was too many because then they could claim that they won the battle instead of giving God the glory (Judges 7:2).

1. What prophet sat on a hill while God sent fire to burn up the army sent to capture him?

• • •

2. In reference to question 1, how many armies did God send fire on?

• • •

3. Fill in the blank: The army that fought with pitchers and lamps shouted, "The sword of the Lord and of _____."

• • •

4. Who had to build a wall with one hand while holding his sword in the other?

5. he fell backward off his chair, broke his neck, and died (1 Samuel 4:18)

6. b) the oxen pulling the cart carrying it stumbled (2 Samuel 6:6)

7. house (2 Samuel 7:2)

8. d) Solomon (1 Kings 8:12, 17–21)

9. Most Holy Place (Hebrews 9:2–4)

10. c) Aaron's staff that had budded (Hebrews 9:4)

11. in heaven (Revelation 11:19)

12. the apostle John (Revelation 11:19)

13. Sinai (Exodus 25:16–22)

14. c) the elders of Israel (1 Samuel 4:3)

15. five gold mice, five gold emerods (1 Samuel 6:4, 11)

5. What military rank did Cornelius, a Gentile convert to Christianity, hold?

• • •

6. What was the first thing God told Gideon to do to reduce the size of his army?

• • •

7. What was the second thing God told Gideon to do to further reduce the size of his army?

• • •

8. How many men ended up in Gideon's army?

• • •

9. What did Paul tell Timothy to fight?

• • •

10. Whom did Joshua see the night before the battle of Jericho?

• • •

11. How many swords did the disciples take with them when they followed Jesus to the Garden of Gethsemane?

12. What rank did Naaman hold in the army of Syria?

• • •

13. According to Revelation 19:14, what are the armies in heaven clothed in?

Armies and Soldiers Answers

1. Elijah (2 Kings 1:9–10)

2. two (2 Kings 1:11-12)

3. Gideon (Judges 7:18)

4. Nehemiah (Nehemiah 4:17–18)

5. centurion (Acts 10:1)

6. tell the ones who were fearful that they could go (Judges 7:3)

7. make them drink water and only keep the ones who knelt down (Judges 7:5)

8. three hundred (Judges 7:6–7)

9. the good fight of faith (1 Timothy 6:12)

10. the commander of the Lord's army (Joshua 5:14)

11. two (Luke 22:38)

12. commander (2 Kings 5:1)

13. fine linen, white and clean (Revelation 19:14)

ARMOR OF GOD

(see also Spiritual Warfare)

All of the armor God gives us covers our front. God has our back.

Match the piece of armor with what it represents:

1. breastplate
2. helmet
3. feet shod
4. girdle
5. sword of the Spirit
6. shield

• • •

a. Word of God
b. salvation
c. righteousness
d. gospel of peace
e. faith
f. truth

Armor of God
Answers

All answers found in Ephesians 6:11–17.

1. c

2. b

3. d

4. f

5. a

6. e

B

BEATITUDES

(see also Sermon on the Mount)

1. From what location did Jesus teach about the Beatitudes?

...

2. Fill in the blanks: Blessed are the _____ ___ _____: for theirs is the kingdom of heaven.

...

3. Fill in the blanks: Blessed are they that _____: for they shall be _____.

...

4. Fill in the blank: Blessed are the _____: for they shall inherit the earth.

...

5. Fill in the blanks: Blessed are they which do _____ and _____ after righteousness: for they shall be _____.

6. Fill in the blanks: Blessed are the _____: for they shall obtain _____.

...

7. Fill in the blanks: Blessed are the _____ ___ _____: for they shall see God.

...

8. Fill in the blank: Blessed are the _____: for they shall be called the children of God.

...

9. Fill in the blank: Blessed are they which are persecuted for _____ sake: for theirs is the kingdom of heaven.

...

10. Fill in the blanks: Blessed are ye, when men shall _____ you, and persecute you, and shall say all manner of evil against you _____, for my sake.

11. Fill in the blanks: Rejoice, and be exceeding glad: for _____ is your _____ in heaven.

Beatitudes Answers

1. a mountain (Matthew 5:1)

2. poor in spirit (Matthew 5:3)

3. mourn, comforted (Matthew 5:4)

4. meek (Matthew 5:5)

5. hunger, thirst, filled (Matthew 5:6)

6. merciful, mercy (Matthew 5:7)

7. pure in heart (Matthew 5:8)

8. peacemakers (Matthew 5:9)

9. righteousness' (Matthew 5:10)

10. revile, falsely (Matthew 5:11)

11. great, reward (Matthew 5:12)

BIBLE

The following books are mentioned in the Bible but are not actual books of the Bible: the book of Nathan the Prophet (2 Chronicles 9:29), the book of Gad the Seer (1 Chronicles 29:29), the book of Jashar (Joshua 10:13), the book of the Acts of Solomon (1 Kings 11:41).

1. What two books of the Bible do not mention God by name?

. . .

2. What letter of the alphabet has the most books that start with it?

. . .

3. What two books have the census of all who returned from Babylon?

. . .

4. What book of the Bible contains the Golden Rule?

. . .

5. What two books of the Bible contain the Lord's Prayer?

6. What book of the Bible mentions the stars singing?

• • •

7. What did John say was the purpose of the Gospel he wrote?

• • •

8. What book of the Bible is named for a tribe of Israel?

• • •

9. How many chapters does the book of Daniel have?

• • •

10. What book of the Bible has more references to angels than any other book of the Bible?

• • •

11. In which two books of the Bible do we read of Michael having a face-to-face confrontation with Satan?

• • •

12. Which book of the Bible contains the story of David and Goliath?

13. How many books of the Bible have only one chapter?

• • •

14. What book of the New Testament is totally dedicated to describing God's love for us?

• • •

15. What is the longest book in the Bible?

• • •

16. What is the longest chapter in the Bible?

• • •

17. What subject does the longest chapter in the Bible deal with?

• • •

18. How many books are in the Old Testament?

• • •

19. How many books are in the New Testament?

• • •

20. What is the last book of the Old Testament?

21. The first five books of the Bible are commonly referred to as the books of
   a) law
   b) history
   c) poetry
   d) history

...

22. What is the shortest psalm?

...

23. Fill in the blank:
The book of Revelation is the revelation of
_____.

...

24. The book of life belongs to whom?

BIBLE Answers

1. Esther, Song of Solomon
2. J (12: Joshua, Judges, Job, Jeremiah, Joel, Jonah, John, James, 1 John, 2 John, 3 John, Jude)
3. Ezra (chapter 2); Nehemiah (chapter 7)
4. Matthew (7:12)
5. Matthew (chapter 6); Luke (chapter 11)
6. Job (chapter 38)
7. "But these are written, that ye might believe that Jesus is the Christ, the Son of God; and that believing ye might have life through his name" (John 20:31)
8. Leviticus
9. 12
10. Revelation (22 references to angels)
11. Jude 9; Revelation 12:7
12. 1 Samuel (chapter 17)
13. five (Obadiah, Philemon, 2 John, 3 John, Jude)
14. 1 John
15. Psalms
16. Psalm 119
17. God's law
18. 39
19. 27
20. Malachi
21. a) law
22. Psalm 117
23. Jesus Christ (Revelation 1:1)
24. the Lamb that was slain (Revelation 13:8)

BIBLE CURIOSITIES

When the seven sons of Sceva tried to exorcise some evil spirits, one of the evil spirits said, "Jesus I know, and Paul I know; but who are you?" (see Acts 19:14–15 NKJV).

1. What portion of Adam's anatomy did God remove to create a companion for the man?

• • •

2. Where did Peter find a coin to pay the temple tax?

• • •

3. What personal item did Ruth's kinsman present to Boaz as an indication he would not redeem Ruth?

• • •

4. Who led a dance of joy wearing only a linen cloth when the ark of the covenant arrived in Jerusalem?

• • •

5. When Jesus healed the Gadarene demoniac, where did the demons go?

6. What king of Israel solved a child custody dispute by proposing that the child be cut in half?

• • •

7. What prophet was taken alive to heaven in a whirlwind?

• • •

8. What did Elisha instruct Captain Naaman to do to rid himself of leprosy?

• • •

9. What young prince was hidden in the temple by his aunt for six years to avoid the wrath of Queen Athaliah?

• • •

10. Who went to sleep while Paul was preaching and fell from a window to his death, but was revived by the apostle?

• • •

11. What did Jesus say He would arrive in when He returns to earth "with power and great glory"?

12. True or False: The Bible says that God hung the earth on nothing.

Bible Curiosities Answers

1. rib (Genesis 2:22)

2. in a fish's mouth (Matthew 17:27)

3. shoe (Ruth 4:6–7)

4. King David (2 Samuel 6:14–15)

5. into a herd of swine (Luke 8:33)

6. Solomon (1 Kings 3:3, 25–27)

7. Elijah (2 Kings 2:11)

8. wash seven times in the Jordan River (2 Kings 5:10)

9. Joash (2 Kings 11:2–3)

10. Eutychus (Acts 20:9–12)

11. a cloud (Luke 21:27)

12. true (Job 26:7 NKJV)

BIBLE DESCRIPTIONS

After reading the following statements, answer a simple question: Who?

1. A choice young man, and a goodly: and there was not among the children of Israel a goodlier person than he: from his shoulders and upward he was higher than any of the people.

• • •

2. He will be a wild man; his hand will be against every man, and every man's hand against him; and he shall dwell in the presence of all his brethren.

• • •

3. This he said, not that he cared for the poor; but because he was a thief, and had the bag, and bare what was put therein.

4. Now he was ruddy, and withal of a beautiful countenance, and goodly to look to.

•••

5. Fill in the blank: Among them that are born of women there hath not risen a greater than _____: notwithstanding he that is least in the kingdom of heaven is greater than he.

•••

6. And, behold, there was a man...which was the chief among the publicans, and he was rich. And he sought to see Jesus who he was; and could not for the press, because he was little of stature.

•••

7. [He] did evil in the sight of the LORD above all that were before him....[He] did more to provoke the LORD God of Israel to anger than all the kings of Israel that were before him.

8. Full of faith and power, [he] did great wonders and miracles among the people .... And all that sat in the council, looking stedfastly on him, saw his face as it had been the face of an angel.

•••

9. To bring...the queen before the king with the crown royal, to shew the people and the princes her beauty: for she was fair to look on.

•••

10. And when Jehu was come to Jezreel...she painted her face, and tired her head, and looked out at a window.

•••

11. [He] wist not that the skin of his face shone while he talked with him.

12. Howbeit the hair of his head began to grow again after he was shaven.

•••

13. And at the end of ten days their countenances appeared fairer and fatter in flesh than all the children which did eat the portion of the king's meat.

•••

14. The same hour was the thing fulfilled. . .and he was driven from men, and did eat grass as oxen, and his body was wet with the dew of heaven, till his hairs were grown like eagles' feathers, and his nails like birds' claws.

•••

15. He hardened his heart, and hearkened not unto them; as the Lord had said.

•••

16. She dwelt under the palm tree. . .between Ramah and Bethel in mount Ephraim: and the children of Israel came up to her for judgment.

17. Because the preacher was wise, he still taught the people knowledge; yea, he gave good heed, and sought out, and set in order many proverbs.

•••

18. Fill in the blank: Let us hear the conclusion of the whole matter: Fear God, and keep his commandments: for this is the whole duty of _____.

•••

19. Her husband, being a just man, and not willing to make her a public example, was minded to put her away privily.

20. Woe is me! for I am undone; because I am a man of unclean lips, and I dwell in the midst of a people of unclean lips: for mine eyes have seen the King, the LORD of hosts.

• • •

21. Fill in the blank: But in all Israel there was none to be so much praised as _____ for his beauty: from the sole of his foot even to the crown of his head there was no blemish in him. And when he polled his head, (for it was at every year's end that he polled it: because the hair was heavy on him, therefore he polled it:) he weighed the hair of his head at two hundred shekels after the king's weight.

• • •

22. Fill in the blank: But _____ found grace in the eyes of the LORD.

Bible Descriptions Answers

1. King Saul (1 Samuel 9:2)

2. Ishmael (Genesis 16:11–12)

3. Judas Iscariot (John 12:4–6)

4. David (1 Samuel 16:12–13)

5. John the Baptist (Matthew 11:11)

6. Zacchaeus (Luke 19:2–3)

7. Ahab (1 Kings 16:30, 33)

8. Stephen (Acts 6:8, 15)

9. Vashti (Esther 1:11)

10. Jezebel (2 Kings 9:30)

11. Moses (Exodus 34:29)

12. Samson (Judges 16:22)

13. Daniel, Hananiah, Mishael, Azaria (Daniel 1:11–15)

14. Nebuchadnezzar (Daniel 4:33)

15. Pharaoh (Exodus 8:15)

16. Deborah (Judges 4:4–5)

17. Solomon
(Ecclesiastes 1:1; 12:9)

18. man (Ecclesiastes 12:13)

19. Joseph (Matthew 1:19)

20. Isaiah (Isaiah 6:5)

21. Absalom
(2 Samuel 14:25–26)

22. Noah (Genesis 6:8)

BIBLICAL MYSTERIES

A mystery in the Bible refers to a previously hidden truth now divinely revealed.

1. True or False: Many of Jesus' parables dealt with the subject of the kingdom of heaven.

• • •

2. True or False: The prophets in the Old Testament knew that the meaning of their prophecies would not always be revealed to them.

3. Why does Paul say that Israel was blinded to the truth of the kingdom of God?

• • •

4. Who said, "Behold, I tell you a mystery"?

• • •

5. Fill in the blank: We shall not all sleep, but we shall all be _____.

• • •

6. Fill in the blanks: In a _____, in the _____ of an eye, at the last trumpet.

• • •

7. True or False: The church is a mystery.

• • •

8. Fill in the blank: Husbands are to love their wives like Christ loved the _____.

9. The last mystery
mentioned in the Bible
concerns
   a) Jesus
   b) the apostle John
   c) the antichrist
   d) Babylon

Biblical Mysteries
Answers

1. true
2. true (1 Peter 1:12)
3. so that the Gentiles could
   be brought in
   (Romans 11:25)
4. Paul (1 Corinthians 15:51)
5. changed
   (1 Corinthians 15:51)
6. moment, twinkling
   (1 Corinthians 15:52)
7. true (Ephesians 3:4–10)
8. church (Ephesians 5:25)
9. d) Babylon
   (Revelation 17:5, 7)

BIBLICAL NUMBERS

1. According to Psalm 90:10,
how many are the days of
our years?

•••

2. How many spies sent into
the Promised Land gave an
unfavorable report?

•••

3. How many were in Jacob's
family (including Joseph's
family) when Jacob moved
to Egypt?

•••

4. The boy's lunch that
Jesus used to feed the five
thousand consisted of what?

•••

5. If someone was too
poor to afford a lamb for a
sacrifice for the birth of their
child, how many turtledoves
could be substituted?

•••

6. How many mites did the
widow give?

7. How many precious stones decorated the front of the high priest's breastplate?

• • •

8. How many men composed Gideon's initial army?

• • •

9. How many people did Jesus meet on the road to Emmaus after His resurrection?

• • •

10. How many Israelites left Egypt?

• • •

11. How many Assyrians did the angel of the Lord slay when Assyria besieged Jerusalem?

• • •

12. How many days did Noah wait after sending out the raven and the dove before he sent out the dove again?

• • •

13. What famous king had seven hundred wives?

14. How many cubits did Jesus say we can add to our stature?

• • •

15. Approximately how many souls were added to the church on the day of Pentecost?

• • •

16. How many days did Daniel and his friends eat "pulse and water"?

• • •

17. How old was Jesus when Mary and Joseph found Him in the temple?

• • •

18. How many people did God tell Elijah there were who had never bowed the knee to Baal?

• • •

19. How many men did Jesus send out to arrive in cities before He did?

• • •

20. How long did the Philistines keep the ark of the covenant?

21. How long was the ark of the covenant kept in Kirjath-jearim?

. . .

22. How many days and nights was Jonah in the belly of the great fish?

. . .

23. How many fish were caught in the net when Jesus told His disciples to cast the net on the right side of the boat?

. . .

24. How many days did the spies Moses sent search in the Promised Land?

Biblical Numbers Answers

1. threescore and ten (70)
2. ten (Numbers 13)
3. seventy (Exodus 1:5)
4. five loaves, two fish (Matthew 14:17)
5. two (Leviticus 12:8)
6. two (Mark 12:42)
7. twelve (Exodus 28:21)
8. 32,000 (Judges 7:3)
9. two (Luke 24:13)
10. the Bible doesn't say (Exodus 13:17)
11. 185,000 (2 Kings 19:35)
12. seven (Genesis 8:10)
13. Solomon (1 Kings 11:3)
14. not a single one (Matthew 6:27)
15. three thousand (Acts 2:41)
16. ten (Daniel 1:12)
17. twelve (Luke 2:42–43)
18. seven thousand (1 Kings 19:18)
19. seventy (Luke 10:1)
20. seven months (1 Samuel 6:1)
21. twenty years (1 Samuel 7:2)
22. three days and three nights (Jonah 1:17)
23. 153 (John 21:6, 11)
24. forty (Numbers 13:25)

BIBLICAL RÉSUMÉS

(see also Occupations)

1. Songwriter, shepherd, harpist

...

2. Spokesperson to Pharaoh, idol maker, priest

...

3. Tender of the garden, namer of animals, father of all mankind

...

4. Slave, messenger, beloved brother

...

5. Ruler, Pharisee, defender of Jesus

...

6. The Lord chose them to stand in His presence, to serve Him, to be His ministers.

7. Everyone in distress, everyone in debt, everyone discontent, about four hundred in number

...

8. Filled with the Spirit of God and wisdom in understanding skilled in all manner of workmanship, designed artistic works

...

9. Works with her hands, provides food for her household, plants a vineyard, helps the poor and needy, makes tapestry

...

10. Priest, father of bad sons, raised Samuel

...

11. Whatever he did, the Lord made it prosper.

...

12. Though I might also have confidence in the flesh. If any other man thinketh that he hath whereof he might trust in the flesh, I more:

circumcised the eighth day, of the stock of Israel, of the tribe of Benjamin, an Hebrew of the Hebrews; as touching the law, a Pharisee; concerning zeal, persecuting the church; touching the righteousness which is in the law, blameless.

Biblical Résumés Answers

1. David (2 Samuel 22:1; 1 Samuel 17:14–15; 1 Samuel 16:23)

2. Aaron (Exodus 5:1; 32:3–4; 29:5)

3. Adam (Genesis 2:15, 20)

4. Onesimus (Philemon 12, 16 NKJV)

5. Nicodemus (John 3:1, 50–51)

6. Levites (2 Chronicles 29:4, 11)

7. David's mighty men (1 Samuel 22:1–2)

8. Bezalel (Exodus 31:2–4 NKJV)

9. the virtuous woman (Proverbs 31:13–22)

10. Eli (1 Samuel 2:11, 12, 18

11. Joseph (Genesis 39:23 NKJV)

12. Paul (Philippians 3:4–6)

BIRDS

(see also Animals Clean/ Unclean, Animals, Misc., Doves)

1. What two types of birds did Noah send out from the ark to see if the waters were receding?

• • •

2. What type of bird brought food to Elijah?

• • •

3. Fill in the blank: They that wait upon the LORD shall renew their strength; they shall mount up with wings like _____.

4. Fill in the blank: In Song of Solomon 2:11–12, the winter is past and the voice of the _____ is heard.

• • •

5. What type of bird did Jesus say that not one falls to the ground without God knowing about it?

• • •

6. True or False: Pelicans are mentioned in the Bible.

• • •

7. Which of the following birds were considered unclean?
a) eagle
b) raven
c) swan
d) all of these

Birds Answers

1. raven, dove (Genesis 8:6–8)

2. ravens (1 Kings 17:4)

3. eagles (Isaiah 40:31)

4. turtledove (Song of Solomon 2:11–12)

5. sparrows (Matthew 10:29)

6. true (Psalm 102:6)

7. d) all of these (Leviticus 11:13–18)

BLESSINGS

(see also Curses)

In Numbers 6:22–27, God told Moses to have the priests pronounce this blessing upon the people: "The LORD bless thee, and keep thee: The LORD make his face shine upon thee, and be gracious unto thee: The LORD lift up his countenance upon thee, and give thee peace."

1. Fill in the blanks: Deuteronomy 28 is a list of blessings that God pronounced upon Israel. One of those blessings says they will be blessed when they ____ ___ and when they ___ ___.

• • •

2. The first blessing in the Bible was pronounced upon what?

3. "Blessed be those who bless you" was part of the blessing that
   a) Laban gave Rebekah
   b) Jacob gave Rachel
   c) Isaac gave Jacob
   d) Jacob gave Leah

• • •

4. The king of Moab was angry at Balaam because Balaam did what?

• • •

5. What was Balaam's excuse for what he did?

• • •

6. Fill in the blanks: When Satan spoke to God about Job, he said that God had blessed the _____ of Job's _____.

• • •

7. According to Psalm 33:12, what nation is blessed?

• • •

8. Whose children rise up and call her blessed?

9. The blessing of the Lord, it maketh
   a) rich
   b) wise
   c) courage
   d) love

• • •

10. What does the Lord say we must do and then He will pour out such blessing upon us that we won't have room to receive it?

• • •

11. When did Jesus tell Peter, "Blessed are you, Simon Bar-Jonah"?

• • •

12. Fill in the blanks: Jesus said, "If ye know these things, blessed are ye if ye _____ _____."

• • •

13. Fill in the blanks: It is more blessed to _____ than to _____.

14. Fill in the blank: James said, "Out of the same _____ proceed blessing and cursing."

• • •

15. To whom did God make the promise that all nations of the earth would be blessed through his descendants?
    a) Abraham
    b) Isaac
    c) Jacob
    d) all of the above

Blessings Answers

1. come in; go out (Deuteronomy 28:6)

2. sea creatures and birds (Genesis 1:21–22)

3. c) Isaac gave Jacob (Genesis 27:29–30)

4. blessed the Israelites instead of cursing them (Numbers 24:10)

5. "What the LORD says, that I must speak." (Numbers 24:13 NKJV)

6. work, hands (Job 1:10)

7. the one whose God is the Lord

8. the virtuous woman (Proverbs 31:10, 28)

9. a) rich (Proverbs 10:22)

10. bring all our tithes into His storehouse (Malachi 3:10)

11. after Peter said, "You are the Christ." (Matthew 16:16–17)

12. do them (John 13:17)

13. give, receive (Acts 20:35)

14. mouth (James 3:10)

15. d) all of the above (Genesis 12:3; 26:4; 28:14)

BLINDNESS, PHYSICAL

(see also Blindness, Spiritual)

1. True or False: In John 9, the man had been blind from birth.

• • •

2. The man was
   a) a musician
   b) a priest
   c) a beggar
   d) a merchant

• • •

3. True or False: A group of Pharisees asked who had sinned for the man to suffer blindness.

• • •

4. Who did Jesus say sinned to cause the man to be born blind?
   a) the man himself
   b) his parents
   c) neither
   d) both

5. True or False: The man was born blind so the works of God could be revealed through him.

• • •

6. Fill in the blank: Jesus said, "As long as I am in the world, I am the _____ of the world.

• • •

7. Jesus cured the man with:
   a) water from the River Jordan
   b) only a touch
   c) water from the pool of Siloam
   d) spit, clay, and water from the pool of Siloam

• • •

8. True or False: This is the only case in which the Bible says Jesus cured a blind man in this manner.

• • •

9. To what group of people did the neighbors take the man after they saw he was healed?

10. True or False: The man's parents were afraid to tell the truth about their son's healing, because anyone who confessed Jesus would be put out of the synagogue.

• • •

11. Fill in the blank: He answered and said, Whether he be a sinner or no, I know not: one thing I know, that, whereas I was _____, now I see.

• • •

12. True or False: The man declared that Jesus is of God.

• • •

13. For his confession of Christ, the man was
   a) forgiven by the Pharisees
   b) honored for his conviction
   c) put out of the synagogue
   d) thrown into prison

• • •

14. True or False: After this happened, Jesus found the man and told him that He is the Son of God.

15. Fill in the blank: The man told Jesus: "Lord, I _____. And he worshipped him."

• • •

16. Who said that he was eyes to the blind, feet to the lame, a father to the poor?
   a) Abraham
   b) Isaiah
   c) Job
   d) Paul

• • •

17. How did Israel defile God's altar?

• • •

18. What prophet asked God to strike the Syrians blind?

• • •

19. How did Jesus heal blind Bartimaeus?

• • •

20. How did Jesus heal the two blind men sitting by the side of the road?

21. How did Jesus heal the blind man in Bethsaida?

• • •

22. Whom did Jesus send to restore Saul's (Paul's) sight?

• • •

23. What sorcerer did Paul strike blind in the name of the Lord?

• • •

24. Whom did the angels strike blind to save Lot?

Blindness, Physical Answers

1. true (John 9:1)

2. c) a beggar (John 9:8)

3. false (John 9:2)

4. c) neither (John 9:3)

5. true (John 9:3)

6. light (John 9:5)

7. d) spit, clay, and water from the pool of Siloam (John 9:6–7)

8. true

9. Pharisees (John 9:13)

10. true (John 9:22–23)

11. blind (John 9:25)

12. true (John 9:33)

13. c) put out of the synagogue (John 9:34)

14. true (John 9:35–38)

15. believe (John 9:38)

16. c) Job (Job 29:15–16)

17. by offering blind animals as sacrifices (Malachi 1:7–8)

18. Elisha (2 Kings 6:18–20)

19. spoke to him
(Mark 10:46–52)

20. touched their eyes
(Matthew 20:30–34)

21. put spit on the man's eyes
and then touched the man's
eyes twice (Mark 8:22–26)

22. Ananias (Acts 9:17–18)

23. Elymas (Bar-Jesus)
(Acts 13:6–11)

24. the men of Sodom
(Genesis 19:11)

BLINDNESS, SPIRITUAL

(see also Blindness, Physical)

*The people that walked
in darkness have seen
a great light.*
ISAIAH 9:2

1. Whom did God say He
had called in righteousness
to open blind eyes?

2. Of whom did Jesus say
that they were the blind
leaders of the blind?

• • •

3. Which of the seven
churches in Revelation did
Jesus say was blind?

• • •

4. Why did God say that He
had blinded His people's eyes
and hardened their hearts?

• • •

5. Who did Paul say had
blinded the perishing to the
gospel?

• • •

6. What blinds the eyes
of the wise and twists the
words of the righteous?

Blindness, Spiritual
Answers

1. His Elect One
(Isaiah 42:1, 6–7)

2. the Pharisees
(Matthew 15:12–14)

3. Laodicea
(Revelation 3:14, 17)

4. lest they should
understand and be healed
(John 12:40)

5. the god of this age
(2 Corinthians 4:4)

6. a bribe
(Deuteronomy 16:19)

BROTHERS

(see also Fathers,
Mothers, Sisters)

1. What two pairs of brothers
were Jesus' disciples?

• • •

2. What is the only
time Isaac and Ishmael
cooperated?

3. Did Samson have any
brothers?

• • •

4. How many brothers did
Abram have?

• • •

5. Which brother of Solomon
tried to take Solomon's
throne and then claimed
sanctuary in the temple?

• • •

6. Which one of his brothers
did Absalom kill to avenge
his sister, Tamar's, honor?

• • •

7. Fill in the blank: Proverbs
17:17 says that a brother is
born for _____.

• • •

8. David was the youngest of
how many brothers?
   a) 6
   b) 7
   c) 8
   d) 9

9. A brother offended is harder to win than what?

• • •

10. Who was born grasping his brother's heel?

• • •

11. What was Jesus' answer to the one who asked Him to make his brother divide the inheritance?

• • •

12. Fill in the blank: 1 John 2:10 says that he who loves his brother abides in the

_____ .

• • •

13. Of which two brothers was it said that one was hairy and one was smooth skinned?

• • •

14. True or False: Goliath had a brother.

• • •

15. On the first trip, how many of Joseph's brothers came to Egypt?

16. On the first trip, what accusation did Joseph make against his brothers to frighten them into telling him more about his father and family?
   a) they had stolen grain
   b) they used false weights and measures
   c) they were spies
   d) they worshipped false gods

• • •

17. True or False: After being away for so long, Joseph could not understand his brothers and had to use an interpreter.

• • •

18. Fill in the blank: Joseph told his brothers, "It was not you who sent me here, but _____."

• • •

19. On the second trip for grain, who else came with the brothers?
   a) Benjamin
   b) Jacob
   c) both Jacob and Benjamin

Brothers Answers

1. Peter and Andrew, James and John (Matthew 4:18–21)

2. when they buried their father, Abraham (Genesis 25:8–9)

3. yes (Judges 16:31)

4. two; Nahor, Haran (Genesis 11:27)

5. Adonijah (1 Kings 1:50)

6. Amnon (2 Samuel 13:28–29)

7. adversity

8. c) 8 (1 Samuel 16:10–11)

9. a strong city (Proverbs 18:19)

10. Jacob (Genesis 25:26)

11. "Who made Me a judge. . .over you?" (Luke 12:14 NKJV)

12. light

13. Esau, Jacob (Genesis 27:11 NKJV)

14. true (2 Samuel 21:19)

15. ten; Benjamin stayed behind (Genesis 42:3–4)

16. c) they were spies (Genesis 42:9)

17. false—he could understand the language (Genesis 42:23)

18. God (Genesis 45:8)

19. a) Benjamin (Genesis 43:8–15)

C

CAPTIVITY, ASSYRIA

(see also Captivity, Babylon; Captivity, Egypt)

1. Which kingdom of Israel did Assyria take captive: northern or southern?

• • •

2. Who was king when Assyria took Israel captive?

• • •

3. True or False: Assyria made Israel their vassal before taking them captive.

• • •

4. Who was king of Assyria at this time?
   a) Sennacherib
   b) Shalmaneser
   c) Nebuchadnezzar
   d) Xerxes

• • •

5. Who did the king of Israel try to get to help him fight Assyria?

6. What happened when the king of Assyria found out?

• • •

7. What happened to the people the king of Assyria sent to Samaria?

• • •

8. What did the king of Assyria do to relieve that situation?

Captivity, Assyria Answers

1. northern

2. Hoshea (2 Kings 17:6)

3. true (2 Kings 17:3)

4. b) Shalmaneser (2 Kings 17:3)

5. King of Egypt (2 Kings 17:4)

6. he put the king of Israel in prison (2 Kings 17:4)

7. lions killed them (2 Kings 17:26)

8. sent one of Israel's priests (2 Kings 17:27)

CAPTIVITY, BABYLON

(see also Captivity, Assyria;
Captivity, Egypt)

*The thirty-seventh year into
the captivity, Evil-Merodach
became king of Babylon. He
took pity on the king of Israel
and not only brought him out
of prison, but also gave him a
prominent seat at his table
(2 Kings 25:27–30).*

1. Which kingdom of Israel
did Babylon take captive:
northern or southern?

• • •

2. True or False: The
Babylonian captivity came
before the Assyrian captivity.

• • •

3. Who was king of Babylon
at this time?

• • •

4. Who was king of Israel at
this time?
   a) Jehoiakim
   b) Hezekiah
   c) Mattaniah
   d) Manasseh

• • •

5. True or False: The king of
Babylon took Israel captive
in two stages.

• • •

6. True or False: The king
of Babylon took all the
treasures from the temple
but left the temple standing.

• • •

7. True or False: Jeremiah
prophesied that the captivity
was coming but the king
wouldn't listen.

• • •

8. True or False: Ezekiel
prophesied while Israel was
captive in Babylon.

• • •

9. True or False: Gedaliah,
the person whom the king
of Babylon appointed as
governor over those who
remained in Israel, was a
Babylonian.

Captivity, Babylon
Answers

2. false (2 Kings 17:1–3; 24:1)

3. Nebuchadnezzar (2 Kings 24:1)

4. a) Jehoiakim (2 Kings 24:1)

5. true (2 Kings 24:14, 25:11)

6. false (2 Kings 25:9)

7. true (Jeremiah 34:1)

8. true (Ezekiel 1:1)

9. false (2 Kings 22:12; 25:22)

CAPTIVITY, EGYPT

(see also Captivity, Assyria; Captivity, Babylon)

The Egyptians made the Israelites' lives bitter with hard bondage (Exodus 1:14).

1. Fill in the blank: Israel became captive in Egypt because "there arose up a new king over Egypt, which knew not _____."

2. This pharaoh was afraid that
   a) Israel would take over Egypt
   b) Israel would join Egypt's enemies and fight against Egypt
   c) both

   •••

3. What did the pharaoh do first to subdue the Israelites?

   •••

4. What were the Israelites compelled to do for Pharaoh?

   •••

5. What happened the more the Israelites were afflicted?
   a) the more they rebelled
   b) the more they multiplied
   c) the more they accepted their lot
   d) the more they plotted against Pharaoh

   •••

6. The Egyptians were in _____ of the Israelites.

7. Fill in the blanks: Pharaoh commanded that every son who was born should be cast into the _____, but every daughter could be _____ _____.

Captivity, Egypt Answers

1. Joseph (Exodus 1:8)
2. b) Israel would join Egypt's enemies and fight against Egypt (Exodus 1:10)
3. set taskmasters over them (Exodus 1:11)
4. build cities (Exodus 1:11)
5. b) the more they multiplied (Exodus 1:12)
6. dread (Exodus 1:12)
7. river, saved alive (Exodus 1:22 NKJV)

CHILDREN

(see also Daughters, Fathers, Mothers, Sons)

We are to teach our children about the Lord diligently— when we sit, when we walk, when we lie down, and when we rise up (Deuteronomy 6:7).

1. How old was the youngest king of Judah when he began to reign?
   a) 7
   b) 8
   c) 10
   d) 12

· · ·

2. How old was the second youngest king of Judah when he began to reign?
   a) 8
   b) 10
   c) 12
   d) 14

· · ·

3. How old was Jarius's daughter when Jesus raised her from the dead?

4. Psalm 127:3 says that children are a _____ from the Lord.
   a) gift
   b) blessing
   c) heritage
   d) curse

• • •

5. Who said, "For this child I prayed"?
   a) Hannah
   b) Sarah
   c) Elizabeth
   d) Mary

• • •

6. In what way should a child be raised up?

• • •

7. What child, when he was called in the night, said, "Speak; for thy servant heareth"?

• • •

8. Where is the following verse found? "Children, obey your parents in the Lord: for this is right."

9. What did these children have in common: Ishmael, Isaac, Samson, John the Baptist, Jesus?

• • •

10. Isaiah 11:6 says, "A little child shall lead them." What will the child lead?
   a) animals
   b) adults
   c) children
   d) a parade

• • •

11. What did the Lord do on behalf of Leah and Rachel?

• • •

12. What ruler killed all the male children two years old and younger in Bethlehem and its surrounding districts?

Children Answers

1. a) 7 (2 Kings 11:1–4)
2. a) 8 (2 Kings 22:1)
3. twelve (Luke 8:42)
4. c) heritage

5. a) Hannah (1 Samuel 1:27)

6. in the way he should go (Proverbs 22:6)

7. Samuel (1 Samuel 3:10)

8. Ephesians 6:1

9. all their births were divinely announced (Genesis 16:11; 17:19; Judges 13:5; Luke 1:13, 31)

10. a) animals

11. He intervened on their behalf so they could conceive (Genesis 29:31; 30:22)

12. Herod (Matthew 2:16–18)

CHURCHES IN ACTS

(see also Churches in Revelation)

1. In what church were the disciples first called Christians?

•••

2. What church was Lydia a part of?
   a) Philippi
   b) Antioch
   c) Thyatira
   d) Corinth

3. True or False: Barnabas was part of the church at Antioch.

•••

4. When certain people told the church in Jerusalem that everyone had to be circumcised to be saved, who rebuked them?
   a) Paul
   b) Barnabas
   c) Peter
   d) all three

•••

5. Who were the leaders at the church of Corinth whom Paul stayed with?

•••

6. What did the apostles appoint in every church?

•••

7. Which church sent Paul and Barnabas on their first missionary journey?

Churches in Acts Answers

1. Antioch (Acts 11:26)

2. c) Thyatira (Acts 16:14)

3. true (Acts 13:1)

4. c) Peter (Acts 15:7)

5. Aquila and Priscilla (Acts 18:1–2)

6. elders (Acts 14:23)

7. Antioch (Acts 13:1–3)

CHURCHES IN REVELATION

(see also Churches in Acts)

1. Put the churches in the order they were written to:
- Smyrna
- Sardis
- Ephesus
- Thyatira
- Laodicea
- Pergamos
- Philadelphia

• • •

2. Which church was told it had left its first love?

3. Which church was told it was lukewarm?

• • •

4. Which church was told they had a Jezebel among them?

• • •

5. Which church was told they dwell where Satan's throne is?

• • •

6. Which church was told they are alive but dead?

Churches in Revelation Answers

1. Ephesus, Smyrna, Pergamos, Thyatira, Sardis, Philadelphia, Laodicea (Revelation 2–3)

2. Ephesus (Revelation 2:1, 4)

3. Laodicea (Revelation 3:14, 16)

4. Thyatira (Revelation 2:18, 20)

5. Pergamos
(Revelation 2:12–13)

6. Sardis (Revelation 3:1)

CITIES OF REFUGE

1. How long did a person who fled to a city of refuge have to stay there?

...

2. How many cities of refuge were there to be altogether?

...

3. How many cities of refuge did Moses set up before the conquest of Canaan?

...

4. Whom were the cities of refuge set up to protect?

...

5. Whom were the cities of refuge protecting people from?

...

6. Who decided if a person could take refuge in a city of refuge?

7. True or False: The cities of refuge were only available to the Israelites.

...

8. How many of the cities of refuge were east of the Jordan?

...

9. Which of these tribes didn't have a city of refuge in their territory?
   a) Naphtali
   b) Judah
   c) Gad
   d) Issachar

Cities of Refuge Answers

1. until the current high priest died (Numbers 35:25)

2. six (Numbers 35:6)

3. three (Deuteronomy 4:41–43)

4. someone who killed someone accidentally (Numbers 35:15)

5. the avenger of blood (Numbers 35:25)

6. the elders of that city (Joshua 20:4)

7. false (Joshua 20:9)

8. three (Joshua 20:8)

9. d) Issachar (Joshua 20:7–8)

CITIES OF THE LEVITES

The Levites were not given an inheritance of land but were scattered throughout the land because they were God's ministers. Each tribe had to give the Levites cities in their territory (Joshua 21:1–3).

Match the city to the tribe who gave it:

1. Hebron
2. Kirjath Arba
3. Gibeon
4. Shechem
5. Eltekeh
6. Tanach
7. Kishion
8. Abdon
9. Kedesh
10. Bezer
11. Ramoth
12. Jokneam

a. Manasseh
b. Judah
c. Zebulun
d. Asher
e. Simeon
f. Ephraim
g. Naphtali
h. Dan
i. Gad
j. Benjamin
k. Reuben
l. Issachar

Cities of the Levites Answers

All answers are found in Joshua 21:9–40 NKJV.

1. b
2. e
3. j
4. f
5. h
6. a
7. l
8. d
9. g
10. k
11. i
12. c

CITIES, MISC.

Nimrod built the city of Babel, which later became Babylon, and the city of Nineveh, which was the capital of Assyria (Genesis 10:8–11). The Assyrians carried the ten northern tribes of Israel into captivity and the Babylonians carried the two southern tribes of Israel into captivity.

1. Which tribe of Israel inherited the land containing the cities of Jericho and Jerusalem?

• • •

2. True or False: Lot was an elder who sat in the gate of Sodom.

• • •

3. In the parable of the good Samaritan, where was the man who was robbed going to and from?

4. The shortest sermon in the Bible consists of eight words: "Yet forty days and _____ shall be overthrown." To what city was that sermon preached?

• • •

5. When Naomi returned from afar with Ruth, to which city did they go?

• • •

6. To what city was Paul traveling when he was struck by the light of Jesus?

• • •

7. In what city did Jesus speak to the woman at the well?

• • •

8. What famous biblical city was also called "the city of palm trees"?
   a) Nazareth
   b) Bethlehem
   c) Jericho
   d) Sodom

• • •

9. What city was originally called Jebus?

10. True or False: There is a city in the Bible named the City of Salt.

Cities, Misc. Answers

1. Benjamin (Joshua 18:21–28)
2. true (Genesis 19:1)
3. to Jericho from Jerusalem (Luke 10:30)
4. Nineveh (Jonah 3:4)
5. Bethlehem (Ruth 1:11–19)
6. Damascus (Acts 9:3–4)
7. Sychar, in Samaria (John 4:5–7)
8. c) Jericho (2 Chronicles 28:15)
9. Jerusalem (Joshua 18:28)
10. true (Joshua 15:62 NKJV)

CLEVER WOMEN

1. What woman helped her son trick his father into giving him a blessing?

• • •

2. What woman tricked her father-in-law into doing his duty by her according to the levirate law?

• • •

3. What excuse did the Hebrew midwives give Pharaoh for not killing the baby boys as they were born?
   a) we fear God and cannot do this
   b) the Hebrew women give birth before we get there
   c) both

• • •

4. The woman who gave birth to Moses and devised the plan to save his life was
   a) Jael
   b) Jehoida
   c) Jochebed
   d) Jezebel

5. True or False: Jael killed the commander of the Canaanite army by nailing his head to the ground.

• • •

6. True or False: Abigail saved her husband from being killed by taking provisions to David and his men.

• • •

7. True or False: Jehosheba saved Joash from being killed by his grandmother.

Clever Women Answers

1. Rebekah (Genesis 27:1–17)

2. Tamar (Genesis 38:24–26)

3. b) The Hebrew women give birth before we get there (Exodus 1:19)

4. c) Jochebed (Exodus 2:1–10, 6:20)

5. true (Judges 4:21)

6. true (1 Samuel 25:2–35)

7. true (2 Kings 11:1–2)

COURAGE

(see also Fear Not!)

1. Who told the Israelites to be of good courage?

• • •

2. Who told Joshua to be of good courage?

• • •

3. True or False: Upon becoming their leader, Joshua told the Israelites that he had courage.

• • •

4. True or False: Joshua told his army that if they had courage, the Lord would fight for them.

• • •

5. Upon what occasion did David tell Solomon to be of good courage?

6. When Hezekiah told his army to be of good courage, what nation was coming after them?
a) Assyria
b) Babylon
c) Egypt
d) Persia

•••

7. Which church did Paul, in his letter to that church, tell to be brave and strong?

Courage Answers

1. Moses (Deuteronomy 31:6)

2. God (Joshua 1:9)

3. false (Joshua 1:18)

4. true (Joshua 10:25)

5. when David instructed Solomon to build the temple (1 Chronicles 22:6–14)

6. a) Assyria (2 Chronicles 32:7)

7. Corinth (1 Corinthians 16:13)

COVENANT, NEW

(see also Covenants)

Jesus said the new covenant is in His blood, which He shed for us (Luke 22:20).

1. To which prophet was God speaking when He said He would make a new covenant with Israel and Judah?

•••

2. God says that in His new covenant He will put His law where?

•••

3. Fill in the blanks: God says in the new covenant He will be their _____ and they shall be His _____.

•••

4. Upon what occasion did Jesus introduce the new covenant to His disciples?

5. Hebrews 8:6 says the new covenant is more

_____.

    a) comprehensive
    b) lasting
    c) excellent
    d) strenuous

• • •

6. True or False: The new covenant is conditional.

• • •

7. Who is the mediator of the new covenant?

• • •

8. Hebrews 13:20 says the new covenant is
    a) powerful
    b) sharper than a two-edged sword
    c) everlasting
    d) b & c

Covenant, New Answers

1. Jeremiah (Jeremiah 31:3)

2. in their minds and write it on their hearts (Jeremiah 31:33)

3. God, people (Jeremiah 31:33)

4. the Last Supper (Luke 22:20)

5. c) excellent

6. False (Hebrews 8:10, 12)

7. Jesus (Hebrews 12:24)

8. c) everlasting

COVENANTS

(see also Covenant, New)

1. True or False: The covenant God made with the Israelites through Moses was conditional.

• • •

2. What covenant did God make with Noah before the flood?

3. God told the Israelites that _____ would serve as a perpetual covenant throughout all their generations.
   a) keeping the Sabbath
   b) honoring their father and mother
   c) having no other gods before Him
   d) not worshipping idols

• • •

4. The lord said the heave offerings were a covenant of what common thing?
   a) grass
   b) water
   c) salt
   d) light

• • •

5. Who made a covenant with his eyes never to look on a young woman?

Covenants Answers

1. true (Exodus 19:5)

2. that he and his family would go on on the ark (Genesis 6:18)

3. a) keeping the Sabbath (Exodus 31:16)

4. c) salt (Numbers 18:19)

5. Job (Job 31:1)

CREATION

(see also Garden of Eden)

1. When did God create "the heaven and the earth"?

• • •

2. Fill in the blank: And the earth was without ____, and void.

• • •

3. What is the Bible's first recorded word from God?

• • •

4. Which of the following was not marked by the "lights in the firmament of

the heaven"?
  a) signs
  b) seasons
  c) days
  d) months

• • •

5. True or False: God called for sea creatures before He spoke the birds into existence.

• • •

6. Fill in the blanks: "God made the beast of the earth after his ____, and cattle after their _____."

• • •

7. How did God create man?
  a) for our pleasure
  b) with our blessing
  c) to our glory
  d) in our image

• • •

8. What did God allow Adam and Eve to eat?
  a) seed-bearing herbs and fruit
  b) grasses
  c) birds
  d) fish

9. How many days of creation were there?

• • •

10. How did God describe everything that he had made?

• • •

11. What reason did God give for creating a companion for Adam?

• • •

12. Put the following list in creation chronological order:
  - animals and man
  - light
  - sun and moon and stars
  - skies and seas
  - rest
  - plants and flowers and trees
  - birds and fish

Creation Answers

1. "In the beginning" (Genesis 1:1)

2. form (Genesis 1:2)

3. "Let" (Genesis 1:3)

4. d) months (Genesis 1:14)

5. true (Genesis 1:20)

6. kind, kind (Genesis 1:25)

7. d) "in our image" (Genesis 1:26)

8. a) seed-bearing herbs and fruit (Genesis 1:29)

9. six (Genesis 1:31)

10. "very good" (Genesis 1:31)

11. "And the Lord God said It is not good that the man should be alone; I will make him an help meet for him." (Genesis 2:18)

12. light, skies and seas, plants and flowers and trees, sun and moon and stars, birds and fish, animals and man, rest (Genesis 1:3–2:3)

CROPS

(see also Fruits, Harvest, Vegetables)

1. Fill in the blanks: Moses told the Israelites that God was bringing them into a good land of _____ and _____. (hint: not milk and honey)

• • •

2. What was sown in the parable of the sower?

• • •

3. Who had a dream about seven heads of plump grain and seven heads of thin grain?

• • •

4. Fill in the blank: In describing the compassion of the Messiah, Isaiah says He will not quench the smoking _____.

• • •

5. Fill in the blank: In Matthew 13:24–30 Jesus tells the parable of the wheat and _____.

6. What did Ruth glean in Boaz's field?

Crops Answers

1. wheat, barley (Deuteronomy 8:8)
2. seed—not specified what kind (Matthew 13:3–4)
3. Pharaoh (Genesis 41:5–7)
4. flax (Isaiah 42:3)
5. tares (Matthew 13:24–30)
6. barley (Ruth 2:17)

CURSES

(see also Blessings)

And Joshua adjured them at that time, saying, Cursed be the man before the LORD, that riseth up and buildeth this city Jericho: he shall lay the foundation thereof in his firstborn, and in his youngest son shall he set up the gates of it.
JOSHUA 6:26

1. God told the Israelites that if they were disobedient their livestock would not what?

• • •

2. God told the disobedient Israelites that they would sow their seed in vain because
   a) it would never grow
   b) birds would eat it
   c) their enemies would eat it
   d) it would poison them

• • •

3. Who cursed the day he was born?

• • •

4. When Shimiel cursed David, what did David's captain call Shimiel?
   a) a donkey's jawbone
   b) a dead dog
   c) an ox goad
   d) a sinner

• • •

5. True or False: God designated a mountain of blessing and a mountain of cursing.

6. The curse of the Lord is on the house of whom?

• • •

7. To whom did God say, "You are cursed more than all cattle, and more than every beast of the field"?

• • •

8. True or False: The Bible says a man hanged on a tree is cursed.

Curses Answers

1. bear offspring
(Deuteronomy 28:18)

2. c) their enemies would eat it (Leviticus 26:16)

3. Job (Job 3:1)

4. b) a dead dog
(2 Samuel 16:9)

5. true
(Deuteronomy 27:12–13)

6. the wicked (Proverbs 3:33)

7. the serpent in the Garden of Eden (Genesis 3:14 NKJV)

8. true
(Deuteronomy 21:22–23)

D

DANIEL

(see also Nebuchadnezzar's Dream Interpreted, Visions)

1. True or False: Daniel's Babylonian name was Belteshazzar.

• • •

2. Fill in the blank: Daniel _____ in his heart that he would not defile himself with the portion of the King's meat.

• • •

3. Choose A or B: Melzar was set over Daniel and his friends by the prince of **a)** Babylon or **b)** eunuchs.

• • •

4. How many days did Daniel and his friends eat the food they requested as a test?
   a) three
   b) seven
   c) ten
   d) fourteen

5. Fill in the blanks: God gave them _____ and skill in all learning and _____.

• • •

6. Fill in the blank: Because Daniel interpreted Nebuchadnezzar's dream, Nebuchadnezzar made Daniel "_____ of the governors over all the wise men of Babylon."

• • •

7. Who was the king of Persia when Daniel was thrown into the lions' den?
   a) Darius
   b) Artaxerxes
   c) Shalmaneser
   d) Sennacherib

• • •

8. Choose A or B: The people who tried to find fault in Daniel were **a)** magicians and sorcerers or **b)** presidents and princes.

• • •

9. True or False: The men knew they couldn't find any

fault against Daniel unless it had to do with the law of Daniel's God.

• • •

10. True or False: The king was tricked into passing a law stating that no one could ask a petition of anyone but him for thirty days.

• • •

11. Fill in the blanks: The king's law was the law of the _____ and _____.

• • •

12. How many times a day did Daniel kneel and pray?
   a) one
   b) two
   c) three
   d) four

• • •

13. True or False: The king was eager to have Daniel thrown into the lions' den.

• • •

14. Who said to Daniel, "Thy God whom thou servest continually, he will deliver thee"?

15. Whom did God send to shut the lions' mouths?

• • •

16. True or False: The king had the men who accused Daniel thrown into the lions' den.

• • •

17. True or False: Daniel was a prince of Judah before he was taken to Babylon.

Daniel Answers

1. true (Daniel 1:7)

2. purposed (Daniel 1:8)

3. b) eunuchs (Daniel 1:11)

4. c) ten (Daniel 1:15)

5. knowledge, wisdom (Daniel 1:17)

6. chief (Daniel 2:48)

7. a) Darius (Daniel 6:1, 16)

8. b) presidents and princes (Daniel 6:4)

9. true (Daniel 6:5)

10. true (Daniel 6:7)

11. Medes, Persians (Daniel 6:8)

12. c) three (Daniel 6:10)

13. false; he did his best to keep Daniel from being thrown into the lions' den (Daniel 6:14)

14. the king (Daniel 6:16)

15. an angel (Daniel 6:22)

16. true (Daniel 6:24)

17. true (Daniel 1:3-4)

DAUGHTERS

When Esau saw that his parents disapproved of his two Hittite wives, he married the daughter of Ishmael (Genesis 28:9).

1. Fill in the blank: Of whose three daughters was it said, "In all the land were found no women so beautiful as the daughters of _____?"

• • •

2. True or False: If a Hebrew man had no sons, his daughters could inherit his land.

3. What was the name of Jacob's only daughter?

• • •

4. Of the four women Jacob had children with, which woman was the mother of his daughter?
   a) Leah
   b) Rachel
   c) Bilhah
   d) Zilpah

• • •

5. Whose daughters helped him repair the walls of Jerusalem?
   a) Ezra
   b) Nehemiah
   c) Shallum
   d) Ezekiel

• • •

6. What evangelist had four daughters who prophesied?

• • •

7. What Old Testament hero gave his daughter upper and lower springs as a wedding present?

8. How many daughters did King Saul have?

Daughters Answers

1. Job (Job 42:15)
2. true (Numbers 27:7)
3. Dinah (Genesis 30:20–21)
4. a) Leah (Genesis 30:20–21)
5. c) Shallum (Nehemiah 3:12)
6. Philip (Acts 21:8–9)
7. Caleb (Judges 1:15)
8. two (1 Samuel 14:49)

DESCRIPTION OF JESUS— REVELATION 1

(see also Jesus)

1. Choose A or B: Jesus was clothed in a garment that reached to His **a)** knees or **b)** feet.

2. Fill in the blank: He was standing in the middle of seven _____.

• • •

3. True or False: There was a brass band around His chest.

• • •

4. His hair was white as
   a) snow
   b) wool
   c) linen
   d) a & b

• • •

5. Fill in the blank: His eyes were like _____ _____.

• • •

6. True or False: His feet were like gold.

• • •

7. His voice was
   a) like thunder
   b) human
   c) musical
   d) like the sound of water

• • •

8. Where were the seven stars located on Him?

9. What went out of His mouth?

. . .

10. What did John compare Jesus' countenance to?

. . .

11. What did John do when he saw this Jesus?

Description of Jesus— Revelation 1 Answers

1. b) feet (verse 13)

2. lampstands (verse13)

3. false; it was golden (verse 13)

4. d) a & b (verse 14)

5. a flame of fire (verse 14)

6. false; they were like brass (verse 15)

7. d) like the sound of water (verse 15)

8. in His right hand (verse 16)

9. a sharp two-edged sword (verse 16)

10. the sun (verse 16)

11. fell at His feet as dead (verse 17)

DISCIPLES OF JESUS

After the resurrection, instead of going to Galilee where Jesus had told him to, Peter went fishing and took Thomas, Nathanel, James, John, and two unnamed disciples with him (John 21:2).

1. Which three disciples were on the Mount of Transfiguration with Jesus?
    a) Peter, James, John
    b) Peter, Andrew, John
    c) Andrew, James, John
    d) James, Andrew, Peter

. . .

2. When Jesus asked, "Who do you say that I am?" which disciple answered, "You are the Christ"?
    a) John
    b) Andrew
    c) Philip
    d) Peter

. . .

3. Which disciple brought his brother to Jesus?
    a) James

b) John
c) Bartholomew
d) Andrew

• • •

4. Which disciple was a tax collector before he followed Jesus?
    a) Nathanael
    b) Matthew
    c) Judas
    d) Simon

• • •

5. Which of the following was not a fisherman when Jesus called him?
    a) Peter
    b) Andrew
    c) James
    d) Nathanael

• • •

6. Which disciple had Iscariot as part of his name?
    a) Simon
    b) Bartholomew
    c) Matthew
    d) Judas

• • •

7. Which disciple demanded proof that Jesus had risen?

a) Matthew
b) Thomas
c) James
d) Peter

• • •

8. Who cut off a man's ear?
    a) Judas
    b) Thomas
    c) Peter
    d) James

• • •

9. Which disciple had Jesus heal his mother-in-law?
    a) John
    b) James
    c) Andrew
    d) Peter

• • •

10. How many disciples were at the cross when Jesus was crucified?
    a) 11
    b) 7
    c) 3
    d) 1

• • •

11. Before he was a disciple of Jesus, who was Andrew a disciple of?

Disciples of Jesus Answers

1. a) Peter, James, John (Matthew 17:1–2)

2. d) Peter (Matthew 16:15–16 NKJV)

3. d) Andrew (John 1:40–41)

4. b) Matthew (Matthew 9:9)

5. d) Nathanael (Matthew 4:18–22; John 1:45–48)

6. d) Judas (Mark 3:19)

7. b) Thomas (John 20:24–25)

8. c) Peter (John 18:10)

9. d) Peter (Matthew 8:14–15)

10. d) 1 (John 19:26)

11. John the Baptist (John 1:40)

DONKEYS

(see also Animals, Misc.)

An empty-headed man will be wise, when a wild donkey's colt is born a man.
JOB 11:12 NKJV

1. What did Balaam's donkey say?
   a) Why have you struck me?
   b) Behold the angel of the Lord.
   c) Was I ever disposed to do this to you?
   d) a & c

• • •

2. Who said, "Does the wild donkey bray when it has grass"?
   a) Bildad
   b) Elihu
   c) Job
   d) Zophar

• • •

3. What Old Testament prophet said that Jesus would ride on a donkey, a colt, a foal of a donkey?

• • •

4. Which Gospel writer records the exact fulfillment of that prophecy?

5. What apostle mentions Balaam and his donkey in the second book he wrote in the New Testament?

• • •

6. When Samaria was under siege by Syria, how many shekels did a donkey's head sell for?
   a) 10
   b) 20
   c) 60
   d) 80

• • •

7. In blessing his sons, which son did Jacob say was a strong donkey?

• • •

8. True or False: The description of one judge of Israel says that he had thirty sons who rode on thirty donkeys.

Donkeys Answers

1. d) a & c (Numbers 22:28, 30)

2. c) Job (Job 6:5)

3. Zechariah (Zechariah 9:9)

4. Matthew (Matthew 21:5)

5. Peter (2 Peter 2:15–16)

6. d) 80 (2 Kings 6:25)

7. Issachar (Genesis 49:14)

8. true (Judges 10:4)

DOVES

(see also Animals, Misc., Animals Clean/Unclean)

1. Which of the following is not associated with a dove?
   a) Moses
   b) Noah
   c) Jesus
   d) Jonah

• • •

2. True or False: When Syria besieged Samaria, there was such a great famine that people actually ate dove droppings.

• • •

3. What does the psalmist say he would do if he had the wings of a dove?

4. True or False: Hosea calls Ephraim a silly dove without sense.

• • •

5. Fill in the blank: Jesus said to be wise as _____ and harmless as doves.

• • •

6. True or False: When Jesus cleansed the temple, there were people there selling doves.

Dove Answers

1. a) Moses (Genesis 8:9; Matthew 3:16; Jonah means "dove")

2. true (2 Kings 6:25)

3. fly away and rest (Psalm 55:6)

4. true (Hosea 7:11)

5. serpents (Matthew 10:16)

6. true (Matthew 21:12)

DREAMS

(see also Dreams Associated with Joseph, Nebuchadnezzar's Dream Interpreted, Visions)

1. Jacob dreamed of a _____ that went to heaven.
   a) staircase
   b) ladder
   c) mountain
   d) chariot

• • •

2. Pharaoh dreamed that seven skinny _____ ate seven fat _____.
   a) cattle
   b) sheep
   c) horses
   d) fish

• • •

3. Who saw a sheet full of creatures and was told to "rise and eat"?
   a) John
   b) Peter
   c) Stephen
   d) James

4. Who was warned in a dream not to go back to Herod?
   a) wise men
   b) shepherds
   c) Joseph
   d) John the Baptist

• • •

5. Who was told in a dream to take a wife, even though she was expecting a child?
   a) Hosea
   b) Joseph
   c) Moses
   d) Jacob

• • •

6. Who was disturbed because she had a dream about Jesus?
   a) Mary Magdalene
   b) Martha
   c) Herodias
   d) Pilate's wife

• • •

7. In Daniel's prophetic dream of kingdoms to come, how many beasts did Daniel see?
   a) 2
   b) 3
   c) 4
   d) 7

Dreams Answers

1. b) ladder
(Genesis 28:10–12)

2. a) cattle (Genesis 41:20)

3. b) Peter (Acts 10:9–13)

4. a) wise men
(Matthew 2:1, 12)

5. b) Joseph (Matthew 1:20)

6. d) Pilate's wife
(Matthew 27:17–19)

7. c) 4 (Daniel 7:3)

DREAMS ASSOCIATED WITH JOSEPH

(see also Dreams)

1. True or False: Joseph's first dream was that animals bowed down to him.

• • •

2. What was Jacob's reaction to Joseph's dream of the sun, moon, and eleven stars bowing to him?

3. How many dreams of his own did Joseph have?

• • •

4. Where were Joseph, the butler, and the bakers when Joseph interpreted their dreams for them?

• • •

5. Whose dream did Joseph interpret first—the baker's or the butler's?

• • •

6. Whose dream had a good interpretation—the baker or the butler?

• • •

7. Which dream did Pharaoh have first—the cows or the grain?

Dreams Associated with Joseph Answers

1. false—sheaves (Genesis 37:7)
2. Jacob rebuked him (Genesis 37:10)
3. two dreams (Genesis 37:5–11)
4. jail (Genesis 40:1–3)
5. the butler's (Genesis 40:9–12)
6. the butler's (Genesis 40:13)
7. cows (Genesis 41:2)

E

EARTHQUAKES

1. What did Korah do that caused God to make the earth open up and swallow him?
   a) he spoke against Moses and Aaron
   b) he rejected the Lord
   c) he went into the Holy of Holies
   d) a & b

• • •

2. Which son of King Saul did God protect by using an earthquake to keep the Philistines away?

• • •

3. True or False: When Elijah was standing on the mountain, God spoke to him out of an earthquake.

• • •

4. Amos dates his words as how many years before the earthquake?
   a) 1
   b) 2
   c) 3
   d) 4

5. True or False: When Jesus was on the cross, the veil of the temple was torn in two during an earthquake.

• • •

6. True or False: The earthquake that occurred when Jesus was on the cross caused graves to open.

• • •

7. True or False: The angel rolling the stone away from Jesus' tomb caused an earthquake.

• • •

8. What apostle was in prison when an earthquake set him free?
   a) Peter
   b) James
   c) John
   d) Paul

Earthquakes Answers

ELIJAH/ELISHA

Choose whether the following description was associated with a) Elijah, b) Elisha, or c) both:

1. parted the Jordan River

• • •

2. continuous supply of oil and meal

• • •

3. cured waters of Jericho with salt

4. raised a boy from the dead

• • •

5. increased widow's oil

• • •

6. fed by birds

• • •

7. cured Naaman's leprosy

• • •

8. called down fire from heaven

• • •

9. prophet's bones bring a dead man back to life

• • •

10. hairy man wearing a leather belt

• • •

11. bald headed

Elijah/Elisha Answers

1. c) both (2 Kings 2:8, 14)

2. a) Elijah (1 Kings 17:14–16)

3. b) Elisha (2 Kings 2:21–22)

81

2 Kings 4:32–37)

4. c) both (1 Kings 17:17–24;

5. b) Elisha (2 Kings 4:2–7)

6. a) Elijah (1 Kings 17:6)

7. b) Elisha (2 Kings 5:10, 14)

(1 Kings 18:36–38)

8. a) Elijah

9. b) Elisha (2 Kings 13:21)

10. a) Elijah (2 Kings 1:8)

11. b) Elijah (2 Kings 2:23)

ENEMIES OF ISRAEL

Many of the Israelites'
enemies had common
ancestors with the Israelites.

Match the enemy with its
ancestor:

1. Amalekites
2. Canaanites
3. Edomites
4. Moabites
5. Ammonites
 6. Midianites
7. Jebusites
8. Amorites
9. Hivites
10. Philistines

11. Egyptians

• • •

a. Noah
b. Esau
c. Lot
d. Abraham (with his second
        wife, Keturah)

• • •

12. The ancestors of what
two warring nations fought
together before they were
born?

• • •

13. What man in the Bible is
specifically referred to as "the
Jews' enemy"?
    a) Pharaoh
    b) Herod
    c) Haman
    d) Judas Iscariot

• • •

14. What enemy of Israel
did King Saul fail to wipe
out after God commanded
him to?

Enemies of Israel Answers

1. b. Esau (Genesis 36:12)

2. a. Noah (Genesis 10:6)

3. b. Esau (Genesis 36:12)

4. c. Lot (Genesis 19:37)

5. c. Lot (Genesis 19:38)

6. d. Abraham (Genesis 25:2–4)

7. a. Noah (Genesis 10:15–19)

8. a. Noah (Genesis 14)

9. a. Noah

10. a. Noah (Genesis 10:14)

11. a. Noah (Genesis 10:6)

12. Israelites (Jacob), Edomites (Esau) (Genesis 25:21–26)

13. c. Haman (Esther 3:10)

14. Amalekites (1 Samuel 15:12–15)

EPHOD

(see also Priests)

1. True or False: The ephod was to be made of the colors gold, blue, purple, and scarlet.

• • •

2. Of what material was the ephod to be made?
   a) linen
   b) cotton
   c) flax
   d) wool

• • •

3. What was the ephod?

• • •

4. How many straps joined the ephod?

• • •

5. How many stones for the ephod were to be inscribed with the names of the tribes of Israel?

• • •

6. What were the stones in question 5 to be made of?

7. How were the tribes to be listed on the stones?

• • •

8. What type of setting were the stones to be in?

• • •

9. In what location were the stones to be attached to the ephod?

• • •

10. True or False: Braided chains of silver were on the ephod.

Ephod Answers

1. true (Exodus 28:6)

2. a) linen (Exodus 28:6)

3. one of the high priest's garments (Exodus 28:4)

4. two straps (Exodus 28:7)

5. two stones (Exodus 28:9)

6. onyx (Exodus 28:9)

7. in order of their birth (Exodus 28:10)

8. gold (Exodus 28:11)

9. shoulders (Exodus 28:12)

10. false; the braided chains were to be made of gold (Exodus 28:14)

EXCUSES

1. What excuse did Adam offer for eating the forbidden fruit in the Garden of Eden?

• • •

2. What excuse did Eve use for eating the forbidden fruit in the garden?

• • •

3. What was Aaron's excuse for shaping a golden calf out of the Israelites' gold earrings?

• • •

4. Why did Laban say he refused to give his daughter Rachel to Jacob after Jacob had worked seven years to fulfill their agreement?

• • •

5. Most of the spies who investigated Canaan said the land could not be taken for what reason?

6. After Jesus healed a man blind from birth, why did the man's parents fail to confirm the healing?

• • •

7. How did Jesus answer the reluctant disciple who said he must first bury his father before following the Master?

• • •

8. In Jesus' parable of the great feast, what excuses were made by businessmen who could not attend?

• • •

9. What excuse for not attending the great feast was offered by a man with a new companion?

• • •

10. Why did the young ruler who asked Jesus about eternal life go away "sorrowful"?

Excuses Answers

1. "The woman whom thou gavest. . .me, she gave me of the tree, and I did eat" (Genesis 3:12 kjv)

2. "The serpent beguiled me, and I did eat" (Genesis 3:13 kjv)

3. the people said, "Make us gods, for we don't know what happened to Moses." (see Exodus 32:23)

4. it wasn't customary in our country to give the younger before the firstborn (Genesis 29:25–26)

5. giants were seen in the land that made the spies look like grasshoppers (Numbers 13:33)

6. they feared the Jews would put them out of the synagogue (John 9:21–22)

7. "Follow Me, and let the dead bury their own dead" (Matthew 8:21–22 nkjv)

8. one bought land and must see it; the other bought oxen and must approve them (Luke 14:18–19)

9. "I have married a wife, and therefore I cannot come" (Luke 14:20 nkjv)

10. he was rich and unwilling to sacrifice to have treasure in heaven (Luke 18:23)

EVERLASTING

1. In Isaiah 9:6–7, what word follows "everlasting"?

• • •

2. Fill in the blank: Psalm 90:2 says that from everlasting to everlasting the Lord is _____.

• • •

3. Fill in the blank: The eternal God is your refuge, and underneath are the everlasting _____.

• • •

4. Fill in the in the blank: John 3:16 says that whoever _____ in Him has everlasting life.

5. To whom did Paul say, "You judge yourselves unworthy of everlasting life"?

• • •

6. Fill in the blank: To reap everlasting life, Paul says we must sow to the _____.

Everlasting Answers

1. Father

2. God

3. arms (Deuteronomy 33:27)

4. believes (John 3:16)

5. Jews (Acts 13:45–46)

6. Spirit (Galatians 6:8)

F

FAITH

(see also God's Faithful,
God's Hall of Fame,
Grace, Hope, Love)

*Because God's faithfulness to us
is so great (Lamentations 3:23),
we can have faith in Him.*

1. Fill in the blank: Faith
is the evidence of things
_____.

• • •

2. Without faith it is
impossible to do what?

• • •

3. Who said he had fought
the good fight and kept the
faith?

• • •

4. Who shall live by faith?

• • •

5. About whom did Jesus say,
"I have not found such great
faith, not even in Israel"?

6. Who said, "Increase our
faith"?

Faith Answers

1. unseen (Hebrews 11:1)
2. please God
   (Hebrews 11:6)
3. Paul (1 Timothy 4:7)
4. the just (Habakkuk 2:4)
5. a centurion
   (Matthew 8:8–10 nkjv)
6. the apostles (Luke 17:5)

FALSE GODS/
GODDESSES

(see also Idols)

*There were two false gods
that had Baal as part of their
name, Baal-Berith (Judges
8:33) and Baal-zebub
(2 Kings 1:3), but they were
not the same false god as Baal.*

1. Where did people worship their false gods?
   a) shrines
   b) high places
   c) temples
   d) a & b

...

2. What princess of Sidon (or Zidon) introduced Baal worship to Israel?
   a) Bathsheba
   b) Athaliah
   c) Jezebel
   d) Abigail

...

3. Samson's death was in a temple to what god?

...

4. Elijah slew 450 prophets of what god?

...

5. True or False: The false gods of the Greeks, Hermes and Zeus, are mentioned in the Bible.

6. What king of Israel was the first to build places for the worship of Chemosh and Molech?
   a) Ahab
   b) Jehu
   c) Solomon
   d) Zimri

...

7. What judge of Israel pulled down his own father's altar to Baal because God commanded him to?
   a) Samson
   b) Othniel
   c) Gideon
   d) Jephthah

...

8. What king had Daniel thrown in the lions' den because Daniel refused to pray to him instead of praying to God?
   a) Nebuchadnezzar
   b) Darius
   c) Cyrus
   d) Belshazzar

Match the false god to the country-people who worshipped it.

9. Succoth Benoth
10. Nergal
11. Ashima
12. Nibhaz and Tartak
13. Adrammelech
14. Ashtoreth
15. Chemosh
16. Dagon

• • •

a. Sidonians
b. Philistines
c. Moabites
d. Avites
e. Babylon
f. Cuth
g. Hamath
h. Sepharvites

False Gods/Goddesses Answers

1. d) a & b (2 Kings 17:29)

2. c) Jezebel (1 Kings 16:31-32)

3. Dagon (Judges 16:23)

4. Baal (1 Kings 18:22, 40)

5. true (Acts 14:12)

6. c) Solomon (1 Kings 11:7)

7. c) Gideon (Judges 6:24-25)

8. b) Darius (Daniel 6:9-16)

9. e. Babylon (2 Kings 17:28-31)

10. f. Cuth (2 Kings 17:28-31)

11. g. Hamath (2 Kings 17:28-31)

12. d. Avites (2 Kings 17:28-31)

13. h. Sepharvites (2 Kings 17:28-31)

14. a. Sidonians (1 Kings 11:5)

15. c. Moabites (1 Kings 11:7)

16. b. Philistines (1 Samuel 5:2)

FAMINES

1. Where did Abram go to escape a famine in his land?

• • •

2. Where did Isaac go to escape famine?

• • •

3. Who managed the store of provisions in Egypt during the seven-year famine?

• • •

4. To what land did Naomi and her husband go to escape famine in Judah?

• • •

5. During David's reign a famine occurred that lasted how many years?
    a) 1
    b) 2
    c) 3
    d) 4

• • •

6. True or False: Famine struck Gilgal during the days of Elijah.

7. True or False: A seven-year famine occurred in Israel during the time of Jeremiah.

• • •

8. True or False: A famine occurred in the early days of the church.

Famines Answers

1. Egypt (Genesis 12:10)

2. the land of the Philistines (Genesis 26)

3. Joseph (Genesis 41:29–30, 56)

4. Moab (Ruth 1:1)

5. c) 3 (2 Samuel 21:1)

6. False; during the days of Elisha (2 Kings 4:38)

7. False; during the time of Elisha (2 Kings 8:1–2)

8. true (Acts 11:28)

FASTING

(see also Prayer)

Is not this the fast that I have chosen? to loose the bands of wickedness, to undo the heavy burdens, and to let the oppressed go free, and that ye break every yoke? Is it not to deal thy bread to the hungry, and that thou bring the poor that are cast out to thy house? when thou seest the naked, that thou cover him; and that thou hide not thyself from thine own flesh? Then shall thy light break forth as the morning, and thine health shall spring forth speedily: and thy righteousness shall go before thee; the glory of the LORD shall be thy reward.
ISAIAH 58:6–8

1. True or False: Ahab humbled himself before the Lord and fasted.

• • •

2. What king proclaimed a fast throughout all Judah before he inquired of the Lord?

3. What caused Nehemiah to fast and pray for many days?

• • •

4. In the days of Nehemiah, the people fasted and repented and then read what?

• • •

5. True or False: After he threw Daniel into the lions' den, Darius fasted.

• • •

6. True or False: When the people of Nineveh repented in the days of Jonah, they fasted.

• • •

7. What did Jesus say hypocrites do to show they are fasting?

Fasting Answers

1. true (1 Kings 21:27–29)

2. Jehoshaphat (2 Chronicles 20:3)

3. the news that the wall of Jerusalem was broken down and burned (Nehemiah 1:2–4)

b) Jubal
c) Tubal-Cain
d) Lamech

• • •

5. Who was David's father?

• • •

6. Who was Peter and
Andrew's father?

• • •

7. Who was the father of
John the Baptist?
    a) Zebedee
    b) Zacchaeus
    c) Zacharias
    d) Zephaniah

• • •

8. Who was the father of
James and John?

• • •

9. When told that his sons
had been killed in battle and
the ark of the covenant had
been taken, what father fell
over backward and died of a
broken neck?

10. Who was Abram's
father?

4. the Book of the Law
(Nehemiah 9:1–3)
5. true (Daniel 6:18)
6. true (Jonah 3:5–7)
7. have a sad countenance
(Matthew 6:16)

FATHERS

(see also Daughters,
Mothers, Sons)

1. Which one of Abram's
brothers was Lot's father?

• • •

2. Who was the father of
Aaron, Miriam, and Moses?

• • •

3. Who was King Saul's
father?
    a) Samuel
    b) Kish
    c) Jesse
    d) Obed

• • •

4. Who was called the father
of all who dwell in tents and
have livestock?
    a) Jabal

11. Who was the father of Shem, Ham, and Japheth?

• • •

12. When Abraham died, where did his sons bury him?

• • •

13. True or False: Hezekiah, a good king, was the father of Manasseh, a bad king.

Fathers Answers

1. Haran (Genesis 11:27)

2. Amram (Exodus 6:20)

3. b) Kish (1 Samuel 9:1–2)

4. a) Jabal (Genesis 4:20)

5. Jesse (Ruth 4:17)

6. Jonah (Matthew 16:17, *Bar* means "son of")

7. c) Zacharias (Luke 1:59)

8. Zebedee (Matthew 4:21)

9. Eli (1 Samuel 4:16–18)

10. Terah (Genesis 11:31)

11. Noah (Genesis 5:32)

12. with Sarah in the cave of Machpelah (Genesis 25:9–10)

13. true (2 Kings 20:21)

FEAR NOT!

(see also Courage)

Match the person to the occasion when someone told them not to fear:

1. Hagar
2. Joseph's brothers
3. Joshua
4. Gideon
5. Solomon
6. Paul

• • •

a. commanded to build the temple
b. afraid of being attacked
c. needed water
d. feared revenge
e. became the leader
f. feared death

Fear Not! Answers

1. c (Genesis 21:17)

2. d (Genesis 50:19)

3. e (Joshua 1:9)

4. f (Judges 6:22–23)

5. a (1 Chronicles 22:11, 13)

6. b (Acts 18:–10)

FEASTS

(see also Offerings,
Sacrifices)

1. Fill in the blank: The Lord called His feasts holy
_____.

•••

2. Fill in the blank: The Sabbath was to be a day of
____.

•••

3. The fourteenth day of the first month was
   a) the Feast of Booths
   b) First Gathering
   c) Passover
   d) Jubilee

•••

4. Choose A or B: During the Passover the Israelites were to do no servile work on **a)** the first and seventh days or **b)** all the days.

•••

5. Fill in the blank: During the Feast of Firstfruits, the priest was to wave a ____ before the Lord.

6. True or False: The Israelites could eat neither bread, parched corn (grain), nor green corn (grain) until they had brought their offering of firstfruits to the Lord.

• • •

7. What was gleaning?

• • •

8. True or False: The Day of Atonement was celebrated on the tenth day of the tenth month.

• • •

9. The Feast of Tabernacles celebration lasted how many days?
    a) 3
    b) 7
    c) 10
    d) 14

• • •

10. The Feast of Booths celebration lasted how many days?
    a) 2
    b) 3
    c) 5
    d) 7

Feasts Answers

1. convocations (Leviticus 23:2)

2. rest (Leviticus 23:3)

3. c) Passover (Leviticus 23:5)

4. a) the first and seventh days (Leviticus 23:7-8)

5. sheaf (Leviticus 23:10-11)

6. true (Leviticus 23:14)

7. the poor were allowed to gather what was left behind after the harvest (Leviticus 23:22)

8. false; it was observed on the tenth day of the seventh month (Leviticus 23:27)

9. b) 7 (Leviticus 23:34)

10. d) 7 (Leviticus 23:41-43)

FIERY FURNACE

(see also Daniel,
Nebuchadnezzar's Dream
Interpreted)

1. The image Nebuchadnezzar erected on the plain of Dura was made of
   a) wood
   b) brass
   c) gold
   d) ivory

• • •

2. Fill in the blank: Anytime the people heard music, they were to _____ the image.

• • •

3. Who told the king that Shadrach, Meshach, and Abednego refused to bow down and worship the image?
   a) magicians
   b) Chaldeans
   c) Jews
   d) princes

• • •

4. Who said, "If it be so, our God whom we serve is able to deliver us from the burning fiery furnace, and he will deliver us out of thine hand, O king"?

• • •

5. True or False: Nebuchadnezzar commanded that the furnace be heated three times hotter than normal.

• • •

6. Who was commanded to bind Shadrach, Meshach, and Abednego?
   a) servants
   b) mighty men
   c) princes
   d) slaves

• • •

7. True or False: The hot fire killed the people who threw Shadrach, Meshach, and Abednego into the fiery furnace.

• • •

8. Who said, "Lo, I see four men loose, walking in the midst of the fire"?

9. Fill in the blank: "The form of the fourth is like the _____ of _____."

• • •

10. True or False: Nebuchadnezzar made a decree that anyone who spoke against the God of Shadrach, Meshach, and Abednego would be hacked to pieces.

Fiery Furnace Answers

1. c) gold (Daniel 3:1)

2. worship (Daniel 3:5)

3. b) Chaldeans (Daniel 3:8–12)

4. Shadrach, Meshach, and Abednego (Daniel 3:16–17)

5. false; he ordered it heated seven times hotter than normal (Daniel 3:19)

6. b) mighty men (Daniel 3:20)

7. true (Daniel 3:22)

8. Nebuchadnezzar (Daniel 3:25)

9. Son, God (Daniel 3:25)

10. true (Daniel 3:29)

FIRSTBORN

And the LORD spake unto Moses, saying, Sanctify unto me all the firstborn, whatsoever openeth the womb among the children of Israel, both of man and of beast: it is mine.
EXODUS 13:1–2

1. Who was the firstborn of David's brothers?
   a) Abinadab
   b) Shammah
   c) Nerushia
   d) Eliab

• • •

2. Who was the firstborn of Jacob's sons?

• • •

3. Who was the firstborn of David's sons?

4. Who was the firstborn of Joseph's sons, Ephraim or Manasseh?

• • •

5. Who was the firstborn, Peter or Andrew?

• • •

6. Who was the firstborn, Rachel or Leah?

• • •

7. About whom is the Bible speaking in the following verse: "Through faith he kept the passover, and the sprinkling of blood, lest he that destroyed the firstborn should touch them."

FIRSTS

1. Who was the first murderer?

• • •

2. Who was the first boat builder?

• • •

3. Who was the first disciple of Jesus?

• • •

4. Who is the first queen mentioned in the Bible?

• • •

5. What is the first verse of the Gospel of John?

• • •

6. Who was the first high priest of Israel?

• • •

7. The first pharaoh mentioned in the Bible was associated with
   a) Moses
   b) Joseph
   c) Jacob
   d) Abraham

Firstborn Answers

1. d) Eliab (1 Samuel 16:6)

2. Reuben (Genesis 35:23)

3. Amnon (2 Samuel 3:2)

4. Manasseh (Genesis 48:17–18)

5. the Bible doesn't say

6. Leah (Genesis 29:18)

7. Moses (Hebrews 11:24, 28)

8. What was the first miracle performed by Jesus?

•••

9. What is the first church mentioned in Revelation?

•••

10. What is the first mention of angels in the Bible?

•••

11. Who was the first shepherd?

•••

12. Who was the first wife of David?

•••

13. Who was the first man to build a city?

•••

14. Who is the first priest mentioned in the Bible?

•••

15. What is the first river mentioned in the Bible?

16. Who were the first people the children of Israel fought after they had left Egypt?

•••

17. What is the first thing someone would encounter when entering the tabernacle?

•••

18. What is the first mention of tithing in the Bible?

•••

19. Who built the first altar?

•••

20. What is the first offering mentioned in the Bible?

•••

21. What was the first thing God created?

•••

22. Who was the first man who didn't die?

•••

23. What was the first thing God told Adam to do?

24. What does the first verse of the New Testament say?

•••

25. Who is the first woman mentioned in the Bible after Eve?

•••

26. Who was Ruth's first husband?

•••

27. What was the first plague on Egypt?

Firsts Answers

1. Cain (Genesis 4:8)
2. Noah (Genesis 6:15)
3. Andrew (John 1:40)
4. the queen of Sheba (1 Kings 10:1)
5. "In the beginning was the Word, and the Word was with God, and the Word was God" (John 1:1).
6. Aaron (Numbers 17:5, 8)
7. d) Abraham (Genesis 12:15, 17)
8. water into wine (John 2:9)
9. Ephesus (Revelation 2:1)
10. cherubim in the Garden of Eden (Genesis 3:24)
11. Abel (Genesis 4:2)
12. Michal (1 Samuel 18:27)
13. Cain (Genesis 4:17)
14. Melchizedek (Genesis 14:18)
15. the river in the midst of the Garden of Eden (Genesis 2:10)
16. Amalekites (Exodus 17:8)
17. bronze altar (Exodus 27:1–2)
18. Abraham gave a tithe to Melchizedek (Genesis 14:18–20)
19. Noah after the flood (Genesis 8:20)
20. fruit of the ground from Cain (Genesis 4:3)
21. light (Genesis 1:3)
22. Enoch (Genesis 5:24)
23. tend the garden and keep it (Genesis 2:15)

24. "The book of the genealogy of Jesus Christ, the Son of David, the son of Abraham. (Matthew 1:1 NKJV).

25. Cain's wife (Genesis 4:17)

26. The Bible doesn't say if it was Mahlon or Chilion (Ruth 1:2, 4)

27. water to blood (Exodus 7:14–25)

FLOOD/NOAH

1. Fill in the blank: Noah's story is recorded in the book of _____.

• • •

2. Noah's story begins in what chapter?

• • •

3. Fill in the blank: In contrast to the wickedness of his generation, "Noah walked _____."

4. After instructing Noah to build an ark, God established what covenant with him?

• • •

5. Can you name Noah's three sons?

• • •

6. What significant event concerning man's life span occurred during Noah's time?

• • •

7. Fill in the blank: "Noah found _____ in the eyes of the Lord."

• • •

8. God instructed Noah to make the ark
   a) 300 cubits long,
      50 cubits wide,
      and 30 cubits high
   b) 400 cubits long,
      50 cubits wide,
      and 60 cubits high
   c) 300 cubits long,
      50 cubits wide,
      and 60 cubits high
   d) 400 cubits long,
      30 cubits wide,
      and 30 cubits high

9. True or False: All the animals went to the ark two by two.

• • •

10. Once the flooding was over, the mountaintops could first be seen after
   a) twelve months
   b) two months
   c) five months
   d) ten months

• • •

11. A dove released by Noah returned with what in her mouth to indicate she had found dry land?

• • •

12. Soon after Noah left the ark, he built
   a) a temple
   b) a home out of driftwood
   c) an altar and sacrificed one of each clean beast
   d) an altar and sacrificed one lamb without blemish

13. True or False: The rainbow no longer represents God's promise not to flood the entire earth.

• • •

14. After the flood, the Bible says that Noah
   a) planted a vegetable garden
   b) planted a vineyard
   c) bred goats and sheep
   d) divided the land equally between his three sons

• • •

15. Noah cursed Canaan because
   a) Ham had seen Noah naked and then told his brothers
   b) Ham worshipped a golden calf
   c) Ham was drunk on wine
   d) Ham had refused to take part in sacrificial ceremonies

16. When they learned about Ham's indiscretion, Shem and Japheth
   a) covered their father without looking upon him
   b) destroyed the golden calf
   c) poured the rest of the wine onto the ground
   d) banished him from the family

Flood/ Noah Answers

1. Genesis
2. Genesis 5
3. with God (Genesis 6:9)
4. Noah and his family could enter the ark (Genesis 6:18)
5. Shem, Ham, and Japheth (Genesis 5:32)
6. During Noah's time, the life span of humans was shortened to 120 years (Genesis 6:3)
7. grace (Genesis 6:8)
8. a) 300 cubits long, 50 cubits wide, and 30 cubits high (Genesis 6:15)
9. false (Genesis 7:2)
10. d) ten months (Genesis 8:5)
11. an olive leaf (Genesis 8:11)
12. c) an altar and sacrificed one of each clean beast (Genesis 8:20)
13. false (Genesis 9:12-13)
14. b) planted a vineyard (Genesis 9:20)
15. a) Ham had seen Noah naked and then told his brothers (Genesis 9:22-25)
16. a) covered their father without looking upon him (Genesis 9:23)

FLOWERS AND PLANTS

(see also Trees)

1. On what day of creation did God create flowers and plants?

• • •

2. What flower did Jesus say was better arrayed than Solomon in all his glory?

• • •

3. Fill in the blank: One of the flowers mentioned in the Bible is the rose of _____.

• • •

4. Isaiah says, "The grass withers and the flowers fall," but what endures forever?

• • •

5. What plants did Moses' mother hide him among?

• • •

6. Hyssop was used to apply what two things?

Flower and Plants Answers

1. day 3 (Genesis 1:12–13)

2. lily of the field (Matthew 6:28–29)

3. Sharon (Song of Solomon 2:1)

4. "the word of our God" (Isaiah 40:6–8 niv)

5. bulrushes (Exodus 2:3)

6. blood, water of purification (Leviticus 14:1–7; Numbers 19:1–19)

FORGIVENESS

1. Fill in the blanks: And forgive us our _____ as we forgive our _____.

• • •

2. God said that if His people humble themselves and pray, He will heal their what?

• • •

3. Fill in the blank: The psalmist said the Lord is good and _____ to forgive.

4. Where is this verse found: Jesus said to him, "I do not say to you, up to seven times, but up to seventy times seven"?

• • •

5. True or False: As soon as Jesus said "up to seventy times seven," He immediately began the parable of the unforgiving servant.

• • •

6. Fill in the blanks: If we confess our sins, He is _____ and _____ to forgive us our sins.

Forgiveness Answers

1. debts, debtors (Matthew 6:12)
2. land (2 Chronicles 7:14)
3. ready (Psalm 86:5)
4. Matthew 18:22 NKJV
5. true (Matthew 18:23)
6. faithful, just (1 John 1:9)

FRIENDS

Two are better than one; because they have a good reward for their labour. For if they fall, the one will lift up his fellow: but woe to him that is alone when he falleth; for he hath not another to help him up.
ECCLESIASTES 4:9–10

1. Who was called the friend of God?

• • •

2. Who was David's good friend?

• • •

3. Fill in the blanks: Proverbs 17:17 says a friend loves at
____ _____.

• • •

4. Who said to Jesus, "He whom you love is sick"?

• • •

5. From what city did Paul escape when his friends let him down over the wall in a huge basket?

6. What three disciples comprised Jesus' inner circle?

• • •

7. Fill in the blank: Can two walk together except they be _____?

Friends Answers

1. Abraham (James 2:23)

2. Jonathan (1 Samuel 18:1)

3. all times (Proverbs 17:17)

4. Mary and Martha (John 11:1–3 NKJV)

5. Damascus (Acts 9:22–25)

6. Peter, James, and John (Matthew 17:1)

7. agreed (Amos 3:3)

G

GARDEN OF EDEN

(see also Creation)

Adam managed to blame both God and Eve for his own sin, saying, "The woman whom thou gavest to be with me, she gave me of the tree, and I did eat" (Genesis 3:12).

1. Where was the forbidden tree located in the garden?

• • •

2. What was the name of the forbidden tree?

• • •

3. What tree stood near the forbidden tree?

• • •

4. How many rivers were in the Garden of Eden?

• • •

5. God banished Adam and Eve from the garden to prevent them from
    a) hiding from Him
    b) killing the serpent
    c) living forever
    d) destroying the forbidden tree

• • •

6. When God cursed the ground, what did He say it would bring forth?

• • •

7. What job was given to cherubim after the expulsion of Adam and Eve from Eden?

• • •

8. Fill in the blank: Ezekiel called the Garden of Eden the Garden of _____.

Garden of Eden Answers

1. in the middle (Genesis 2:9)

2. the tree of knowledge of good and evil (Genesis 2:9)

3. the tree of life (Genesis 2:9)

4. one (Genesis 2:10)

5. c) living forever (Genesis 3:22)

3. How many gems were on the high priest's breastplate?

• • •

4. The list of gems in Ezekiel 28 was associated with
   a) the new Jerusalem
   b) the temple
   c) the Garden of Eden
   d) Jesus' robes in heaven

• • •

5. How many layers of gemstones make up the foundation of the new Jerusalem?

6. thorns and thistles (Genesis 3:17–18)

7. guardians of Eden and the tree of life (Genesis 3:24)

8. God (Ezekiel 28:13)

GEMS/PRECIOUS STONES

"And the twelve gates were twelve pearls; every several gate was of one pearl" (Revelation 21:21). *Imagine a city gate made of one single pearl. That is one big pearl!*

1. Fill in the blank: The virtuous woman is said to have a price above

_____.

• • •

2. Which of the following is NOT a gemstone found on the breastplate of the high priest?
   a) sapphire
   b) turquoise
   c) amethyst
   d) garnet

Gems/Precious Stones Answers

1. rubies (Proverbs 31:10)

2. d) garnet (Exodus 28:17–21)

3. twelve (Exodus 28:21)

4. c) the Garden of Eden (Ezekiel 28:13)

5. twelve layers (Revelation 21:19–20)

GENEALOGIES

1. Matthew's genealogy of Jesus begins with which most ancient individual?
    a) Abraham
    b) Adam
    c) David
    d) Moses

• • •

2. Each group of Matthew's genealogy of Jesus has how many generations?

• • •

3. True or False: Luke's genealogy of Jesus traces Jesus' ancestors back to Adam.

• • •

4. What is the difference in Jesus' genealogies presented in Matthew and Luke?

• • •

5. Whom did Paul urge not to give heed to fables and endless genealogies?

• • •

6. Who is the only woman mentioned in both Jesus' genealogy and God's Hall of Fame?

• • •

7. Where is the first genealogy listed in the Bible?

• • •

8. The genealogy in question 7 starts with whom and ends with whom?

Genealogies Answers

1. a) Abraham (Matthew 1:2)

2. fourteen generations (Matthew 1:17)

3. true (Luke 3:38)

4. one genealogy is through His foster father, Joseph, and the other is through His mother, Mary

5. Timothy (1 Timothy 1:4)

6. Rahab (Matthew 1:5; Hebrews 11:31)

7. Genesis 5

8. Adam, Noah

GEOGRAPHY

(see also Mountains, Rivers, Valleys, Wilderness)

1. Upon what mountain did Elijah defeat the prophets of Baal?

• • •

2. What patriarch went out not knowing where he went?

• • •

3. When God told Jonah to go to Nineveh, to what city did Jonah try to flee?

• • •

4. What was Abram's point of origin?

• • •

5. From what location did Moses send the twelve spies into the Promised Land?

• • •

6. From what city did Samson carry off the gates after the Philistines tried to lock him in?

7. At what site did the Lord confound the language of the earth?

• • •

8. Where was Ezekiel when he began to prophesy?

• • •

9. Where was the Garden of Gethsemane located?

• • •

10. Where did Lazarus and his sisters live?

• • •

11. When Moses fled from Egypt, to what country did he go?

• • •

12. Out of what city was Paul lowered in a basket over the wall?

• • •

13. Where was the Pool of Bethesda, and what was special about it?

14. What are Pishon, Gihon, Hiddekel, and Euphrates?

• • •

15. Where were the two disciples headed when Jesus walked with them after His resurrection?

• • •

16. Toward the end of his life, Jeremiah was taken captive to what country?

• • •

17. Where was Eve in the Garden of Eden when the serpent spoke to her?

• • •

18. Where was Adam when the serpent spoke to Eve?

• • •

19. What was the "great city," or capital, of Assyria?

• • •

20. From what mountain was Moses given a look into the Promised Land?

21. When Moses died, in what land did God bury him?

• • •

22. Where did Paul meet Aquila and Priscilla?

• • •

23. Of what significance was Mount Hor to Aaron?

• • •

24. To what city did Jesus lead His disciples just before His ascension?

• • •

25. What did Abraham name the place where God told him to sacrifice Isaac?

Geography Answers

1. Mount Carmel (1 Kings 18:19)

2. Abraham (Hebrews 11:8)

3. Tarshish (Jonah 1:3)

4. Ur of the Chaldeans (Genesis 11:31)

5. wilderness of Paran (Numbers 13:3)

GIANTS

1. 2 Samuel 21:22 said there were four born to the giant in
a) Gaza
b) Gath
c) Gad
d) Gethsemane

• • •

2. True or False: One of the reasons the Israelites refused to enter the Promised Land was because there were giants there.

• • •

3. Which of the following were NOT giants?
a) Emim
b) Anakim
c) Thummim
d) Zamzummim

6. Gaza (Judges 16:1–3)

7. Babel (Genesis 11:9)

8. Babylon (Ezekiel 1:3 NIV)

9. on the lower slopes of the Mount of Olives (Matthew 26:30–36; Mark 14:26–32)

10. Bethany (John 11:1)

11. Midian (Exodus 2:15)

12. Damascus (Acts 9:19–25)

13. by the Sheep Gate in Jerusalem—an angel stirred up the water, and the first one in after that would be healed (John 5:2–4)

14. the four rivers that flowed out of the Garden of Eden (Genesis 2:10–14)

15. Emmaus (Luke 24:13)

16. Egypt (Jeremiah 43:7–8)

17. in the center (Genesis 2:9, 3:6)

18. standing right next to her (Genesis 3:6)

19. Nineveh (Genesis 10:11–12 NIV; Jonah 3:3)

20. Mount Nebo (Deuteronomy 32:48–49)

21. in the land of Moab (Deuteronomy 34:6)

22. Corinth (Acts 18:1–2)

23. he died and was buried there (Numbers 20:25–28)

24. Bethany (Luke 24:50)

25. Jehovah-jireh: the Lord will provide (Genesis 22:14)

4. True or False: Og, king of Bashan, was a giant.

• • •

5. According to 1 Samuel 17:4, how tall was Goliath?

Giants Answers

1. b) Gath (2 Samuel 21:22)
2. true (Numbers 13:33)
3. c) Thummim (Deuteronomy 2:10–11, 20)
4. true (Deuteronomy 3:11)
5. six cubits and a span

GIDEON

(see also Judges)

1. Gideon's story is found in what book of the Bible?

• • •

2. Fill in the blank: The angel of the Lord who appeared to Gideon said, "The Lord is with you, mighty _____."

3. What question did Gideon ask of the Lord?
   a) "If our home is deserving, will your peace rest on it?"
   b) "If the Lord is with us, who can go against us?"
   c) "If the Lord is with us, why has all this happened to us?"
   d) "If we believe in the Lord, will you stay in our house?"

• • •

4. True or False: Gideon said that he was of the weakest clan in Manasseh, and he was the least in his family.

• • •

5. When the angel's staff touched it, what happened to the offering that Gideon had prepared?

• • •

6. Fill in the blanks: Gideon was told to destroy his father's altar to _____ and cut down the Asherah _____ .

7. As a first test whether God would save Israel under Gideon's leadership, what was to happen overnight to the wool fleece?

• • •

8. True or False: Satisfied with the first sign, Gideon gathered his army to defeat the Midianites.

• • •

9. In reducing Gideon's army, what test eliminated the most number of men?

• • •

10. After the tests, how many men did Gideon have left in his army?

• • •

11. In the Midianite's dream that Gideon overheard, what happened to the Midianite's tent?
   a) a burning lantern consumed it
   b) a flood from the Jordan River washed it away
   c) a round loaf of barley bread overturned it

   d) a statue with feet of clay fell on it

• • •

12. Fill in the blank: The Israelite battle cry was "A sword for the Lord and for _____!"

• • •

13. When did Gideon's army attack?
   a) at daybreak
   b) at high noon
   c) at sunset
   d) during the night

• • •

14. True or False: The men of the tribe of Ephraim were angry that Gideon had not called them when he went to fight the Midianites.

• • •

15. When the Israelites asked Gideon to rule over them, how did he respond?
   a) he reluctantly agreed to do so
   b) he said he was exhausted and his grandson would rule instead

c) he said his father, Joash, should rule

d) he said the Lord would rule over them

Gideon Answers

1. Judges

2. warrior (Judges 6:12 NIV)

3. c) "If the Lord is with us, why then has all this happened to us?" (Judges 6:13 NKJV)

4. true (Judges 6:15)

5. fire consumed it (Judges 6:21)

6. Baal, pole (Judges 6:25 NIV)

7. "dew on the fleece only" (Judges 6:37)

8. false; he asked for a second sign (Judges 6:39)

9. those who were afraid went home; (22,000 of 32,000 went home; Judges 7:3)

10. three hundred (Judges 7:8)

11. c) a round loaf of barley bread overturned it (Judges 7:13)

12. Gideon (Judges 7:20)

13. d) during the night (Judges 7:19)

14. true (Judges 8:1)

15. d) he said the Lord would rule over them (Judges 8:22–23)

GIFTS

The Scribes and Pharisees had a practice called Corban which they claimed allowed them to take what they owed their parents and claim they gave it as a gift to God (Mark 7:11).

1. True or False: Rebekah's family gave gifts to Abraham's servant so that he would take her as Isaac's bride.

• • •

2. Why did Abraham give gifts to his children by Keturah?

• • •

3. Fill in the blank: The gifts the people gave to Aaron for his use as high priest became _____ gifts.

4. True or False: Esau kept the gifts Jacob gave to him.

• • •

5. When Elisha refused to take gifts from Naaman, who took the gifts?

• • •

6. Who brought Solomon spices, gold, and precious stones?

• • •

7. Who gave Jesus a gift of very costly perfume?

• • •

8. True or False: When the king made Esther his queen, he proclaimed a Feast of Esther and gave gifts.

• • •

9. On the Feast of Purim, the Jews gave gifts to
   a) each other
   b) God
   c) their servants
   d) the poor

10. Proverbs 6:34–35 says many gifts will not appease whom?
   a) a righteous judge
   b) an evil king
   c) a jealous husband
   d) a greedy child

• • •

11. James 1:17 says every good gift comes from where?

• • •

12. Fill in the blank: Every man is a _____ to one who gives gifts.

• • •

13. True or False: The Bible says that even evil people know how to give good gifts.

• • •

14. Once every year Solomon received tribute from Tarshish that included
   a) apes
   b) peacocks
   c) sheep
   d) a & b

Gifts Answers

1. false; Abraham had sent gifts with the servant to give to Rebekah and her family (Genesis 24:53)

2. because he sent them away from Isaac (Genesis 25:6)

3. holy (Exodus 28:38)

4. true (Genesis 33:11)

5. Gehazi, Elisha's servant (2 Kings 5:20)

6. The queen of Sheba (1 Kings 10:1–2)

7. Mary, sister of Martha and Lazarus (John 12:2–3)

8. true (Esther 2:18)

9. d) the poor (Esther 9:22)

10. c) a jealous husband (Proverbs 6:34–35 niv)

11. above (James 1:17)

12. friend (Proverbs 19:6)

13. true (Matthew 7:11)

14. d) a & b (1 Kings 10:22–23)

GIFTS OF THE SPIRIT

1. In Peter's sermon on the day of Pentecost, what did he offer those who repented and were baptized in Christ's name?

• • •

2. Which gift did Paul say the church at Corinth was misusing?

• • •

3. Fill in the blank: God is not the author of _____ but of peace.

• • •

4. Paul says that the Spirit distributes gifts how?

• • •

5. Fill in the blank: Paul said he preferred the church would _____ rather than speak in tongues.

• • •

6. Fill in the blank: Paul wrote to the Romans: "We have different gifts, according to the _____."

7. According to Paul, those blessed with the gift of generosity should give with
   a) cheerfulness
   b) simplicity
   c) mercy

• • •

8. Fill in the blank: Paul told the Romans those with the gift of prophecy should prophesy "according to the _____."

• • •

9. To what church did Paul send these words: "But one and the same Spirit works all these things, distributing to each one individually as He wills"?

• • •

10. According to Paul, what is the supreme gift of the Spirit to believers?

• • •

11. Put these gifts in the order Paul listed them in 1 Corinthians 12:28 (NKJV):
   - helps
   - varieties of tongues

- teachers
- apostles
- miracles
- prophets
- administrations
- gifts of healing

Gifts of the Spirit Answers

1. The gift of the Holy Spirit (Acts 2:38)
2. speaking in tongues (1 Corinthians 14:2)
3. confusion (1 Corinthians 14:33)
4. as He wills (1 Corinthians 12:11 NKJV)
5. prophesy (1 Corinthians 14:5)
6. grace given to each of us (Romans 12:6 NIV)
7. b) simplicity (Romans 12:8)
8. proportion of faith (Romans 12:6)
9. Corinth (1 Corinthians 12:11 NKJV)

10. love
tongues
administrations, varieties of
gifts of healing, helps,
teachers, miracles,
11. apostles, prophets,

(1 Corinthians 12:31; 13:13)

GLORY OF GOD

1. Psalm 19:1 says, "The
_____ declare the
glory of God "
    a) worlds
    b) nations
    c) heavens
    d) people

• • •

2. Romans 1:23 says man
changed the glory of the
incorruptible God into
    a) an image of corruptible
       man
    b) birds
    c) creeping things
    d) all of the above

• • •

3. When the tabernacle was
finished and the glory of
the Lord filled it, who could

enter the tabernacle?
    a) the high priest
    b) no one
    c) Aaron
    d) Moses

• • •

4. The glory of the Lord
departed from Israel when:
    a) the ark of the covenant
       was taken
    b) they were taken into
       captivity
    c) they refused to go into
       the Promised Land
    d) they lost their battle

• • •

5. When the glory of the
Lord filled the temple
Solomon built, the priests
    a) sacrificed a bull
    b) had to leave
    c) declared a feast
    d) burned incense

• • •

6. According to 1 Chronicles
16:24, we are to declare the
Lord's glory to
    a) all people
    b) each other
    c) the heathen
    d) the nations

7. "For all have sinned, and come short of the glory of God" is found in:
    a) Romans 3:23
    b) Romans 4:23
    c) Romans 5:23
    d) Romans 6:23

• • •

8. John says the people who saw Jesus beheld His glory, which was full of
    a) God's love
    b) God's Spirit
    c) grace and truth
    d) goodness and truth

• • •

9. The last part of the Lord's Prayer says God's glory is
    a) forever
    b) everlasting
    c) eternal
    d) unending

• • •

10. Psalm 24 says that God is the _____ of glory.
    a) Lord
    b) King
    c) Prince
    d) Author

Glory of God Answers

1. c) heavens

2. d) all of the above

3. b) no one (Exodus 40:35)

4. a) the ark of the covenant was taken (1 Samuel 4:17, 22)

5. b) had to leave (1 Kings 8:6, 10–11)

6. c) the heathen

7. a) Romans 3:23

8. c) grace and truth (John 1:14)

9. a) forever (Matthew 6:13)

10. b) King (Psalm 24:10)

GOD'S FAITHFUL

1. Of whom does the Bible say, "In all this _____ sinned not, nor charged God foolishly"?
    a) Nehemiah
    b) Job
    c) John
    d) Moses

2. Shadrach, Meshach, and Abednego were thrown into the fiery furnace because they refused to
   a) pray to the king
   b) bow down to the king's statue
   c) stop praying to their God
   d) all of the above

• • •

3. About whom is the Bible speaking when it says that among men whose thoughts were only evil continually, this person found grace in the eyes of the Lord?
   a) Noah
   b) Abraham
   c) David
   d) Moses

• • •

4. About whom was God speaking when He said, "He has a different spirit in him and has followed Me fully"?
   a) Job
   b) Caleb
   c) David
   d) Moses

5. Which of the following is *not* listed by name in Hebrews 11, God's hall of fame for His faithful?
   a) Abel
   b) Joseph
   c) Rahab
   d) Elijah

• • •

6. About which of Noah's ancestors does the Bible say he "walked with God" and "God took him"?
   a) Seth
   b) Methuselah
   c) Enoch
   d) Lamech

• • •

7. When Abraham proved his faithfulness to God by preparing to sacrifice Isaac, what did God provide as a sacrifice instead?
   a) a lamb
   b) a bullock
   c) a ram
   d) a goat

• • •

8. About whom did Jesus say, "I have not found so great faith, no, not in Israel"?

a) John the Baptist
b) the centurion with the sick servant
c) Jarius
d) the man with the demon-possessed son

•••

9. How many years did Noah spend preparing the ark as God told him?
   a) 10
   b) 50
   c) 75
   d) 100

•••

10. What prophet who devoutly feared God hid one hundred prophets from Jezebel?
   a) Elijah
   b) Elisha
   c) Obadiah
   d) Isaiah

God's Faithful Answers

1. b) Job (Job 1:22)
2. b) bow down to the king's statue (Daniel 3:12)
3. a) Noah (Genesis 6:5, 8)
4. b) Caleb (Numbers 14:24 NKJV)
5. d) Elijah
6. c) Enoch (Genesis 5:24)
7. c) a ram (Genesis 22:13)
8. b) the centurion with the sick servant (Matthew 8:5, 10–14)
9. d) 100 (Genesis 5:32; 7:11)
10. c) Obadiah (1 Kings 18:3–4)

GOD'S HALL OF FAME— HEBREWS 11

(see also Faith, God's Faithful, Righteous People)

1. Who are the only two women mentioned in this list?

•••

2. How many judges from the book of Judges are listed?

3. Who is the first person mentioned in this list?

• • •

4. Who is the last person mentioned by name in this list?

• • •

5. Who has the most written about him on this list?

• • •

6. True or False: Moses' parents are mentioned.

• • •

7. Fill in the blank: God said the world was not _____ of these.

• • •

8. How many people are mentioned by name on this list?

God's Hall of Fame— Hebrews 11 Answers

1. Sarah, Rahab (verses 11, 31)
2. three judges: Gideon, Samson, Jephthah (Barak was not a judge)
3. Abel (verse 4)
4. Samuel (verse 32)
5. Abraham
6. true (verse 23)
7. worthy (verse 38)
8. sixteen people

GOD'S LAW

1. In Matthew 5:17, what did Jesus say He came to do to the Law and the Prophets?

• • •

2. What does Numbers 32:23 say will happen if you sin?

• • •

3. What does Jesus say keeping God's commandments is proof of?

• • •

4. What did God, through His prophet Samuel, say is "better than sacrifice"?

5. On what two command-ments did Jesus say hang all the Law and the Prophets?

• • •

6. What is the first of the Ten Commandments?

• • •

7. How many days are we to labor?

• • •

8. According to the Ten Commandments, what will happen if you honor your father and mother?

• • •

9. What is the first thing listed that we should not covet, per the Ten Commandments?

• • •

10. According to Psalm 19, what of the Lord's are true and righteous?

• • •

11. What did the people think would happen to them if God, instead of Moses, spoke to them?

12. What kind of stone were the Israelites not to use when building an altar?

• • •

13. What psalm mentions the law of the Lord in every verse?

• • •

14. What, according to Psalm 19, are God's laws to be desired more than?

• • •

15. According to Psalm 1:2, what man does God bless?

• • •

16. Where did Moses tell the Israelites they were to write God's commandments?

• • •

17. How long did the unintentional slayer have to stay in the city of refuge?

• • •

18. According to Paul, from what curse has Christ redeemed us?

19. To what food does Psalm 19 compare God's law?

• • •

20. What does Galatians 6:2 say we are to do to fulfill the law of Christ?

• • •

21. What does God promise in Isaiah 58:13–14 to those who keep His Sabbath?

• • •

22. What will we have if, as Joshua 1:8 says, we meditate on the Book of the Law day and night and do all that is in it?

• • •

23. What does Psalm 103:17–18 say is everlasting to those who keep God's covenants?

• • •

24. What does James call the law of the Lord?

• • •

25. For whom does Paul say the law is not intended?

God's Law Answers

1. fulfill them (Matthew 5:17)

2. you will be found out (Numbers 32:23)

3. loving Him (John 14:15)

4. obedience (1 Samuel 15:22)

5. "Thou shalt love the Lord thy God with all thy heart, and with all thy soul, and with all thy mind" and "Thou shalt love thy neighbor as thyself" (Matthew 22:37, 39)

6. "Thou shalt have no other gods before me" (Exodus 20:3)

7. six (Exodus 20:9)

8. your days will be long (Exodus 20:12)

9. neighbor's house (Exodus 20:17)

10. judgments (Psalm 19:9)

11. they would die (Exodus 20:19)

12. hewn stone (Exodus 20:25)

13. Psalm 119

GOD'S LITTLE THINGS

1. Fill in the blank: Because Rahab believed in God and hid the Israelite spies, God told her she would not perish in Jericho if she bound a _____ in her window.
   a) new rope
   b) loom
   c) bundle of straw
   d) scarlet thread

• • •

2. How many stones did David take out of the brook when he went to fight Goliath?
   a) 3
   b) 4
   c) 5
   d) 6

• • •

3. Shamgar was a judge of Israel who used what to slay six hundred Philistines?
   a) an ox goad
   b) the jawbone of an ass
   c) a sling
   d) a shepherd's staff
4. To show that Aaron was

14. much fine gold (Psalm 19:10)
15. one whose delight is in the law of the Lord (Psalm 1:2)
16. on their doorposts (Deuteronomy 6:9)
17. until he stood before the congregation for judgment and until the death of the one who was high priest at that time (Joshua 20:6)
18. curse of the law (Galatians 3:13)
19. honey (Psalm 19:7–10)
20. bear one another's burdens (Galatians 6:2)
21. they would find joy in the Lord (Isaiah 58:13–14)
22. a prosperous way and good success (Joshua 1:8)
23. His mercy (Psalm 103:17–18)
24. the perfect law of liberty (James 1:25)
25. the righteous (1 Timothy 1:9)

His choice for high priest,
God made Aaron's rod
   a) longer
   b) shorter
   c) turn into a snake
   d) blossom

• • •

5. Samson used what to slay a
thousand of Israel's enemies?
   a) an ox goad
   b) donkey's jawbone
   c) a sling
   d) a shepherd's staff

• • •

6. When a prophet's widow
needed money to save her
sons, Elisha multiplied her
last pot of
   a) oil
   b) corn
   c) meal
   d) wheat

• • •

7. When Jesus needed to pay
the temple tax, He directed
Peter to find a coin where?
   a) in a nearby field
   b) in the mouth of a fish
   c) in the middle of the road
   d) in a tree

8. When the poor widow
gave her two mites, she gave
   a) what the temple
     required
   b) money that she had
     found
   c) all she had
   d) what the priest told her
     to give

• • •

9. When Moses asked the
people to bring offerings for
the making of the tabernacle,
they brought gold
   a) bracelets
   b) earrings
   c) rings
   d) all of the above

• • •

10. When Elisha succeeded
Elijah, what did he receive
of Elijah's as a symbol of his
succession?
   a) a mantle
   b) a rod
   c) a ring
   d) a robe

God's Little Things Answers

1. d) scarlet thread
(Joshua 2:18)

2. c) 5 (1 Samuel 17:40)

3. a) an ox goad
(Judges 3:31)

4. d) blossom
(Numbers 17:1–8)

5. b) a donkey's jawbone
(Judges 15:16)

6. a) oil (2 Kings 4:1–7)

7. b) in the mouth of a fish
(Matthew 17:24–27)

8. c) all she had
(Mark 12:42–44)

9. d) all of the above
(Exodus 35:5, 21–22)

10. a) a mantle
(2 Kings 2:9–13)

GOD'S WORD

1. There is one psalm in the Bible in which each verse contains a reference to God's Word as His law. That psalm is
   a) Psalm 1
   b) Psalm 19
   c) Psalm 23
   d) Psalm 119

• • •

2. In the parable of the sower, the Word of God is likened to
   a) the sower
   b) fertilizer
   c) the seed
   d) the receptive ground

• • •

3. In the list of the armor of God in Ephesians 6, the Word of God is the
   a) breastplate
   b) helmet
   c) shield
   d) sword

4. Which Gospel begins by saying the Word was in the beginning with God and was God?

   a) Matthew

   b) Mark

   c) Luke

   d) John

...

5. Hebrews 4:12 says the Word of God is

   a) quick

   b) powerful

   c) sharper than a two-edged sword

   d) all of the above

...

6. Jeremiah 23:29 says the Word of God is like a

   a) fire

   b) hammer

   c) rock

   d) a & b

...

7. Hebrews 11:3 says something was framed by the Word of God. What was it?

   a) the worlds

   b) the heavens

   c) mankind

   d) all of the above

8. Psalm 119:105 says the Word of God is a

   a) river

   b) lamp

   c) rock

   d) path

...

9. The Bible says that the Word became flesh and

   a) came to die

   b) dwelt among us

   c) came to earth

   d) was rejected

...

10. God said that when His Word goes out, it will not return

   a) void

   b) again

   c) ever

   d) to heaven

God's Word Answers

1. d) Psalm 119

2. c) the seed (Luke 8:11)

3. d) sword (Ephesians 6:17)

4. d) John (John 1:1)
(Hebrews 4:12)

5. d) all of the above
(Jeremiah 23:29)

6. d) a & b
(Hebrews 11:3)

7. a) the worlds

8. b) lamp (Psalm 119:105)
(John 1:14)

9. b) dwelt among us

10. a) void (Isaiah 55:11)

GRACE

(see also Faith)

God's
Riches
At
Christ's
Expense

1. Fill in the blank: Ephesians 2:8 says grace is the _____ of God.

2. To whom was Paul speaking when he said grace came through the kindness and love of God?

• • •

3. Who found grace in the eyes of the Lord?

• • •

4. Who became strong in spirit, filled with wisdom, and the grace of God was upon him?

• • •

5. Fill in the blank: John said Jesus was full of grace and _____.

• • •

6. In Acts 4:33, whom was great grace upon?

• • •

7. How is each one of us given grace?

• • •

8. Fill in the blanks: Grace allows us to "serve God acceptably with reverence and _____ _____."

9. Fill in the blank: Peter tells us to grow in grace and _____ of our Lord and Savior Jesus Christ.

Grace Answers

1. gift (Ephesians 2:8)

2. Titus (Titus 3:4, 7)

3. Noah (Genesis 6:8)

4. Jesus (Luke 2:40)

5. truth (John 1:14)

6. the apostles

7. according to the measure of Christ's gift (Ephesians 4:7)

8. godly fear (Hebrews 12:28 NKJV)

9. knowledge (2 Peter 3:18)

H

HARVEST

(see also Crops)

1. Who said, "While the earth remains, seedtime and harvest. . .shall not cease"?

• • •

2. What book of the Bible contains this verse: "A time to plant, and a time to pluck what is planted"?

• • •

3. Fill in the blank: "The harvest is past, the summer is ended, and we are not _____!"

• • •

4. Who said, "The harvest truly is plentiful, but the laborers are few"?

• • •

5. What are we to ask the Lord of the harvest to do?

• • •

6. Fill in the blank: The fields are already _____ for harvest.

Harvest Answers

1. God (Genesis 8:22)

2. Ecclesiastes (Ecclesiastes 3:2 nkjv)

3. saved (Jeremiah 8:20 nkjv)

4. Jesus (Matthew 9:37 nkjv)

5. send out laborers (Matthew 9:38)

6. white (John 4:35)

HEALING

1. Whom did Jesus heal in Capernaum, from a distance?

• • •

2. Why was the lame man Jesus healed by the pool near the Sheep Gate criticized by the Jews?

• • •

3. When ten lepers approached Jesus for healing, what instructions did He give them?

4. What did Jesus say when He healed the woman who had suffered with a crooked back for eighteen years?

• • •

5. What did Naaman have to do to be healed?

• • •

6. About whom was Moses speaking when he said, "Please heal her, O God, I pray!"

• • •

7. Which disciple had a mother-in-law whom Jesus healed?

• • •

8. What of Jesus' did a woman with an issue of blood touch, hoping to be healed?

• • •

9. True or False: Jesus' disciples couldn't heal a demon-possessed boy.

• • •

10. What was the name of the pool where Jesus healed the paralyzed man?

11. What was wrong with the man whose friends let him down through the roof?

• • •

12. How many friends were there in question 11?

Healing Answers

1. a nobleman's son (John 4:46, 50–53)

2. he was carrying his bed on the Sabbath (John 5:8–10)

3. "Go shew yourselves unto the priests" (Luke 17:12–14)

4. "Woman, thou art loosed from thine infirmity" (Luke 13:11–13)

5. wash in the Jordan River seven times (2 Kings 5:10)

6. Miriam (Numbers 12:10–13 NKJV)

7. Peter (Matthew 8:14–15)

8. the hem of his garment (Matthew 9:20)

9. true (Matthew 17:16)

10. Bethesda (John 5:2)

11. he was paralyzed (Mark 2:3)

12. four friends (Mark 2:3)

g. Esther 2:16
h. Ezekiel 8:14
i. Exodus 13:4
j. Nehemiah 2:1

HEBREW CALENDAR

Match the month of the Hebrew calendar to the Bible verse that mentions it:

1. Zif
2. Nisan
3. Abib
4. Sivan
5. Tammuz
6. Elul
7. Ethanim
8. Bul
9. Tebeth
10. Adar

• • •

a. Nehemiah 6:15
b. Esther 8:9
c. 1 Kings 6:1
d. Esther 9:21
e. 1 Kings 6:38
f. 1 Kings 8:2

Hebrew Calendar Answers

1. c
2. j
3. i
4. b
5. h
6. a
7. f
8. e
9. g
10. d

HELL

1. Who provoked God to the point where He said the fire of His anger would burn in the lowest hell?

2. Who said, "Hell is naked before Him"?

• • •

3. Who said, "The wicked shall be turned into hell"?

• • •

4. True or False: The psalmist said God is with us even in hell.

• • •

5. Whose house does Proverbs say is the way to hell?

• • •

6. True or False: The Bible says hell has gates.

• • •

7. Fill in the blank: Mark 9:44 says that in hell the _____ never dies and _____ is never quenched.

• • •

8. Of whom was David speaking in Psalm 16:10 when he said, "You will not leave my soul in hell"?

9. True or False: The Bible says that hell has keys.

• • •

10. Fill in the blank: When death and hell are cast into the lake of fire, the apostle John says this is the second _____.

Hell Answers:

1. the Israelites (Deuteronomy 32:21–23)

2. Job (Job 26:6)

3. David (Psalm 9:17 NKJV)

4. true (Psalm 139:8)

5. the immoral woman (Proverbs 7:5, 27 NKJV)

6. true (Matthew 16:18)

7. worm, fire (Mark 9:43)

8. Jesus (Acts 2:25–27)

9. true (Revelation 1:18)

10. death (Revelation 20:14)

HERBS AND SPICES

*Can that which is unsavoury
be eaten without salt?
or is there any taste in
the white of an egg?*
JOB 6:6 KJV

1. Who was turned into a pillar of salt?

• • •

2. True or False: When a conqueror wanted to ruin the place he conquered, he sowed the land with salt.

• • •

3. Jesus said that the Pharisees tithed even their spices—mint, anise, and cummin—but neglected what?

4. Which two Gospels say the women brought spices to Jesus' tomb?

• • •

5. What feast was associated with bitter herbs?

6. To what is the writer of Song of Solomon comparing his spouse when he lists the following spices: saffron, cinnamon, frankincense?

• • •

7. What spice mixed with wine was offered to Jesus on the cross?

• • •

8. What spicy herb did the complaining Israelites recall from their years of slavery in Egypt?

Herbs and Spices Answers

1. Lot's wife (Genesis 19:26)

2. true (Judges 9:45)

3. the weightier matters of the law: justice, mercy, faith (Matthew 23:23)

4. Mark and Luke (Mark 16:1; Luke 24:1)

5. Passover (Exodus 12:8)

6. a garden (Song of Solomon 4:12–14)

7. myrrh (Mark 15:23)

8. garlic (Numbers 11:4–8)

HEROD

Herod was a title like Caesar or Pharaoh. There are several Herods mentioned in the New Testament. The Herod mentioned in connection with Jesus and John the Baptist is not the same Herod mentioned in Acts.

1. When Herod was harassing the church, which of Jesus' disciples did he kill with a sword?

• • •

2. Why did John the Baptist preach against Herod?

• • •

3. Who was the woman in Herod's life?

• • •

4. Who did Herod think Jesus was?

5. What prophecy did Herod fulfill when Jesus was a baby?

• • •

6. What was the occasion when Herod agreed to behead John the Baptist?

• • •

7. Who actually asked for John the Baptist to be beheaded?

• • •

8. What did that person do with the head of John the Baptist?

• • •

9. What was Herod's title as a ruler?

• • •

10. What happened when Herod allowed the people to say his was the voice of a god and not a man?

Herod Answers

1. James, the brother of John
(Acts 12:1–2)

2. Herod was living with his
brother Philip's wife
(Mark 6:18)

3. Herodias (Mark 6:17)

4. John the Baptist come
back to life (Mark 6:14)

5. he had all the male
children in Bethlehem killed
(Matthew 2:14–18)

6. Herod's birthday
(Matthew 14:6)

7. Herodias's daughter
(Matthew 14:6–8)

8. gave it to her mother
(Matthew 14:11)

9. tetrarch (Luke 3:1 NKJV)

10. an angel struck him and
he was eaten by worms and
died (Acts 12:23)

HOLY

(see also Unholy)

1. God says we are to be holy
because...?

• • •

2. In heaven, who never
ceases day and night to say,
"Holy, holy, holy, Lord God
Almighty"?
   a) angels
   b) the four living creatures
   c) the saved
   d) Jesus

• • •

3. What shepherd was God
speaking to when He said,
"The place where you stand
is holy ground"?

• • •

4. Which of the Ten
Commandments contains
the word "holy"?

• • •

5. In order to be able to
distinguish between holy
and unholy things, what
were the Israelites NOT to

do when they went into the tabernacle?
  a) wear their shoes
  b) drink wine
  c) talk
  d) eat food

•••

6. Fill in the blank: Psalm 48:1 says God is greatly to be praised in His holy _____.

•••

7. Fill in the blank: Hebrews 9:24 says that Christ has not entered holy places made with _____.

Holy Answers

1. He is holy (1 Peter 1:16)

2. b) the four living creatures (Revelation 4:8)

3. Moses (Exodus 3:5 NKJV)

4. the fourth: "Remember the Sabbath day" (Exodus 20:8)

5. b) drink wine (Leviticus 10:9)

6. mountain (Psalm 48:1)

7. hands (Hebrews 9:24 NKJV)

HOLY SPIRIT

1. In Genesis 1:2, what was the Spirit of the Lord doing?

•••

2. Who tried to buy the gifts of the Holy Spirit?

•••

3. What name did Jesus use for the Holy Spirit?

•••

4. After Pentecost, how did the apostles impart the Holy Spirit?

•••

5. Through the laying on of whose hands did Timothy receive the Holy Spirit?

•••

6. What did Jesus tell the disciples that the Holy Spirit would specifically do?

7. On what New Testament occasion were the Holy Spirit, God the Father, and Jesus all present at the same time?

• • •

8. How did the Holy Spirit empower Moses' seventy elders?

• • •

9. What does 1 Corinthians 2:12 say that the Holy Spirit is not the spirit of?

• • •

10. The Holy Spirit bears witness with us that we are what to God?

• • •

11. What does God say in Genesis 6:3 that His Spirit will not always do?

• • •

12. What are five symbols of the Holy Spirit?

• • •

13. According to the prophet Joel, what would the Holy Spirit enable young men and young women to do?

14. Using Paul's belt (or "girdle"), what message from the Holy Spirit did Agabus give Paul?

• • •

15. According to Paul, what will we not fulfill if we walk in the Spirit?

• • •

16. What does Romans 8:26 say that the Holy Spirit does for us?

• • •

17. According to Acts 8:39, what did the Holy Spirit do with Philip?

• • •

18. What three things did Paul tell Timothy that God has given us, as opposed to a spirit of fear?

• • •

19. How do those who do not have God's Spirit consider the things of God?

20. What did Jesus do to the disciples, after His resurrection, before He gave them His Spirit?

• • •

21. According to Paul, in whom have we been marked with a seal?

• • •

22. According to Paul, for what four things are the Holy Spirit–inspired scriptures profitable?

• • •

23. What should we not do to the Holy Spirit?

• • •

24. According to Paul, how should we endeavor to keep the unity of the Spirit?

• • •

25. According to John, what does the Holy Spirit help us do?

• • •

26. What was the first immediate effect on Jesus'

disciples upon receiving the Holy Spirit?

Holy Spirit Answers

1. moving upon the face of the waters (Genesis 1:2)

2. Simon the sorcerer (Acts 8:18–19)

3. Comforter (kjv), Advocate (niv) (John 15:26)

4. by the laying on of hands (Acts 8:17)

5. Paul (2 Timothy 1:6)

6. abide with them forever (John 14:15–17)

7. Jesus' baptism (Matthew 3:16–17)

8. they prophesied (Numbers 11:25)

9. this world (1 Corinthians 2:12)

10. His children (Romans 8:16)

11. strive with men (Genesis 6:3)

12. water (John 7:38–39), wind (John 3:8), seal (Ephesians 1:13), dove (Matthew 3:16), fire (Acts 2:3)

13. see visions, prophesy (Joel 2:28–32; Acts 2:16–21)

14. that Paul would be bound by the Jews in Jerusalem and delivered to the Gentiles (Acts 21:11)

15. the lust of the flesh (Galatians 5:16)

16. makes intercession for us (Romans 8:26)

17. caught him away (Acts 8:39)

18. power, love, and a sound mind (2 Timothy 1:7)

19. as foolishness (1 Corinthians 2:14)

20. He breathed on them (John 20:22)

21. the promised Holy Spirit (Ephesians 1:13)

22. doctrine, reproof, correction, instruction in righteousness (2 Timothy 3:16)

23. quench Him (1 Thessalonians 5:19)

24. with the bond of peace (Ephesians 4:3)

25. test the spirits (1 John 4:1–3)

26. they began to speak in different languages (tongues) (Acts 1:13; 2:4)

HONEY/ HONEYCOMB

When Jesus appeared to His disciples after His resurrection and they couldn't believe it was really Him, He ate some broiled fish and some honeycomb to prove to them that He was real (Luke 24:41–43).

1. True or False: There is a story in the Bible about honey in a lion's carcass.

• • •

2. What does the psalmist say is sweeter than honey and the honeycomb?

• • •

3. True or False: The second time Joseph's brothers went down to Egypt, they brought Joseph honey.

4. What land was flowing with milk and honey?

• • •

5. True or False: Manna tasted like honey.

• • •

6. Honey was not to be used in any offering
a) at all
b) made by fire
c) that involved meats
d) none of the above

• • •

7. What does the song of Moses in Deuteronomy 32 say God would draw honey from?
a) a tree
b) a beehive
c) a rock
d) a plant

• • •

8. When King Saul commanded his hungry army not to eat some honey they found, who ate it anyway?
a) all his army
b) Jonathan

c) their enemies
d) Saul ate it himself

• • •

9. Fill in the blank: Honey drips from the _____ of an immoral woman.

• • •

10. What does Proverbs 16:24 say are like honeycomb?

• • •

11. What did God command Ezekiel to eat that Ezekiel said tasted like honey in sweetness?

• • •

12. Who was described as eating locusts and wild honey?

• • •

13. What did the apostle John eat that was as sweet as honey in his mouth but made his stomach bitter?

Honey/Honeycomb Answers

1. true (Judges 14:8)
2. the law of the Lord (Psalm 19:7–10)
3. true (Genesis 43:11)
4. the Promised Land (Exodus 3:8)
5. true (Exodus 16:31)
6. b) made by fire (Leviticus 2:11)
7. c) a rock (Deuteronomy 32:13)
8. b) Jonathan (1 Samuel 14:25–29)
9. lips (Proverbs 5:3)
10. pleasant words (Proverbs 16:24)
11. a scroll (Ezekiel 3:3)
12. John the Baptist (Matthew 3:4)
13. a little book (Revelation 10:9)

HONOR

Now unto the King eternal, immortal, invisible, the only wise God, be honour and glory for ever and ever. Amen.
1 TIMOTHY 1:17

1. "Honor thy father and mother" is the first commandment to contain what?

• • •

2. Who is without honor in his own country?

• • •

3. In addition to honor, what other two things do the living creatures in heaven give to Him who sits on the throne?
   a) wisdom and power
   b) glory and thanks
   c) strength and beauty
   d) love and glory

• • •

4. True or False: When the king told Haman that he delighted to honor someone, Haman knew the king meant Mordecai.

5. Fill in the blank: Psalm 96:6 says honor and _____ are before the Lord.

. . .

6. True or False: Psalm 66:2 says we are to sing out the honor of God's name.

. . .

7. Fill in the blank: Proverbs 15:33 says that before honor is _____.

. . .

8. Fill in the blank: According to Peter, we are to honor all _____.

Honor Answers

1. a promise (Ephesians 6:1–3)

2. a prophet (Matthew 13:57)

3. b) glory and thanks (Revelation 4:9)

4. false (Esther 6:6)

5. majesty (Psalm 96:6)

6. true (Psalm 66:2)

7. humility (Proverbs 15:33 NKJV)

8. people (1 Peter 2:17 NKJV)

HOPE

(see also Faith, Love)

Why art thou cast down, O my soul? and why art thou disquieted within me? hope thou in God: for I shall yet praise him, who is the health of my countenance, and my God.
PSALM 42:11

1. Fill in the blank: For surely there is a _____ and your hope will not be cut off.

. . .

2. There is more hope for a fool than a
a) drunkard
b) man wise in his own eyes
c) slothful man
d) man caught in a woman's net

3. It is good that one should hope and wait quietly for what?

• • •

4. Fill in the blank: Paul said hope does not _____.

• • •

5. Fill in the blank: Hope that is _____ is not hope.

• • •

6. Fill in the blank: Paul's definition of hope is "eagerly awaiting with _____."

• • •

7. True or False: In Paul's list of seven "ones" in Ephesians 4:4–6, hope is not listed.

• • •

8. Fill in the blank: Christ in you, the hope of _____.

• • •

9. Paul says we are to wear the hope of salvation as a
   a) breastplate
   b) girdle
   c) helmet
   d) shield

10. Fill in the blank: Peter says our hope is a _____ hope.

Hope Answers

1. hereafter (Proverbs 23:18)
2. b) man wise in his own eyes (Proverbs 26:12)
3. the salvation of the Lord (Lamentations 3:26)
4. disappoint (Romans 5:5)
5. seen (Romans 8:24)
6. perseverance (Romans 8:25)
7. false
8. glory (Colossians 1:27)
9. c) helmet (1 Thessalonians 5:8)
10. living (1 Peter 1:3 NKJV)

HUMBLING EXPERIENCES

(see also Punishments)

Wherefore let him that thinketh he standeth take heed lest he fall.
1 CORINTHIANS 10:12 KJV

1. To whom was the prophet Nathan speaking when he pointed out this king's sin with the words, "Thou art the man"?
   a) Saul
   b) David
   c) Solomon
   d) Jeroboam

• • •

2. The king who threw Daniel into the lions' den couldn't change the bad law that he had passed because
   a) he didn't want to
   b) the people who tricked him into it wouldn't let him
   c) he thought it would make him look weak
   d) the law of his land said he couldn't

3. Jesus told Peter that he would deny Him three times before the cock crowed how many times?
   a) 1
   b) 2
   c) 3
   d) 4

• • •

4. Moses wasn't allowed to go into the Promised Land because
   a) he was too old
   b) he didn't want to
   c) he let the people turn away when they first got there
   d) he struck the rock for water instead of speaking to it

• • •

5. When Miriam spoke against Moses, she was struck with leprosy for
   a) 40 days
   b) 7 days
   c) the rest of her life
   d) 1 year

6. Who thought the king was going to honor him and instead ended up having to honor his worst enemy?
   a) Haman
   b) Mordecai
   c) Absalom
   d) Ahab

• • •

7. Why did the Lord finally reject Saul from being king?
   a) Saul prophesied with the prophets
   b) Saul tried to kill David
   c) Saul rejected the word of the Lord
   d) Saul went to the witch of Endor

• • •

8. When Elisha's servant lied to Naaman and took gifts from him, the servant was struck with
   a) blindness
   b) deafness
   c) muteness
   d) Naaman's leprosy

• • •

9. When Nebuchadnezzar claimed glory instead of giving the glory to God, he became mad and
   a) tore his clothes
   b) lived like a wild animal
   c) lived in a cave
   d) b & c

• • •

10. When Herod allowed the people to say that his voice was the voice of a god, the angel of the Lord struck him
   a) blind
   b) deaf
   c) mute
   d) dead

Humbling Experiences Answers

1. b) David (2 Samuel 12:7)

2. d) the law of his land said he couldn't (Daniel 6:7–15)

3. b) 2 (Mark 14:72)

4. d) he struck the rock for water instead of speaking to it (Numbers 20:7–12)

5. b) 7 days (Numbers 12:1–2, 14–15)

6. a) Haman (Esther 6:6–11)

(answers, printed upside-down)

7. c) Saul rejected the word
of the Lord
(1 Samuel 15:26)

8. d) Naaman's leprosy
(2 Kings 5:20–27)

9. b) lived like a wild animal
(Daniel 4:24–25, 30–33)

10. d) dead (Acts 12:20–23)

HUSBANDS

(see also Wives)

Adam was the only man who went to sleep single and woke up married.

1. How did Isaac meet Rebekah?

• • •

2. Where did Isaac take Rebekah when he met her?
   a) to her home
   b) to his tent
   c) to his mother, Sarah's, tent
   d) to Abraham's tent

3. Who was Bathsheba's first husband?

• • •

4. Who was Naomi's husband?

• • •

5. True or False: Peter was married.

• • •

6. Who was Hannah's husband?
   a) Ezekiel
   b) Elkanah
   c) Elijah
   d) Eleazar

• • •

7. Which prophet did God tell to take a wife of harlotry?
   a) Hosea
   b) Joel
   c) Amos
   d) Obadiah

• • •

8. True or False: Elisha was married.

9. True or False: Moses had two wives.

• • •

10. Lapidoth was the husband of a
   a. prophetess
   b. judge
   c. harlot
   d. a & b

Husbands Answers

1. Abraham's servant brought her to him (Genesis 24:64–65)

2. c) to his mother, Sarah's, tent (Genesis 24:67)

3. Uriah (2 Samuel 11:3)

4. Elimelech (Ruth 1:1–2)

5. True (Luke 4:38)

6. b) Elkanah (1 Samuel 1:1–2)

7. a) Hosea (Hosea 1:2)

8. false

9. true (not at the same time) (Exodus 2:21; Numbers 12:1)

10. d) a & b (Judges 4:4–5)

I

IDOLS

And the man Micah had an house of gods, and made an ephod, and teraphim, and consecrated one of his sons, who became his priest.
JUDGES 17:5

1. Besides Aaron, who else made golden calves for Israel to worship?

• • •

2. In the list of the Ten Commandments, what number is the commandment to have no graven images?

• • •

3. Hezekiah destroyed what popular idol?
   a) the brass snake Moses made in the wilderness
   b) the golden calf Aaron made
   c) Baal
   d) Ashtaroth

4. What idol of the Philistines fell facedown in front of the ark of the covenant?
   a) Molech
   b) Chemosh
   c) Beelzebub
   d) Dagon

• • •

5. Into what did King Josiah transform the places of idolatry?
   a) cemeteries
   b) meadows
   c) wastelands
   d) potters' fields

• • •

6. When Jacob was leaving Laban, which one of Jacob's family members stole Laban's idols?

• • •

7. What were men building when God confused their speech and language?
   a) an altar
   b) a tower
   c) a castle
   d) a temple

8. True or False: Some of the graven images people worshipped were made of wood.

• • •

9. True or False: Ahab, king of Israel, had his own graven image.

• • •

10. What happened to the golden calf Aaron made?

• • •

11. The only mention of an idol in the New Testament is the goddess Diana, whose shrine was in what city?
    a) Philippi
    b) Macedonia
    c) Ephesus
    d) Colosse

• • •

12. What was the name of the silversmith who made shrines of Diana and started a riot to get rid of Paul?
    a) Demas
    b) Diotrephes
    c) Demetrius
    d) Dumah

13. True or False: The worshippers of Diana thought her image fell down from Zeus.

• • •

14. Fill in the blank: Jeremiah said that the people had become _____ with their idols.

• • •

15. Zechariah said that idols speak
    a) falsely
    b) not at all
    c) delusion
    d) truth

• • •

16. The Corinthian church was divided over what having to do with idols?

• • •

17. Who said, "Little children, keep yourselves from idols"?

• • •

18. Fill in the blank: Revelation 9:20 says that idols can neither _____ nor _____ nor _____.

Idols Answers

1. Jeroboam
(1 Kings 12:25–29)

2. two (Exodus 20:4)

3. a) the brass snake Moses
made in the wilderness
(2 Kings 18:1, 4)
(1 Samuel 5:1–3)

4. d) Dagon
(2 Kings 23:13–14)

5. a) cemeteries

6. Rachel (Genesis 31:34)

7. b) a tower (Genesis 11:4–9)
(2 Chronicles 24:18 NKJV)

8. true

9. true (1 Kings 16:33)

10. it was burned, ground to
powder, mixed with water,
and the people were forced
to drink it (Exodus 32:20)
(Acts 19:24–28)

11. c) Ephesus
(Acts 19:24)

12. c) Demetrius

13. true (Acts 19:35)

14. insane
(Jeremiah 50:38 NKJV)

15. c) delusion
(Zechariah 10:2 NKJV)

16. eating meat offered to
idols (1 Corinthians 10:28)

17. John (1 John 5:21)

18. see, hear, walk
(Revelation 9:20)

IMAGE OF GOD

*And God said,
Let us make man in our
image, after our likeness.*
GENESIS 1:26

1. Hebrews 1:3 says that Jesus
is the express image of what?

• • •

2. Romans 8:29 says we
are to be conformed to the
image of who?

• • •

3. Who said, "Man is the
image and glory of God"?

• • •

4. To whom was Jesus speaking when He said, "He who
has seen Me has seen the
Father"?

5. Fill in the blank: "Who, being in the form of God, did not consider it _____ to be equal with God."

• • •

6. Fill in the blank: Psalm 139:14 says, "I am _____ and _____ made."

• • •

7. Who said, "In Him we live and move and have our being"?

Image of God Answers

1. His person (Hebrews 1:3)

2. God's Son (Romans 8:29)

3. Paul (1 Corinthians 11:7)

4. Philip (John 14:8–9 NKJV)

5. robbery (Philippians 2:6 NKJV)

6. fearfully, wonderfully (Psalm 139:14 NKJV)

7. Paul (Acts 17:28 NKJV)

J

JACOB AND ESAU

1. The Bible says that Esau sold Jacob his birthright because he thought
   a) Jacob was entitled to it
   b) he would die from hunger and would have no use for it
   c) Isaac favored Jacob and would deny the birthright to Esau
   d) Jacob would eventually return his rights to him

• • •

2. What did Jacob use to purchase Esau's birthright?

• • •

3. What did Jacob wear to make his father, whose eyes were dim with age, think he was hairy like Esau?

• • •

4. God promised Jacob that
   a) he would be the father of kings
   b) all who hated him would be cursed
   c) he would have seven hundred wives
   d) he would be greater than Abraham

• • •

5. True or False: Jacob was renamed Israel.

• • •

6. Where can you find Esau's story in the Bible?

• • •

7. Who was Esau's mother?

• • •

8. Esau liked to
   a) sail
   b) fish
   c) study the Torah
   d) hunt

• • •

9. True or False: When he took his first wife, Esau pleased his parents by choosing a godly woman who strengthened his faith in the one true God.

• • •

10. After Jacob stole Esau's blessing, Isaac blessed Esau by saying

a) Esau would serve his brother, asserting his independence from time to time
b) God would grant him riches
c) Esau's faith would soon grow
d) Jacob would pay for his duplicity by serving him

• • •

11. True or False: Although at first Esau was angry with Jacob for stealing his birthright and blessing, he did not let the sun set on his anger.

• • •

12. What did Esau do when he saw that Jacob was obedient to Isaac by marrying women from their extended family?

• • •

13. How many men did Esau have with him when he reunited with Jacob?

• • •

14. True or False: As soon as Jacob saw Esau, he drew his sword.

15. When Esau saw Jacob, he
a) drew his sword
b) ran toward him and kissed him
c) instructed his men to kill Jacob
d) demanded recompense for Jacob's deceit

• • •

16. Jacob called himself Esau's
a) servant
b) master
c) brother
d) kinsman

• • •

17. What did Esau initially say about Jacob's gifts?

• • •

18. Fill in the blank: "So Esau returned that day on his way unto _____."

• • •

19. True or False: Isaac died before his twin sons were reconciled.

Jacob and Esau
Answers

1. b) he would die from hunger and would have no use for it (Genesis 25:32)

2. a bowl of pottage/bean soup (Genesis 25:31, 34)

3. the skins of goat kids (Genesis 27:16)

4. a) he would be the father of kings (Genesis 35:11–12)

5. true (Genesis 32:27–28; 35:9–10)

6. Genesis 25–36

7. Rebekah, Isaac's wife (Genesis 25:20–26)

8. d) hunt (Genesis 25:27)

9. false (Genesis 26:34–35)

10. a) Esau would serve his brother, asserting his independence from time to time (Genesis 27:40)

11. false; Esau planned to kill Jacob soon after their father died (Genesis 27:41)

12. he married a descendant of Ishmael (Genesis 28:9)

13. four hundred (Genesis 33:1)

14. false; he bowed seven times (Genesis 33:3)

15. b) ran toward him and kissed him (Genesis 33:4)

16. a) servant (Genesis 33:5); he also called him "my lord" (Genesis 33:8, 14–15)

17. he didn't want to accept them, protesting he had enough (Genesis 33:9)

18. Seir (Genesis 33:16)

19. false; they both buried him (Genesis 35:28–29)

JEREMIAH

Then I said, I will not make mention of [God], nor speak any more in his name. But his word was in mine heart as a burning fire shut up in my bones, and I was weary with forbearing, and I could not stay.
JEREMIAH 20:9

1. True or False: God told Jeremiah that He had ordained him before he was born.

• • •

2. True or False: Jeremiah's family supported his ministry.

• • •

3. When the priests and prophets tried to kill Jeremiah, who saved him?

• • •

4. Whom did the Lord put to death because he spoke against Jeremiah and the Lord?
    a) the king of Israel
    b) a false prophet
    c) a foreign king
    d) Jeremiah's servant

5. What happened after the king burned the scroll of God's word?

• • •

6. Where did the captains of the remnant of Judah take Jeremiah when the Babylonians conquered Israel?

Jeremiah Answers

1. true (Jeremiah 1:5)

2. false (Jeremiah 12:6)

3. the princes and the people (Jeremiah 26:16)

4. b) a false prophet (Jeremiah 28:11–17)

5. Jeremiah wrote another one with added words (Jeremiah 36:32)

6. Egypt (Jeremiah 43:5–7)

JESUS

1. Who was promised that he would not die until he saw the Messiah come?

•••

2. When someone called Jesus "good Master," what did Jesus reply?

•••

3. Who was Caesar when Jesus was born?

•••

4. Why was Jesus in Jerusalem when He got separated from His parents?

•••

5. How long did Jesus' parents search before they found Him?

•••

6. Who are the five women mentioned in Jesus' genealogy in Matthew 1?

•••

7. From what mountain did Jesus talk about the end times?

8. What did the people shout when Jesus rode into Jerusalem on Palm Sunday?

•••

9. When the chief priests and elders demanded to know by what authority Jesus taught, what question did Jesus use to confound them?

•••

10. According to Paul, how was Jesus in the wilderness with Moses and the children of Israel?

•••

11. How many days had Lazarus lain in the tomb before Jesus arrived at the site?

•••

12. How did Pilate's wife describe Jesus?

•••

13. When Jesus sent forth His twelve disciples the first time, what did He give them the power and authority to do?

14. Which of the following are not ancestors of Jesus?
- Jeconiah
- Salmon
- Zerubbabel
- Jeroboam
- Saul
- Aminadab
- Hezekiah
- Daniel
- Obed

...

15. Did Jesus ever sing?

...

16. Fill in the blank: John said Jesus was full of grace and _____.

...

17. What did Paul say should happen at the name of Jesus?

...

18. What are the four ways Luke says the young boy Jesus grew?

...

19. In John 14:6, what three things did Jesus say He is?

20. When Satan tempted Jesus, what is the one place he didn't take Him?
a) wilderness
b) sea
c) a mountain
d) the temple

Jesus Answers

1. Simeon (Luke 2:25–26)
2. "There is none good but... God" (Mark 10:18)
3. Augustus (Luke 2:1)
4. for the Feast of Passover (Luke 2:41)
5. three days (Luke 2:46)
6. Tamar, Rahab, Ruth, Bathsheba (Uriah's wife), Mary (Matthew 1 NIV)
7. Mount of Olives (Matthew 24:3)
8. "Hosanna to the son of David: Blessed is He that cometh in the name of the Lord" (Matthew 21:9)
9. "The baptism of John, whence was it? from heaven, or of men?" (Matthew 21:24–25)

JESUS SAYS, "I AM"

Jesus used the expression "I am" a lot.

1. What phrase completes Jesus' statement beginning "I am meek. . ."?

• • •

2. When asked directly, "Whom say ye that I am?" how did Peter reply?

• • •

3. How does Jesus' promise "I am with you always" end?
   a) "and My peace I leave with you."
   b) "even unto the end of the world"
   c) "for where I go you cannot come"
   d) "until we drink together in my Father's kingdom"

• • •

4. Fill in the blank: I am the light of the world: he that followeth me shall not walk in darkness, but shall have the light of _____.

10. as the spiritual Rock that followed them (1 Corinthians 10:4)

11. four days (John 11:17)

12. a just or innocent man (Matthew 27:19)

13. power and authority over all demons and to cure diseases (Luke 9:1)

14. Jeroboam, Saul, Daniel (Matthew 1 NKJV)

15. yes (Matthew 26:30)

16. truth (John 1:14)

17. every knee should bow (Philippians 2:10)

18. in wisdom, in stature, in favor with God and man (Luke 2:52)

19. way, truth, life

20. b) sea (Matthew 4:1–11)

5. How did Jesus reply when His critics said that He was under fifty years old and could not have seen Abraham?

...

6. In speaking of sheep, how did Jesus describe Himself?
   a) "I am come that they might have life"
   b) "I am the door of the sheep"
   c) "I am the good shepherd"
   d) all of the above

...

7. True or False: Jesus said, "I am the resurrection, and the life" while speaking to Martha about her brother Lazarus who had died.

...

8. After saying, "I am the way, the truth, and the life," how many ways did Jesus list that a man could come to the Father?

...

9. After saying, "I am the vine," how did Jesus describe His Father?

a) as good ground
b) as the husbandman
c) as the sower of fertile seed
d) as winds and water

...

10. Fill in the blank: Jesus said, "I am the vine, ye are the _____."

Jesus Says, "I Am" Answers

1. "...and lowly in heart" (Matthew 11:29)

2. "Thou art the Christ" (Mark 8:29)

3. b) "even unto the end of the world" (Matthew 28:20)

4. life (John 8:12)

5. "Before Abraham was, I am" (John 8:58)

6. d) all of the above (John 10:7, 10–11)

7. true (John 11:23–25)

8. one (John 14:6)

9. b) as the husbandman (John 15:1)

10. branches (John 15:5)

JESUS—ARREST AND TRIAL

1. True or False: When the cock crowed the third time, Jesus was blindfolded.

• • •

2. Jesus told His apostles it was written that He would be reckoned among whom?
   a) the firstborn
   b) the leaders of nations
   c) the Levites
   d) the transgressors

• • •

3. What was the name of the garden where Jesus prayed?

• • •

4. Choose A or B: When Jesus prayed in the garden, He asked that the hour might **a)** pass from Him or **b)** come quickly.

• • •

5. Fill in the blank: The spirit indeed is willing, but the flesh is _____.

6. How many times did Jesus pray the same words?

• • •

7. What did Jesus tell those who came to arrest Him at night?
   a) "Nothing is secret that shall not be made manifest."
   b) "The children of this world are wiser than the children of light."
   c) "This is your hour, and the power of darkness."
   d) "You keep your wrath in secret until the appointed time."

• • •

8. When Jesus stated that He was the one they sought, what happened to the band of men who came to arrest Him?
   a) they heard the voices of angels
   b) they rushed forward and bound Jesus
   c) they went backward and fell to the ground
   d) they were momentarily struck blind by a great light

9. Which ear of Malchus did Peter cut off with the sword?

•••

10. Fill in the blanks: Jesus told Peter, "Put up again thy_____ into his place: for all they that take the _____ shall perish with the _____."

•••

11. True or False: When Jesus announced at the Last Supper that He would be betrayed by one of the Twelve, most of the apostles suspected Judas.

•••

12. How did Judas identify Jesus to the multitude that came to arrest Him?

•••

13. How many pieces of silver did the chief priests and elders pay Judas to betray Jesus?

•••

14. Fill in the blank: Judas said, "I have sinned in that I have betrayed the innocent _____."

15. Why did the priests use the betrayer's money to buy a field rather than put it in the treasury?

•••

16. How did Judas kill himself?
   a) cast himself down from a high place
   b) fell on his sword
   c) hanged himself
   d) hung a millstone from his neck and drowned in the sea

•••

17. The chief priests bought the potter's field to use for what purpose?

•••

18. In addition to Aceldama, the potter's field was also known by what other name?

•••

19. Why did the chief priests and elders who brought Jesus to Pontius Pilate's judgment hall not enter it themselves?

20. What was one of the charges that the crowd brought against Jesus when He was before Pilate?
   a) He brought Gentiles into the temple
   b) He claimed a kingdom not of this world
   c) He claimed He would destroy the temple in forty days
   d) He objected to giving tribute to Caesar

• • •

21. What did the chief priests say when Pilate told them to judge Jesus according to their law?

• • •

22. What three-word question did Pilate ask when Jesus said, "To this end was I born. . .that I should bear witness unto the truth"?

• • •

23. True or False: Pilate sent Jesus to Herod because Jesus was from Judaea.

24. Fill in the blank: When Pilate asked if he should crucify their king, the chief priests said, "We have no king but _____."

• • •

25. Whose wife said she had suffered many things in a dream because of Jesus?
   a) the wife of Caiaphas
   b) the wife of Herod
   c) the wife of Pilate
   d) the wife of the chief of the Praetorian guard

• • •

26. When the soldiers mocked Jesus, what did they put in His right hand?

• • •

27. What did the guards say when they mocked Jesus and saluted Him?
   a) "Behold the man!"
   b) "Bow down and worship us!"
   c) "Hail, King of the Jews!"
   d) "Tell us the color of your robe!"

25. c) the wife of Pilate (Matthew 27:17, 19)

24. Caesar (John 19:15)

23. false; He was from Galilee (Luke 23:5, 7)

22. "What is truth?" (John 18:38)

21. "It is not lawful for us to put any man to death" (John 18:31)

20. d) He objected to giving tribute to Caesar (Luke 23:2)

19. they did not want to defile themselves; this would have kept them from eating the Passover (John 18:28)

18. the field of blood (Matthew 27:8; Acts 1:19)

17. to bury strangers in (Matthew 27:7)

16. c) hanged himself (Matthew 27:5)

15. it was not lawful because it was the price of blood (Matthew 27:6)

14. blood (Matthew 27:4)

13. thirty (Matthew 27:3)

12. with a kiss (Matthew 26:49)

11. false; they each asked if it was them (Matthew 26:22)

10. sword, sword, sword (Matthew 26:52)

9. his right ear (John 18:10)

8. c) they went backward and fell to the ground (John 18:6)

7. c) "This is your hour, and the power of darkness" (Luke 22:53)

6. three (Matthew 26:44)

5. weak (Matthew 26:41)

4. a) pass from Him (Mark 14:35)

3. Gethsemane (Matthew 26:36)

2. d) the transgressors (Luke 22:37)

1. false; He looked at Peter (Luke 22:61)

Jesus—Arrest and Trial Answers

28. What did Herod hope to see Jesus do?

26. a reed (Matthew 27:29)

27. c) "Hail, King of the Jews!" (Mark 15:18)

28. some miracle (Luke 23:8)

JESUS— CRUCIFIXION

Put the following events in their chronological order (questions 1–14):

a) Jesus is crucified between two robbers

b) the soldiers divide Jesus' garments

c) Jesus says, "Today you will be with Me"

d) Jesus says, "I thirst"

e) Jesus dismisses His spirit

f) Jesus says, "Father, forgive them"

g) the robbers revile Jesus; one repents

h) darkness

i) Jesus says, "It is finished"

j) Jesus says, "My God, My God, why have you forsaken Me?"

k) offer of stupefying drink is refused

l) the Jews mock Jesus

m) Jesus says, "Woman, behold your son!"

n) Jesus says, "Father, into Your hands I commit My spirit"

• • •

15. Who helped Jesus to carry His cross?
a) Peter
b) a Roman soldier
c) Simon of Cyrene
d) a slave

• • •

16. The sign Pilate put on Jesus' cross said "The King of the Jews" in how many languages?
a) 1
b) 2
c) 3
d) 4

• • •

17. Fill in the blank: Although one man ran for vinegar, the others said, "Let be, let us see whether Elias [Elijah] will come to _____ him."

18. What method was used to raise vinegar to Jesus' lips?
   a) a cup raised by the centurion
   b) a sponge raised on a hyssop reed
   c) a linen cloth soaked in vinegar
   d) none; the soldiers forbade giving Him vinegar

•••

19. Following the death of Jesus, what happened at the temple?
   a) no stone was left upon another
   b) the cherubim fell face down
   c) the Pharisees gnashed their teeth and tore their clothes
   d) the veil of the temple was torn from top to bottom

•••

20. True or False: Tombs were opened and saints came forth and marched to Golgotha as witnesses of Jesus' holiness.

21. Fill in the blank: The centurion said, "_____ this was the Son of God."

•••

22. The centurion's statement about Jesus being the Son of God was made shortly after what event?
   a) the earthquake
   b) when he pierced Jesus' side
   c) when Jesus was found to be dead
   d) when they came for the body of Jesus

•••

23. True or False: Some of the women who viewed the crucifixion from afar had followed Jesus from Galilee and ministered to Him.

•••

24. Why did the Jews want the bodies taken down from the crosses before sunset?

•••

25. What method was used to ensure the two men crucified with Jesus were dead?

26. Fill in the blank: "They shall look on him whom they_____."

• • •

27. Who buried Jesus?

• • •

28. Who rolled the big stone across the tomb after Jesus' body had been placed in it?
   a) chief priests and Pharisees
   b) Joseph of Arimathea
   c) soldiers who crucified Him
   d) temple guards

Jesus—Crucifixion Answers

1. k) (Mark 15:23)

2. a) (Mark 15:24–28)

3. f) (Luke 23:34)

4. b) (Mark 15:24)

5. l) (Mark 15:29–32)

6. g) (Mark 15:32; Luke 23:40–42)

7. c) (Luke 23:43 NKJV)

8. m) (John 19:26–27 NKJV)

9. h) (Matthew 27:45)

10. j) (Mark 15:34–36 NKJV)

11. d) (John 19:28)

12. i) (John 19:30)

13. n) (Luke 23:46 NKJV)

14. e) (Mark 15:37)

15. c) Simon of Cyrene (Matthew 27:32)

16. c) 3 (Luke 23:38; John 19:19–20)

17. save (Matthew 27:49)

18. b) a sponge on a hyssop reed (Mark 15:36; John 19:29)

19. d) the veil of the temple was torn from top to bottom (Matthew 27:51)

20. false; they went into the holy city, Jerusalem (Matthew 27:53)

21. Truly (Matthew 27:54)

22. a) the earthquake (Matthew 27:54)

23. true (Mark 15:40–41)

24. so the bodies would not remain on the cross on the Sabbath day (John 19:31)

25. soldiers broke their legs (John 19:32)

26. pierced (John 19:37)

27. Joseph of Arimathea and Nicodemus (John 19:38–42)

28. b) Joseph of Arimathea (Matthew 27:57–60)

JESUS— RESURRECTION AND ASCENSION

1. On the first day of the week, as the women went to anoint Jesus' body with spices, what question did they ask each other?

• • •

2. Who rolled the stone away?
   a) an angel
   b) the women
   c) Jesus' disciples
   d) Roman soldiers

• • •

3. Fill in the blanks: The two men in glowing clothes at the empty tomb asked the women, "Why do you look for the _____ among the _____?"

4. What was left in the tomb?
   a) nothing
   b) the linen clothes
   c) some spices
   d) an angel

• • •

5. How did the disciples react when Mary Magdalene and the other women told them Jesus was alive?
   a) with disbelief
   b) with rejoicing

• • •

6. When the chief priests and elders learned about the empty tomb, what did they do to the soldiers who were guarding it?
   a) sent them to a far country
   b) shut them in prison
   c) beat them and commanded them not to speak about the matter
   d) gave them money

• • •

7. True or False: The two men on the road to Emmaus who walked and talked with Jesus never realized who He was.

8. When the disciples gathered on the evening of the first day of the week after Jesus' resurrection, why did they have the doors locked?

•••

9. True or False: Thomas, who said, "Unless I see the nail marks in his hands. . .I will not believe," was a disciple of Jesus but not an apostle.

•••

10. After Jesus arose, whom did He ask three times, "Do you love me?"

•••

11. Fill in the blank: Jesus said, "Therefore go and make disciples of all _____, baptizing them in the name of the Father and of the Son and of the Holy Spirit."

•••

12. Jesus was taken up into heaven in the vicinity of what small city?

Jesus—Resurrection and Ascension Answers

1. "Who will roll the stone away from the entrance of the tomb?" (Mark 16:3 NIV)

2. a) an angel (Matthew 28:2)

3. living, dead (Luke 24:5)

4. b) the linen clothes (John 20:6)

5. a) with disbelief (Luke 24:11)

6. d) gave them money (Matthew 28:12)

7. false; "their eyes were opened and they recognized him" (Luke 24:31 NIV)

8. they feared the Jewish leaders (John 20:19)

9. false; he was one of the Twelve (John 20:24–25 NIV)

10. Peter (John 21:17)

11. nations (Matthew 28:19 NIV)

12. Bethany (Luke 24:50–51)

JOB

1. When Job was tested, how many sons and daughters did he have?

...

2. True or False: Job was so concerned about sin that he made sacrifices to the Lord on behalf of his sons, lest they had unintentionally sinned.

...

3. Why did Satan say that Job had been faithful to God?

...

4. Where had Satan been before he approached God?

...

5. The oxen and donkeys and all but one servant tending them were slaughtered by
   a) Egyptians
   b) Assyrians
   c) Chaldeans
   d) Sabeans

6. The sheep and all but one of the servants tending them were destroyed by
   a) a pack of wolves
   b) fire falling from heaven
   c) Chaldeans
   d) a flood

...

7. The camels and all but one servant were killed by whom?

...

8. Job's children were killed by
   a) Assyrians
   b) fire
   c) wind
   d) hail

...

9. True or False: Job's children were still small when they were mortally wounded.

...

10. True or False: Job shaved his head when he found out about his losses.

11. Fill in the blanks: Job said, "_____ came I out of my mother's womb, and _____ shall I return thither: the LORD gave, and the LORD hath taken away; blessed be the name of the LORD."

• • •

12. When Satan placed boils on him, Job scratched them with
   a) broken pottery
   b) his fingernails
   c) the dull edge of a knife
   d) the tip of a stick

• • •

13. How many friends arrived to comfort Job?

• • •

14. What were their names?

• • •

15. True or False: Job's friends didn't speak to him for seven days and seven nights.

• • •

16. The Lord told Job's visitors that He was

a) pleased with them
b) willing to prosper them
c) angry that they were unsuccessful at teaching Job new skills
d) angry about their unfaithfulness to Him

Job Answers

1. he had ten children—seven sons and three daughters (Job 1:2)

2. true (Job 1:5)

3. Satan claimed Job had been faithful only because the Lord had blessed him—because he had never been tested (Job 1:10–11)

4. Satan had been roaming to and fro upon the earth (Job 1:7)

5. d) Sabeans (Job 1:15)

6. b) fire falling from heaven (Job 1:16)

7. Chaldeans (Job 1:17)

8. c) wind (Job 1:18–19)

9. false (Job 1:4, 13)

10. true (Job 1:20)

11. Naked, naked (Job 1:21)

12. a) broken pottery (Job 2:8)

13. Three friends came to comfort him (Job 2:11)

14. Eliphaz, Bildad, and Zophar (Job 2:11)

15. true (Job 2:13)

16. d) angry about their unfaithfulness to Him (Job 42:7)

JOHN THE BAPTIST

All four Gospels quote Isaiah 40:3 in describing the prophet as one who would "prepare the way for the Lord."

1. Fill in the blank: Isaiah wrote, "A voice of one calling: 'In the _____ prepare the way for the LORD.'"

•••

2. What was the name of the angel who announced John the Baptist's birth to his father?
a) Gabriel
b) Michael

3. Because of his unbelief, what condition struck John's father until the time his son, John the Baptist, was named?

•••

4. Who were the parents of John the Baptist?
a) Ananias and Sapphira
b) Aquila and Priscilla
c) Cleophas and Mary
d) Zacharias and Elisabeth

•••

5. Fill in the blank: "He shall go before him in the spirit and power of Elias [Elijah] . . .to make ready a people _____ for the Lord."

•••

6. Choose A or B: John had the same name as **a)** his grandfather or **b)** none of his relatives.

•••

7. How did John's father tell others his newborn son's name?

8. Who was the Caesar when John the Baptist began preaching?
    a) Caligula
    b) Claudius
    c) Nero
    d) Tiberius

...

9. Fill in the blank: John the Baptist told soldiers, "Don't extort money and don't accuse people falsely—be content with your _____."

...

10. Fill in the blanks: John said he baptized with water, but the one who came after would baptize with the _____ _____.

...

11. According to the Gospel of John, what expression did John the Baptist use to describe Jesus?
    a) Everlasting Rabbi
    b) Lamb of God
    c) Son of Man
    d) Word with God

12. In speaking of Jesus (the one who would come after), what did John say he was unworthy to do?
    a) eat at the same table
    b) place a fan in His hand
    c) unloose the shoes of Jesus
    d) wear the robe of Jesus

...

13. What expression did John the Baptist use to describe the Pharisees and Sadducees?
    a) brood of vipers
    b) children of the Most High
    c) sons of Beelzebul
    d) leaders with uncircumcised hearts

...

14. According to Jesus, who is greater than John the Baptist?

...

15. True or False: Herod the tetrarch believed Jesus was John the Baptist raised from the dead.

16. What was the name of the woman who John the Baptist said was not lawful for Herod to have?

• • •

17. How was the woman's husband, Philip, related to Herod?

• • •

18. At first, why did Herod not have John the Baptist killed?

a) Herod feared John the Baptist would come back to life
b) Herod feared the people
c) it pleased Herod to make sport of John the Baptist at his royal banquets
d) the high priest warned Herod not to kill a holy man

• • •

19. What event was Herod celebrating when John the Baptist was beheaded?

20. True or False: After John the Baptist's death, Herod his had body burned.

John the Baptist Answers

1. wilderness (Isaiah 40:3 NIV)

2. a) Gabriel (Luke 1:19)

3. he could not speak (Luke 1:13, 20)

4. d) Zacharias and Elisabeth (Luke 1:5, 13)

5. prepared (Luke 1:17)

6. b) none of his relatives (Luke 1:61)

7. he wrote it on a writing tablet (Luke 1:63)

8. d) Tiberius (Luke 3:1–3)

9. pay (Luke 3:14 NIV)

10. Holy Spirit (Mark 1:8)

11. b) "Lamb of God" (John 1:29)

12. c) unloose the shoes of Jesus (Mark 1:7)

13. a) "brood of vipers" (Matthew 3:7)

14. whoever is least in the kingdom of heaven" (Matthew 11:11).

15. true (Matthew 14:1–2)

16. Herodias (Matthew 14:3–4)

17. Philip was Herod's brother (Matthew 14:3–4)

18. b) Herod feared the people (Matthew 14:5)

19. Herod's birthday (Matthew 14:6)

20. false; the disciples buried the body (Matthew 14:12)

JONAH

1. Jonah was asked to go to Nineveh by whom?

• • •

2. Jonah was instructed to tell the Ninevites that
   a) they had found grace in the eyes of the Lord
   b) the Lord was against their wickedness
   c) they were to build an ark to prepare for an oncoming flood
   d) they were to build a temple in God's honor

3. Jonah boarded a ship to Tarshish because
   a) Tarshish was on the way to Nineveh
   b) he had been told to take a priest from Tarshish with him
   c) he wanted to flee from the Lord
   d) he needed a catch of fish to take along as food

• • •

4. What happened to the sea after Jonah boarded the ship?

• • •

5. True or False: The Bible says that Jonah was swallowed by a whale.

• • •

6. Fill in the blank: But I will sacrifice unto thee with the voice of thanksgiving; I will pay that that I have vowed. _____ is of the LORD.

• • •

7. Jonah told the Ninevites that they had how many days left before God would destroy them?

8. After the Ninevites heard the message from God delivered by Jonah, they
    a) threw Jonah out of town
    b) stoned Jonah
    c) fasted and wore sackcloth
    d) proclaimed the Lord was greater than Baal

• • •

9. True or False: The king of Nineveh resisted God's call to repentance.

• • •

10. Nineveh's repentance angered Jonah because
    a) Nineveh wasn't part of his own country
    b) his ex-wife lived in Nineveh
    c) success meant he would be required to join the priesthood
    d) the Ninevites didn't invite him to their revival service

• • •

11. True or False: Jonah asked God to take his life.

12. Why did Jonah remain near Nineveh?

• • •

13. The plant that shaded Jonah as he waited was a
    a) cactus
    b) Venus fly trap
    c) gourd
    d) cypress tree

• • •

14. The plant was destroyed by
    a) a bolt of lightning
    b) a worm
    c) a lack of flies to eat
    d) harsh sunlight

• • •

15. God made and destroyed the plant to show Jonah what?

Jonah Answers

1. the Lord (Jonah 1:1–2)

2. b) the Lord was against their wickedness (Jonah 1:2)

3. c) he wanted to flee from the Lord (Jonah 1:3)

JUDGES

1. True or False: The Lord raised up judges to deliver the Israelites from their enemies.

• • •

2. Choose A or B: Othniel, the first judge of Israel, was the son of **a)** Joshua's brother or **b)** Caleb's brother.

• • •

3. Choose A or B: Ehud went against Eglon, the king of **a)** Moab or **b)** Edom.

• • •

4. True or False: Shamgar killed six hundred Philistines with a spear.

• • •

5. The person who campaigned to make himself a judge was
   a) Abimelech
   b) Tola
   c) Jair
   d) Jephthah

4. a great wind caused the sea to rage (Jonah 1:4)

5. false; he was swallowed by a fish (Jonah 1:17)

6. Salvation (Jonah 2:9)

7. forty (Jonah 3:4)

8. c) fasted and wore sackcloth (Jonah 3:5)

9. false (Jonah 3:6); for his entire decree, see verses 6–9.

10. a) Nineveh wasn't part of his own country (Jonah 4:2)

11. true (Jonah 4:3)

12. he wanted to see what would happen to the city (Jonah 4:5)

13. c) gourd (Jonah 4:6)

14. b) a worm (Jonah 4:7)

15. "Then said the LORD, Thou hast had pity on the gourd, for the which thou hast not laboured, neither madest it grow; which came up in a night, and perished in a night: And should not I spare Nineveh, that great city, wherein are more than sixscore thousand persons that cannot discern between their right hand and their left hand, and also much cattle?" (Jonah 4:10–11)

6. True or False: Abimelech was the son of Gideon, also known as Jerub-baal.

...

7. Jephthah made a vow to the Lord that he would sacrifice
   a) forty bullocks
   b) an unblemished ram
   c) the first thing that came out of his house to meet him
   d) a pair of turtledoves

...

8. Choose A or B: Ibzan was from **a)** Bethlehem or **b)** Jerusalem.

...

9. True or False: Abdon had fifteen sons.

...

10. Fill in the blank: After each judge died, the children of Israel did _____ in the sight of the Lord.

11. Jabin was the king of
    a) Canaan
    b) the Philistines
    c) Ammon
    d) Edom

...

12. True or False: Jabin was the captain of Sisera's army.

...

13. Fill in the blanks: Deborah dwelt under a _____ _____.

...

14. True or False: Barak told Deborah he would go fight only if she went with him.

...

15. Fill in the blank: Deborah told Barak that the Lord would sell Sisera into the hand of a _____.

...

16. Heber was a
    a) Kenite
    b) Moabite
    c) Edomite
    d) Philistine

17. True or False: Sisera fled to the tent of Heber and Heber's wife, Jael, because there was peace between Jabin and Heber.

• • •

18. How did Jael welcome Sisera when he arrived at her tent?

• • •

19. True or False: Jael killed Sisera by suffocating him with a pillow while he was asleep.

• • •

20. Who said, "Praise ye the LORD for the avenging of Israel"?

Judges Answers

1. true (Judges 2:16)
2. b) Caleb's brother (Judges 3:9)
3. a) Moab (Judges 3:15)
4. false; he used an ox goad (Judges 3:31)
5. a) Abimelech (Judges 9:1–2)
6. true (Judges 9:1 NLT)
7. c) the first thing that came out of his house to meet him (Judges 11:30–31)
8. a) Bethlehem (Judges 12:8)
9. false; he had forty sons (Judges 12:13–14)
10. evil (Judges 13:1)
11. a) Canaan (Judges 4:2)
12. false; Sisera was the captain of Jabin's army (Judges 4:2)
13. palm tree (Judges 4:5)
14. true (Judges 4:8)
15. woman (Judges 4:9)
16. a) Kenite (Judges 4:11)
17. true (Judges 4:17)
18. she covered him with a mantle and gave him milk to drink (Judges 4:18–19)
19. false; she pounded a tent peg, or nail, into his head (Judges 4:21)
20. Deborah and Barak (Judges 5:1–2)

K

KINGDOM OF GOD

1. If we seek first the kingdom of God, what will be added unto us?

• • •

2. Fill in the blanks: The kingdom of God is like a man who sowed _____ _____ in his field.

• • •

3. Fill in the blank: The kingdom of God is like a _____ seed.

• • •

4. Fill in the blank: The kingdom of God is like a _____ hidden in a field.

• • •

5. True or False: The kingdom of God is never compared to leaven.

• • •

6. The kingdom of God is like a merchant seeking beautiful
   a) vessels
   b) gems
   c) pearls
   d) ships

• • •

7. True or False: The kingdom of God is compared to a dragnet.

• • •

8. True or False: The kingdom of God is compared to a king.

• • •

9. True or False: In the kingdom of God, few are called but all respond.

• • •

10. True or False: The kingdom of God is compared to marriage.

Kingdom of God Answers

1. all these things
(Matthew 6:31–33)

2. good seed
(Matthew 13:24–30)

3. After the kingdom split into the ten northern tribes (Israel) and the two southern tribes (Judah), who was the first king of the northern tribes?
a) Jehu
b) Ahab
c) Jeroboam
d) Jotham

• • •

4. After the kingdom split, how many kings did the ten northern tribes have before they were taken into captivity?
a) 20
b) 25
c) 30
d) 35

• • •

5. What nation took the ten northern tribes into captivity?
a) Assyria
b) Syria
c) Babylon
d) Egypt

3. mustard (Matthew 13:31–32)
4. treasure (Matthew 13:44)
5. false (Matthew 13:33)
6. c) pearls (Matthew 13:45–46)
7. true (Matthew 13:47–48)
8. true (Matthew 18:23–35)
9. false (Matthew 20:16)
10. true (Matthew 22:2)

KINGS OF ISRAEL

(see also Kings of Judah; Kings of the United Kingdom; Kings, Pagan)

1. Who was the first king of Israel?

• • •

2. What was the shortest reign of a king of Israel?
a) 1 day
b) 3 days
c) 5 days
d) 7 days

6. Who was king when the ten northern tribes were taken into captivity?
   a) Ahab
   b) Zimri
   c) Hoshea
   d) Omni

• • •

7. After the kingdom split, what was the longest period of time that a king reigned over Israel?
   a) 30 years
   b) 31 years
   c) 40 years
   d) 41 years

• • •

8. What son of a king of Judah married the daughter of a king of Israel?
   a) Rehoboam
   b) Hezekiah
   c) Jehoram
   d) Manasseh

• • •

9. What wicked king and queen killed Naboth so they could steal his vineyard?

10. What king drove his chariot furiously?

• • •

11. Who does the Bible say did evil in the sight of the Lord more than all who were before him?

• • •

12. What ruler followed Joash as king of Israel?

• • •

13. What king got a withered hand because he tried to have a prophet arrested?

• • •

14. Who was king of Israel for only seven days?

• • •

15. How did Omri become king of Israel?

• • •

16. What king of Israel reigned at the same time as a king of Judah with the same name?

Kings of Israel Answers

1. Saul
(1 Samuel 9:1–2, 15–16)

2. d) 7 days (1 Kings 16:15)

3. c) Jeroboam
(1 Kings 11:31)

4. a) 20

5. a) Assyria (2 Kings 17:6)

6. c) Hoshea (2 Kings 17:6)

7. d) 41 years
(2 Kings 14:23)

8. c) Jehoram
(2 Chronicles 21:1, 6)

9. Ahab and Jezebel
(1 Kings 21)

10. Jehu (2 Kings 9:20)

11. Ahab (1 Kings 16:30)

12. Jeroboam
(2 Kings 13:13)

13. Jeroboam II
(1 Kings 13:4)

14. Zimri (1 Kings 16:15)

15. Zimri, who was king, killed himself (1 Kings 16:18), and Tibni, Omri's rival, died (1 Kings 16:22)

16. Jehoash (2 Kings 13:10–11; 2 Kings 12:2)

KINGS OF JUDAH

(see also Kings of Israel; Kings of the United Kingdom; Kings, Pagan)

Jehoram was such a bad king that the Bible says, "He reigned in Jerusalem eight years and, to no one's sorrow, departed. However they buried him in the City of David, but not in the tombs of the kings" (2 Chronicles 21:20 NKJV). He was only forty years old when he died.

1. Who was the first king of Judah?

• • •

2. What king's grandmother tried to kill all of her grandchildren so she could be queen?
a) Joash
b) Hezekiah
c) Manasseh
d) Josiah

3. Like Ahab, which king built up a grove for the worship of false gods?
   a) Asa
   b) Manasseh
   c) Jeconiah
   d) Jehoram

• • •

4. How many times was David anointed king?
   a) 1
   b) 2
   c) 3
   d) 4

• • •

5. What prophet, along with Zadok the priest, anointed Solomon king?
   a) Elijah
   b) Elisha
   c) Isaiah
   d) Nathan

• • •

6. Who was the king when the kingdom split into the ten northern tribes (Israel) and the two southern tribes (Judah)?
   a) Solomon
   b) Rehoboam
   c) Hezekiah
   d) David

7. About what boy king does the Bible say there was none before him or after him "that turned to the LORD with all his heart"?
   a) Joash
   b) Jehoram
   c) Jehu
   d) Josiah

• • •

8. Uzziah was one of the really good kings of Judah, but God struck him with leprosy because he
   a) accidentally killed someone
   b) took God's name in vain
   c) burned incense in the temple
   d) b & c

• • •

9. What king had a brother named Adonijah who tried to steal his throne?
   a) David
   b) Solomon
   c) Asa
   d) Jotham

10. Who was king when the kingdom of Judah was taken into Babylonian captivity?
    a) Hezekiah
    b) Manasseh
    c) Jehoiakim
    d) Hazael

•••

11. Why did God give Solomon riches, wealth, and honor?

•••

12. Who was the youngest king of Judah?

•••

13. When the golden shields Solomon had made for the temple were stolen, with what did King Rehoboam replace them?

•••

14. What king was responsible for bringing a guaranteed water supply to Jerusalem?

•••

15. What youngest son of Jehoram was made king

of Judah because all of his brothers were killed?

•••

16. What king of Judah cleared the temple of objects used to worship Baal?

•••

17. What king of Judah was blinded by his captors?

•••

18. Whose reign of fifty-five years was the longest of the kings of Judah?

•••

19. Who took away the treasures of Jerusalem during the reign of Rehoboam?

Kings of Judah Answers

1. Saul (1 Samuel 10:21–24)

2. a) Joash (2 Chronicles 22:10–11)

3. b) Manasseh (2 Kings 21:1–3)

18. Manasseh (2 Kings 21:1)

19. Shishak, king of Egypt (1 Kings 14:25–26)

KINGS OF THE UNITED KINGDOM

(see also Kings of Israel; Kings of Judah; Kings, Pagan)

One from among thy brethren shalt thou set king over thee: thou mayest not set a stranger over thee, which is not thy brother.
DEUTERONOMY 17:15

1. How many kings did the United Kingdom of Israel have before it split into the northern and southern kingdoms?

...

2. Name the kings in question 1.

...

3. When God was giving Moses instructions concerning the king, who did God say was to choose the king?

4. c) 3 (1 Samuel 16:13; 2 Samuel 2:4; 5:3)

5. d) Nathan (1 Kings 1:34)

6. b) Rehoboam (1 Kings 12:19–21)

7. d) Josiah (2 Kings 23:24–25)

8. c) burned incense in the temple (2 Chronicles 26:19–20)

9. b) Solomon (1 Kings 1:5, 17–18)

10. c) Jehoiakim (2 Chronicles 36:5–6)

11. because He was pleased that Solomon asked for wisdom (2 Chronicles 1:11–12)

12. Joash was seven years old when he became king (2 Kings 11)

13. bronze shields (1 Kings 14:27)

14. Hezekiah (2 Kings 20:20, 2 Chronicles 32:30)

15. Ahaziah (2 Chronicles 22:1)

16. Josiah (2 Kings 23:4, 16)

17. Zedekiah (Jeremiah 39:7)

4. God told Moses that the king was not to multiply
a) horses
b) wives
c) gold and silver
d) all of the above

• • •

5. What was the first thing a king was supposed to do when he became king?

• • •

6. Whose feelings were hurt because Israel wanted a king?

• • •

7. What king solicited the services of the witch of Endor?

• • •

8. What king of Israel notably had three hundred concubines?

• • •

9. What king's wife despised him for dancing before the Lord?

• • •

10. How did King Saul die?

11. How long was David king of Judah before he also became king of Israel?

• • •

12. When David was made king of Judah, who was made king of Israel?

Kings of the United Kingdom Answers

1. four

2. Saul, David, Solomon, Rehoboam (1 Samuel 10:21–24; 2 Samuel 5:2–3; 1 Kings 4:1; 1 Kings 12:1)

3. God (Deuteronomy 17:15)

4. d) all of the above (Deuteronomy 17:16–17)

5. write a copy of the Law (Deuteronomy 17:18)

6. Samuel (1 Samuel 8:6–7)

7. Saul (1 Samuel 28:7–25)

8. Solomon (1 Kings 11:3)

9. David (2 Samuel 6:16)

10. he deliberately fell on a sword (1 Samuel 31:4)

11. seven years, six months
(2 Samuel 5:5)

12. Ishbosheth
(2 Samuel 2:10)

a) Jericho
b) Zion
c) Jerusalem
d) Salem

• • •

KINGS, PAGAN

(see also Kings of Israel,
Kings of Judah, Kings of
the United Kingdom)

1. Balak, who hired Balaam
to curse the Israelites, was
king of the
   a) Moabites
   b) Amorites
   c) Hittites
   d) Edomites

• • •

2. King Hiram (or Huram),
from whom Solomon
got materials to build the
temple, was king of
   a) Tyre
   b) Sidon
   c) Tyre and Sidon
   d) Syria

• • •

3. Melchizedek was a priest,
but he was also king of

4. The king of Babylon who
took the southern kingdom
of Judah captive was
   a) Darius
   b) Nebuchadnezzar
   c) Cyrus
   d) Belshazzar

• • •

5. The king of what country
took the northern kingdom
of Israel captive?
   a) Egypt
   b) Assyria
   c) Syria
   d) Samaria

• • •

6. The name of the king
who allowed the Israelites
to return to Jerusalem from
their captivity in
Babylon was
   a) Nebuchadnezzar
   b) Darius
   c) Cyrus
   d) Ezra

7. The king who saw the handwriting on the wall was
   a) Belshazzar
   b) Nebuchadnezzar
   c) Darius
   d) Cyrus

• • •

8. Who saved a king's life after he overheard two eunuchs plotting against the king?

• • •

9. What king threw Daniel into the lions' den?

• • •

10. What king did Saul refuse to kill in direct disobedience to God's command?

11. What caused King Xerxes to have the book of chronicles of his reign read to him?
   a) it was a yearly ritual started by his wise advisers
   b) Haman requested it
   c) he could not sleep
   d) he was bothered by a question from Queen Esther

• • •

12. Whom did King Xerxes ask, "What should be done for the man the king delights to honor?"

• • •

13. What name applies to a line of wicked kings from the time of Jesus through the apostle Paul?

13. Herod: Herod the Great (Matthew 2:1–20), Herod Antipas (Mark 8:15), Herod Agrippa I (Acts 12), Herod Agrippa II (Acts 25)

12. Haman (Esther 6:6 NIV)

11. c) he could not sleep (Esther 6:1)

10. Agag (1 Samuel 15:8–9)

9. Darius (Daniel 5:31; 6:16–23)

8. Mordecai (Esther 2:21–23)

7. a) Belshazzar (Daniel 5:1–5)

6. c) Cyrus (Ezra 1:1–2)

5. b) Assyria (2 Kings 17:6)

4. b) Nebuchadnezzar (2 Chronicles 36:6)

3. d) Salem (Genesis 14:18)

2. a) Tyre (2 Chronicles 2:3)

1. a) Moabites (Numbers 22:1–6)

Kings, Pagan
Answers

L

LAMB OF GOD

(see also Jesus)

1. Who called Jesus the Lamb of God?

• • •

2. Fill in the blank: Isaiah prophesied the Messiah would be led as a lamb to the _____.

• • •

3. Fill in the blanks: Peter said Christ is a lamb without _____ and without _____.

• • •

4. Fill in the blanks: John described the Lamb he saw in heaven as having seven _____ and seven _____.

• • •

5. When John first saw the Lamb in heaven, what was the Lamb doing?

6. Fill in the blank: Satan was _____ by the blood of the Lamb.

• • •

7. True or False: The Bible says that the Book of Life is actually the Lamb's Book of Life.

• • •

8. The supper of the Lamb in heaven celebrates what occasion?

Lamb of God Answers

1. John the Baptist (John 1:29)

2. slaughter (Isaiah 53:7)

3. blemish, spot (1 Peter 1:19 NKJV)

4. horns, eyes (Revelation 5:6)

5. standing (Revelation 5:6)

6. overcome (Revelation 12:11)

7. true (Revelation 13:8)

8. His marriage (Revelation 19:9)

LAW OF MOSES

And he said, The LORD came from Sinai, and rose up from Seir unto them; he shined forth from mount Paran, and he came with ten thousands of saints: from his right hand went a fiery law for them.

DEUTERONOMY 33:2

1. Fill in the blanks: Jesus said not a _____ or _____ will pass away from the Law until it is fulfilled.

• • •

2. True or False: When the Israelites stood before the mountains of blessing and cursing, Joshua read the Book of the Law to them.

• • •

3. Upon which two commandments did Jesus say all of the Law and the Prophets hang?

• • •

4. Fill in the blanks: Jesus said He came not to _____ the Law but to _____ it.

5. Fill in the blanks: Paul says the Law was our _____ to bring us to Christ.

• • •

6. God told Joshua that if Joshua meditated on the Book of the Law day and night he would have
  a) salvation
  b) good success
  c) victory in battle
  d) a good family

• • •

7. Which of the following did not read the Book of the Law to his people?
  a) Josiah
  b) Jeroboam
  c) Ezra
  d) Jehoshaphat

• • •

8. True or False: When Moses went up on Mount Sinai, seventy of the elders went with him and saw God.

• • •

9. Fill in the blank: Jesus came to _____ those under the Law.

Law of Moses Answers

1. jot, tittle (Matthew 5:18)

2. true (Joshua 8:33–35)

3. love the Lord your God; love your neighbor (Matthew 22:37–40)

4. destroy, fulfill (Matthew 5:17)

5. tutor (Galatians 3:24 nkjv)

6. b) good success (Joshua 1:8)

7. b) Jeroboam (2 Kings 23:2; 2 Chronicles 17:9; Nehemiah 8:1–3)

8. true (Exodus 24:9–10)

9. redeem (Galatians 4:4–5)

LEAVING EGYPT

1. True or False: Immediately after the Exodus, the Israelites believed in God and in the leadership of His servant, Moses.

2. After the Lord brought His people out of Egypt, they immediately
   a) celebrated Passover
   b) prayed
   c) built a temple
   d) sang and danced

• • •

3. True or False: At one point, Pharaoh agreed to let the men go, but not the women and children.

• • •

4. The Passover is known by what other name?
   a) Festival of Dedication
   b) Festival of Tabernacles
   c) Festival of Unleavened Bread
   d) Pentecost

• • •

5. True or False: The Israelite people escaped Egypt with nothing but the clothes they could carry.

6. For how many years did the Israelite people live in Egypt?
    a) 70
    b) 430
    c) 969
    d) the Bible does not specify the number of years

...

7. Fill in the blank: The Lord told Moses to _____ all the firstborn.

...

8. When the Israelites left Egypt, why did God keep them from going through the land of the Philistines?
    a) it was full of giants
    b) it was too far away
    c) it was at war
    d) it was hard to find

...

9. Whose bones did Moses take when the Israelites left Egypt?

10. Fill in the blanks: "The LORD went before them by day in a pillar of a ____... and by night in a pillar of ____."

...

11. What did Moses stretch over the sea to divide the waters?

...

12. Fill in the blank: "The children of Israel went into the midst of the sea upon the ____ ground."

...

13. How did the Lord trouble the hosts of Egypt?
    a) He took off their chariot wheels
    b) He caused their horses to founder
    c) He made them fall out of their chariots
    d) He struck them blind

...

14. Fill in the blank: The waters returned and covered the hosts of Pharaoh and there remained "not so much as ___ of them."

Leaving Egypt Answers

1. true (Exodus 14:31)

2. d) sang and danced (Exodus 15:1–21)

3. true (Exodus 10:11)

4. c) Festival of Unleavened Bread (Exodus 12:17)

5. false; they left with silver, gold, clothing, flocks, and herds (Exodus 12:34–38)

6. b) 430 (Exodus 12:40)

7. sanctify (Exodus 13:1–2)

8. c) it was at war (Exodus 13:17)

9. Joseph's bones (Exodus 13:19)

10. cloud, fire (Exodus 13:21)

11. his hand (Exodus 14:21)

12. dry (Exodus 14:22)

13. a) He took off their chariot wheels (Exodus 14:25)

14. one (Exodus 14:28)

LEPERS

(see also Healing)

1. Who was stricken with leprosy because she spoke against her brother's wife?

•••

2. What otherwise good king was stricken with leprosy for burning incense in the temple?

•••

3. True or False: When God caused the army of Syria to flee, four lepers looted the camp of the Syrians.

•••

4. When Naaman was healed of his leprosy, what did he take two mule loads of back to Syria?

•••

5. According to Leviticus 14:17–18, where on the body was a cleansed leper to be anointed?
   a) right ear, right thumb, right big toe
   b) head
   c) left ear, left thumb, left big toe
   d) a & b

6. What prophet did Jesus mention in connection with lepers?
   a) Elijah
   b) Elisha
   c) Isaiah
   d) Jeremiah

• • •

7. How many of the ten lepers whom Jesus cleansed came back to thank Him?

• • •

8. True or False: One of those ten lepers was a Samaritan.

• • •

9. True or False: The first person Jesus healed when He finished the Sermon on the Mount was a leper.

Lepers Answers

1. Miriam (Numbers 12:10)
2. Uzziah (2 Chronicles 26:19)
3. true (2 Kings 7:3, 8)
4. earth (2 Kings 5:17)
5. d) a & b (Leviticus 14:17–18)
6. b) Elisha (Luke 4:27)
7. one (Luke 17:12–16)
8. true (Luke 17:12–16)
9. true (Matthew 8:1–3)

LEVITES

(see also Cities of Levites, Priests)

Levites were the descendants of Jacob's son Levi and were the tribe of Levi. All priests were Levites, but not all Levites were priests. Priests had to be directly descended from Aaron.

1. True or False: When Aaron made the golden calf, only the tribe of Levi stood with Moses against the sinning Israelites.

• • •

2. Why did God separate out the Levites to be His priests and ministers?

199

3. According to 2 Chronicles 31:17, how old were the Levites to be when they started their service in the temple?

   a) 10
   b) 15
   c) 20
   d) 30

...

4. For the purposes of carrying the tabernacle and all its furnishings, the Levites were divided into how many groups?

...

5. True or False: One group was responsible to carry the curtains of the tabernacle and the ark of the covenant.

...

6. Which of the following was not a group of Levites assigned to transport the tabernacle?

   a) Gershonites
   b) Kohathites
   c) Merarites
   d) Nadabites

7. True or False: It was the responsibility of the gatekeepers in the temple to count all the serving vessels in the temple.

...

8. Which of the following was not a duty of the Levites?

   a) purifying all holy things
   b) helping the priests
   c) standing every morning and evening to thank and praise God
   d) offering burnt offerings

Levites Answers

1. true (Exodus 32:26)

2. He substituted them for every firstborn (Numbers 3:12–13)

3. c) 20 (2 Chronicles 31:17)

4. three (Numbers 3:23–37)

5. false (Numbers 3:25–31)

6. d) Nadabites (Numbers 3:25–37)

7. true (1 Chronicles 9:28)

8. d) offering burnt offerings (1 Chronicles 23:28–30)

LIGHT

1. Who fought a battle with torches hidden in pitchers?

• • •

2. Fill in the blank: John said if we walk in the light as Jesus is in the light, we have _____ one with another.

• • •

3. Who said, "Ye are the light of the world"?

• • •

4. Why are we to let our light shine before men?

• • •

5. Fill in the blanks: Jesus said people do not light a lamp and put it under a _____ but on a _____.

• • •

6. To whom was Jesus speaking when He said, "I am the light of the world"?

7. What do the seven lampstands in Revelation 1:20 represent?

• • •

8. Fill in the blank: Proverbs 15:30 says that the light of the eyes rejoices the _____.

• • •

9. True or False: According to Proverbs 29:13, the Lord gives light to the poor man but not the oppressor.

• • •

10. Fill in the blanks: Paul said that when the Lord comes, He will bring to light the _____ things of _____.

Light Answers

1. Gideon (Judges 7:15–16)

2. fellowship (1 John 1:7)

3. Jesus (Matthew 5:14)

4. so they will glorify God (Matthew 5:16)

5. basket, lampstand
(Matthew 5:15 nkjv)

6. Pharisees (John 8:12–13)

7. the seven churches
(Revelation 1:20)

8. heart (Proverbs 15:30)

9. false (Proverbs 29:13)

10. hidden, darkness
(1 Corinthians 4:5)

LIONS

Benaiah, who was one of David's mighty men, first killed two lionlike men of Moab and then killed an actual lion in a pit on a snowy day (1 Chronicles 11:22).

1. What famous Old Testament person killed a lion with his bare hands?

• • •

2. When Jacob blessed his sons, which one did he say was a lion's whelp?
   a) Reuben
   b) Joseph
   c) Dan
   d) Judah

3. When Moses blessed the tribes before his death, which tribe did he say was a lion's whelp?
   a) Reuben
   b) Joseph
   c) Dan
   d) Judah

• • •

4. When Moses blessed the tribes before his death, which tribe did he say dwelt like a lion?
   a) Gad
   b) Issachar
   c) Joseph
   d) Levi

• • •

5. How many lions did Solomon have decorating his throne?

• • •

6. How many lions did Solomon have decorating the steps up to his throne?

• • •

7. In 1 Kings 13, a prophet was killed by a lion because the prophet did what?

202

8. True or False: When the king of Assyria tried to settle foreigners in Samaria, God sent lions to kill them.

• • •

9. Fill in the blank: Job said the old lion perishes for lack of _____.

• • •

10. Who is described as a roaring lion seeking whom he may devour?

• • •

11. Fill in the blank: In Revelation 5:5, Jesus is described as the Lion of the tribe of _____.

• • •

12. In the kingdom of God, the lion will lie down with the
   a) cow
   b) lamb
   c) goat
   d) calf

• • •

13. Fill in the blank: Isaiah 11:7 says that in the kingdom of God the lion will eat _____ like an ox.

14. Who does Proverbs say is as bold as a lion?

• • •

15. True or False: One of the four faces on the living creatures that Ezekiel saw was like a lion.

• • •

16. True or False: One of the four faces on the living creatures that John saw in Revelation was like a lion.

• • •

17. To whom was Ezekiel speaking when he said, "What is your mother? A lioness"?

Lions Answers

1. Samson (Judges 14:5–6)

2. d) Judah (Genesis 49:9)

3. c) Dan (Deuteronomy 33:22)

4. a) Gad (Deuteronomy 33:20)

5. two (1 Kings 10:19)

6. twelve (1 Kings 10:20)

7. disobeyed God (1 Kings 13)

8. true (2 Kings 17:24–25)

9. prey (Job 4:11 NKJV)

10. Satan (1 Peter 5:8)

11. Judah (Revelation 5:5)

12. d) calf (Isaiah 11:6–7)

13. straw (Isaiah 11:7 NKJV)

14. the righteous (Proverbs 28:1)

15. true (Ezekiel 1:10)

16. false; these creatures didn't have four faces (Revelation 4:6–7)

17. the princes of Israel (Ezekiel 19:1–2 NKJV)

LITTLE-KNOWN PEOPLE IN THE BIBLE

Priscilla and Aquila were a couple whom Paul stayed with when he was in Corinth (Acts 18:1–3).

Match these people with their descriptions:
1. Apollos

2. Shiphrah
3. Ethbaal
4. Nimrod
5. Demas
6. Bezaleel
7. Orpah
8. Simon the Cyrene
9. Silas
10. Puah
11. Phoebe
12. Og
13. Lamech
14. Eleazar
15. Drusilla
16. Sennacherib
17. Doeg
18. Cyrus
19. Asaph
20. Keturah
21. Tamar
22. Bartholomew
23. Epaphras
24. Epaphroditus
25. Potiphar
26. Mephibosheth
27. Eliab
28. Athaliah
29. Joanna
30. Iddo

• • •

a. forsook Paul
b. deaconess
c. carried Jesus' cross

d. accompanied Paul

e. designed and built the tabernacle

f. high priest after Aaron died

g. Hebrew midwife

h. servant of King Saul

i. the mighty hunter

j. a preacher of the Gospel

k. king of Bashan

l. Persian ruler who allowed Nehemiah to rebuild Jerusalem

m. king of Zidon, father of Jezebel

n. writer of psalms, supervisor of music

o. Ruth's sister-in-law

p. Hebrew midwife

q. Noah's father

r. wife of Felix

s. king of Assyria

t. disciple of Jesus

u. faithful minister of Christ

v. captain of Pharaoh's guard

w. Abraham's second wife

x. Paul's fellow worker

y. ancestress of Jesus

z. David's older brother

aa. daughter of Ahab and Jezebel

bb. wife of Chuza, Herod's steward

cc. the Seer

dd. Jonathan's son

Little-Known People in the Bible Answers

1. j (Acts 18:24–25)

2. g or p. (Exodus 1:15)

3. m (1 Kings 16:31)

4. i (Genesis 10:9)

5. a (2 Timothy 4:10)

6. e (Exodus 35:30–35)

7. o (Ruth 1:4)

8. c (Mark 15:21)

9. d (Acts 16:25)

10. p or g (Exodus 1:15)

11. b (Romans 16:1)

12. k (Deuteronomy 4:47)

13. q (Genesis 5:28–29)

14. f (Deuteronomy 10:6)

15. r (Acts 24:24)

16. s (2 Kings 18:13)

17. h (1 Samuel 21:7)

18. l (Ezra 1:1)

19. n (1 Chronicles 16:4–6; Psalm 50)

20. w (Genesis 25:1)

21. y (Matthew 1:3)

22. t (Matthew 10:3)

23. u (Colossians 1:7)

24. x (Philippians 2:25)

25. v (Genesis 39:1)

26. dd (2 Samuel 4:4)

27. z (1 Samuel 17:28)

28. aa (2 Kings 8:18; 2 Chronicles 22:2–3)

29. bb (Luke 8:3)

30. cc (2 Chronicles 9:29)

LOVE

For I am persuaded, that neither death, nor life, nor angels, nor principalities, nor powers, nor things present, nor things to come, nor height, nor depth, nor any other creature, shall be able to separate us from the love of God, which is in Christ Jesus our Lord.

ROMANS 8:38–39

1. What did Jesus call "the first and great commandment"?

• • •

2. Fill in the blank: Jesus said, "Greater love hath no man than this, that a man lay down his life _____."

• • •

3. Fill in the blank: Jesus told His disciples: "This is my commandment, That ye love one another, as _____."

4. Fill in the blanks: "For God so loved the _____, that he gave his only begotten _____, that whosoever believeth in him should not perish, but have _____."

• • •

5. In what New Testament book do we find these words: "Owe no man any thing, but to love one another: for he that loveth another hath fulfilled the law"?

• • •

6. How did Paul express the futility of speaking "with the tongues of men and of angels" without charity?

• • •

7. Fill in the blank: "And though I bestow all my goods to feed the poor, and though I give my body to be burned, and have not charity, it _____."

8. Name the most enduring virtue according to 1 Corinthians 13:
   a) faith
   b) hope
   c) charity/love

• • •

9. Who wrote these words: "Behold, what manner of love the Father hath bestowed upon us, that we should be called the sons of God"?

• • •

10. Fill in the blank: "We love him, because he _____."

• • •

11. When God told the Israelites, "I have loved you" what did they reply?

• • •

12. Fill in the blank: Proverbs 10:12 says that loves covers all _____.

13. Better is a dinner of herbs where love is than what?

...

14. What chapter in the Bible is called the Love Chapter?

...

15. What book of the Bible deals exclusively with God's love for us?

Love Answers

1. "Thou shalt love the Lord thy God with all thy heart, and with all thy soul, and with all thy mind" (Matthew 22:37–38)

2. for his friends (John 15:13)

3. I have loved you (John 15:12)

4. world, Son, everlasting life (John 3:16)

5. Romans (Romans 13:8)

6. one becomes as "sounding brass, or a tinkling cymbal" (1 Corinthians 13:1)

7. profiteth me nothing (1 Corinthians 13:3)

8. c) charity / love (1 Corinthians 13:13)

9. John (1 John 3:1)

10. first loved us (1 John 4:19)

11. "In what way have You loved us?" (Malachi 1:2 nkjv)

12. sins (Proverbs 10:12)

13. a fatted calf with hatred (Proverbs 15:17 nkjv)

14. 1 Corinthians 13

15. 1 John

LUCIFER

1. What is the only book of the Bible that mentions Lucifer?

...

2. Where did Lucifer fall from?

3. What did Lucifer do to the nations?

• • •

4. How many times does Lucifer say "I will"?

• • •

5. True or False: Lucifer said, "I will ascend into heaven."

• • •

6. Where did Lucifer say he would exalt his throne?

• • •

7. True or False: Lucifer said, "I will be like the Most High."

• • •

8. What will become of Lucifer?

• • •

9. What question will those who see Lucifer ask?

Lucifer Answers

1. Isaiah

2. heaven (Isaiah 14:12)

3. weakened them (Isaiah 14:12 nkjv)

4. five times (Isaiah 14:13–14)

5. true (Isaiah 14:13)

6. above the stars of God (Isaiah 14:13)

7. true (Isaiah 14:14)

8. God will bring him down to Sheol (Isaiah 14:15 nkjv)

9. "Is this the man that made the earth to tremble, that did shake kingdoms?" (Isaiah 14:16)

LYING

1. True or False: In the early church, a couple fell down dead for lying to the Holy Spirit.

•••

2. True or False: In the list of things that are an abomination to the Lord in Proverbs 6:16–19, lying is not mentioned.

•••

3. Who commanded people to tell lies about Naboth in order to steal his vineyard?
   a) Jezebel
   b) Ahab
   c) Ahab and Jezebel
   d) the captain of Ahab's army

•••

4. What was the lie that the serpent told Eve?
   a) you will not die
   b) you will be like God
   c) you will rule the world
   d) a & b

•••

5. Fill in the blank: A lying tongue is but for a _____.

•••

6. Ziba told David a lie about Ziba's master, who was
   a) Saul
   b) Jonathan
   c) Mephibosheth
   d) David's brother Eliab

•••

7. What does Ephesians 4:25 say we are to do with lying?

•••

8. Whom did Paul tell the Thessalonians was coming with "all power and signs and lying wonders"?
   a) the lawless one
   b) Satan
   c) the antichrist
   d) a false prophet

•••

9. To whom was Jesus speaking when He said the devil was the father of liars?

10. What does Revelation 21:8 say that all liars will have their part in?

Lying Answers

1. true (Acts 5:3–10)

2. false (Proverbs 6:16–19)

3. a) Jezebel (1 Kings 21:9)

4. d) a & b (Genesis 3:4–5)

5. moment
(Proverbs 12:19 nkjv)

6. c) Mephibosheth
(2 Samuel 16:1–4)

7. put it away
(Ephesians 4:25)

8. a) the lawless one
(2 Thessalonians 2:9)

9. Jews (John 8:22, 44)

10. the lake that burns with fire and brimstone (Revelation 21:8)

M

MANNA

(see also Wilderness Wanderings)

1. Fill in the blank: The Lord said, "I will rain _____ from heaven."

• • •

2. True or False: The Israelites had to gather three times as much manna the day before the Sabbath.

• • •

3. True or False: Nobody went out to gather manna on the Sabbath.

• • •

4. What happened to the manna if the Israelites left it overnight?

• • •

5. Choose A or B: a) The Lord or b) people called this mysterious food manna.

6. True or False: The Israelites ate manna until they entered the Promised Land.

• • •

7. God sent manna in response to what specific complaint of the Israelites?

• • •

8. True or False: The Israelites were limited to how much manna they could gather each day.

• • •

9. True or False: *Manna* means "What is it?"

• • •

10. When the Jews told Jesus that their forefathers had eaten manna, what was His response?

• • •

11. Which of the seven churches in Revelation was told they would have hidden manna to eat?

Manna Answers

1. bread (Exodus 16:4)

2. false; they had to gather twice as much (Exodus 16:5)

3. false (Exodus 16:25–27)

4. it spoiled and bred worms (Exodus 16:20)

5. b) the people (Exodus 16:31)

6. true (Exodus 16:35)

7. "You have brought us into this wilderness to kill us with hunger" (see Exodus 16:3)

8. true (Exodus 16:4–5)

9. true (Exodus 16:15 nkjv)

10. "I am the bread of life" (John 6:30–35)

11. Pergamos (Revelation 2:12, 17)

MELCHIZEDEK

Melchizedek is mentioned in both the Old and the New Testaments.

1. Fill in the blank: The first mention of Melchizedek is in association with

_____.

• • •

2. True or False: Melchizedek was a king and a priest.

• • •

3. True or False: Tithing is mentioned in association with Melchizedek.

• • •

4. True or False: Genesis is the only book of the Old Testament that mentions Melchizedek.

• • •

5. In the New Testament, who is considered to be a priest after the order of Melchizedek?

6. True or False: Hebrews is the only book of the New Testament to mention Melchizedek.

Melchizedek Answers

1. Abram (Genesis 14:17–20)

2. true (Genesis 14:18)

3. true (Genesis 14:20)

4. false (Psalm 110:4)3. true (Genesis 14:20)

5. Jesus (Hebrews 5:5–6)

6. true (Hebrews 7)

MESSIANIC NAMES

(see also Jesus)

1. Fill in the blanks: Others called Jesus the son of ____, but Jesus called Himself the son of _____.

• • •

2. Fill in the blank: Paul referred to Jesus as the last _____.

3. What name for Jesus meaning "anointed one" did Daniel use when writing about the end times?

• • •

4. What name for Jesus meaning "anointed one" did the angel use when speaking to the shepherds?

• • •

5. Fill in the blanks: In Revelation 1:8, Jesus says He is the _____ and the _____; the beginning and the end.

• • •

6. Zechariah 3:8 calls the Messiah God's servant and the
   a) Rod
   b) Measuring Line
   c) Branch
   d) Morning Star

• • •

7. Fill in the blank: The very first mention of the Messiah in the Bible calls Him the _____.

8. Fill in the blank: In Luke 1:69, Zacharias calls the Messiah the _____ of salvation.

• • •

9. Fill in the blank: Revelation 5:5 calls Jesus the _____ of the tribe of Judah.

• • •

10. Choose A or B: Matthew said Jesus was called **a)** the Nazarite or **b)** the Nazarene.

• • •

11. Fill in the blank: Isaiah 9:6 says that the Messiah is called the Prince of _____.

• • •

12. Fill in the blanks: Jesus is the _____ shepherd, the _____ shepherd, and the _____ shepherd.

• • •

13. True or False: Balaam called the Messiah "a Star [that] shall come out of Jacob."

14. Fill in the blank: Malachi says the Sun of Righteousness shall arise with _____ in His wings.

• • •

15. Fill in the blank: Jesus said He is the _____ and we are the branches.

• • •

16. Fill in the blank: Revelation 3:14 says Jesus is the _____, faithful and true.

• • •

17. Which of the following is not on the list in Isaiah 9:6–7?
  a) Wonderful
  b) Counselor
  c) Bright and Morning Star
  d) the Mighty God

• • •

18. In John 1:1, what does John call Jesus?

• • •

19. When Jacob was blessing his sons, in which son's blessing was the reference "until Shiloh comes"?

Messianic Names Answers

1. David, man (Mark 10:46–52; Matthew 24:37)
2. Adam (1 Corinthians 15:45)
3. Messiah (Daniel 9:25)
4. Christ (Luke 2:11)
5. Alpha, Omega (Revelation 1:8)
6. c) Branch (Zechariah 3:8)
7. seed (Genesis 3:15)
8. horn (Luke 1:69)
9. Lion (Revelation 5:5)
10. b) Nazarene (Matthew 2:23)
11. Peace (Isaiah 9:6)
12. Chief, Good, Great (1 Peter 5:4; John 10:11; Hebrews 13:20)
13. true (Numbers 24:17 nkjv)
14. healing (Malachi 4:2)
15. vine (John 15:1, 5)
16. Witness (Revelation 3:14 nkjv)
17. c) Bright and Morning Star (Isaiah 9:6–7)
18. the Word (John 1:1)
19. Judah (Genesis 49:10)

MESSIANIC PROPHECIES

1. What minor prophet predicted that the Messiah would be betrayed for thirty pieces of silver?

• • •

2. What minor prophet's book contains the prophecy that the Messiah would be born in Bethlehem?

• • •

3. What was the fulfillment of the prophecy "Out of Egypt have I called my son"?

• • •

4. Who wrote the prophecy "I am poured out like water, and all my bones are out of joint"?

5. When Jesus prophesied that the temple would be destroyed, what description did He use?

• • •

6. What famous relative of Jesus did Isaiah and Malachi both foretell?

• • •

7. When Jesus prophesied about His death, which minor prophet did He say was a sign?

• • •

8. When Jacob pronounced his blessing on Judah, what prophecy did that blessing contain?

• • •

9. When did Jesus say that the disciples would be witnesses to Him?

• • •

10. Where in the Old Testament is the prophecy about Jesus being bruised for our iniquities?

11. What minor prophet prophesied about the outpouring of God's Spirit at Pentecost?

• • •

12. To what time in the Old Testament did Jesus compare the time when the Son of Man will return?

• • •

13. What does Zechariah say will happen when the Messiah's foot touches the Mount of Olives?

• • •

14. To whom was David referring when he wrote, "Mine own familiar friend, in whom I trusted, which did eat of my bread, hath lifted up his heel against me"?

• • •

15. Which of the four Gospels mentions more about fulfilled prophecies than the other Gospels?

16. What king did God promise that his kingdom would have no end because the Messiah would be descended from him?

• • •

17. Which prophet said, "They will look on Me whom they pierced"?

• • •

18. True or False: Isaiah prophesied about Christ's triumphal entry into Jerusalem.

• • •

19. Who wrote, "As a sheep before its shearers is silent, so He opened not His mouth"?

• • •

20. Which psalm describes the crucifixion?

• • •

21. True or False: Jesus' being betrayed by a friend is mentioned in Psalms and Zechariah.

22. Psalm 69:21 mentions what that was offered to Jesus on the cross?

• • •

23. True or False: The soldiers' casting of lots for Jesus' clothes was a fulfillment of prophecy.

• • •

24. True or False: Jesus' being buried in someone else's tomb was a fulfillment of prophecy.

• • •

25. Psalm 69:9 is a prophecy about
    a) Jesus' kingdom
    b) Jesus' birth
    c) Jesus' power over nature
    d) Jesus' cleansing of the temple

Messianic Prophecies Answers

1. Zechariah (Zechariah 11:12–13)

2. Micah (Micah 5:2)

3. Joseph fled to Egypt with Mary and Jesus to escape Herod (Matthew 2:15)

4. David (Psalm 22:14)

5. not one stone would be left upon another (Matthew 24:2)

6. John the Baptist (Isaiah 40:3; Malachi 3:1)

7. Jonah (Matthew 12:39–40)

8. that the Messiah would be a descendant of Judah (Genesis 49:8–12)

9. after the Holy Spirit came upon them (Acts 1:8)

10. Isaiah (53:5)

11. Joel (Joel 2:28–29)

12. the days of Noah (Matthew 24:37)

13. the mountain will split in two (Zechariah 14:4)

14. Judas Iscariot (Psalm 41:9; Acts 1:16)

15. Matthew

16. David (2 Samuel 7:16)

17. Zechariah (Zechariah 12:10 NKJV)

18. false; it was Zechariah (Zechariah 9:9)

19. Isaiah (Isaiah 53:7 NKJV)

20. Psalm 22

21. true (Psalm 41:9; Zechariah 13:6)

22. gall and vinegar (Psalm 69:21)

23. true (Psalm 22:18)

24. true (Isaiah 53:9)

25. d) Jesus' cleansing of the temple (Psalm 69:9)

MIRACLES OF JESUS

1. Jesus' first recorded miracle was at Cana of Galilee. What was it?

• • •

2. At the marriage feast in Cana of Galilee, to whom did Jesus say, "Mine hour is not yet come"?
   a) His disciples
   b) His mother
   c) the bridegroom
   d) the governor of the feast

3. How many fish were caught in the net in the miracle of the filling of the fishnets?

• • •

4. Before the miracle of the filling of the fishnets, why did Jesus enter the boat and ask Peter to thrust a little way from the land?

• • •

5. After catching a great multitude of fish, what did Simon Peter say?
   a) "Can any man forbid that we eat this food?"
   b) "Depart from me; for I am a sinful man."
   c) "The Gentiles shall hear the word of the Gospel."
   d) "Thou art the Son of God."

• • •

6. Before Jesus calmed the sea, what was He doing?

• • •

7. What did Jesus say to calm the sea?

8. How did the disciples react when Jesus calmed the angry winds and water on the Sea of Galilee?

• • •

9. True or False: The five thousand were fed with five loaves and two fish.

• • •

10. Who found the boy with the loaves and fishes?
   a) a shepherd
   b) Andrew
   c) Jesus
   d) Simon Peter

• • •

11. How many baskets of food were left over after the feeding of the five thousand?

• • •

12. After Jesus sent the multitude away and the disciples crossed by ship to the other side without Jesus, what did they see in the fourth watch of the night?

13. True or False: The same number of loaves and fish were used to feed the four thousand as the five thousand.

• • •

14. Choose A or B: During the arrest of Jesus, Simon Peter cut off the **a)** left or **b)** right ear of Malchus.

Miracles of Jesus Answers

1. turning water into wine (John 2:1–11)

2. b) His mother (John 2:3–4)

3. one hundred and fifty and three (John 21:11)

4. to teach the people (Luke 5:3)

5. b) "Depart from me; for I am a sinful man" (Luke 5:8)

6. sleeping in the boat (Mark 4:38)

7. "Peace, be still" (Mark 4:39)

8. "They marvelled, saying. . . Even the winds and the sea obey him!" (Matthew 8:26–27)

9. true (Mark 6:38)

10. b) Andrew (John 6:8–9)

11. twelve (John 6:13)

12. Jesus walking on the sea, but they supposed it was a spirit and cried out (Mark 6:48–49)

13. false; this time there were seven loaves and "a few" fish (Matthew 15:34)

14. b) right (John 18:10)

MIRACLES, MISC.

1. What two people had time altered for them?

• • •

2. What two Old Testament men didn't die?

• • •

3. What miracle was performed by both Peter and Paul?
   a) making someone go blind

b) casting out demons
c) curing a lame man
d) b & c

• • •

4. What Old Testament prophet fed one hundred men with twenty loaves of bread and had some left over?

• • •

5. Who cured bad water with salt?

• • •

6. On what mountain was Moses when he saw the burning bush?
    a) Carmel
    b) Horeb
    c) Sinai
    d) Moriah

Miracles, Misc. Answers

1. Joshua, Hezekiah (Joshua 10:12–13; 2 Kings 20:10–11)

2. Elijah, Enoch (2 Kings 2:1, 11; Genesis 5:24)

3. c) curing a lame man (Acts 3:4–8; 14:8–10)

4. Elisha (2 Kings 4:38, 42–44)

5. Elisha (2 Kings 2:21–22)

6. b) Horeb (Exodus 3:1)

MONEY

(See also Wealth)

1. Who paid Judas Iscariot to betray Jesus?

• • •

2. What happened to the thirty pieces of silver after Judas threw them back at the Pharisees?

• • •

3. Where can a treasure be put so that moth and rust do not corrupt it, and thieves cannot steal it?

• • •

4. Why does Jesus say a man cannot serve God and mammon (material wealth)?
    a) He will be a hypocrite with a sad countenance
    b) He will hate the one and love the other

c) He hides his wealth to preserve it

d) He will spoil those of his household

...

5. Fill in the blanks: "For what is a man profited, if he shall gain the _____ _____, and lose his own soul?"

...

6. Rather than seeking food, drink, and clothing, what should believers seek first?

...

7. Fill in the blank: The poor widow put _____ mites in the temple treasury.

...

8. Why did Jesus say the poor widow had given more than the rich people?

   a) Scribes and Pharisees had devoured her house

   b) She had gone to the moneychangers for coins without Caesar's image

c) Their hearts were not right, but her heart was right

d) they gave of their abundance, but she gave all she had

...

9. The moneychangers had made the temple a den of thieves, but it should have been called what kind of house by all nations?

...

10. True or False: The just man who invites the poor, maimed, lame, and blind to dinner will receive recompense at the resurrection.

...

11. After the rich ruler said he had obeyed all of the commands from his youth until the present, what did Jesus tell him to do?

...

12. How much did Joseph's brothers sell him for?

13. How much gold did the queen of Sheba give Solomon?

• • •

14. True or False: A denarius was a week's wage.

Money Answers

1. the chief priests (Matthew 26:14–16)

2. they were used to buy a potter's field (Matthew 27:7)

3. in heaven (Matthew 6:19–21)

4. b) he will hate the one and love the other (Matthew 6:24)

5. whole world (Matthew 16:26)

6. the kingdom of God (Matthew 6:31, 33)

7. two (Mark 12:42)

8. d) they gave out of their abundance, but she gave all she had (Mark 12:44)

9. a house of prayer (Mark 11:17)

10. true (Luke 14:12–14)

11. sell everything he had and give it to the poor (Luke 18:22)

12. twenty shekels of silver (Genesis 37:28 NKJV)

13. 120 talents (1 Kings 10:10)

14. false; a day's wage (Matthew 20:2)

MOSES

1. What five books of the Bible did Moses write?

• • •

2. True or False: Moses' story begins in the book of Genesis.

• • •

3. Why did Pharaoh decree that all the Hebrew baby boys be killed?

• • •

4. Moses' basket floating in the river was found by
   a) Pharaoh's servant
   b) Pharaoh's daughter

c) Pharaoh

d) Pharaoh's daughter's handmaiden

. . .

5. True or False: When he was a young man, Moses had no idea he was an adopted Hebrew.

. . .

6. After he was grown, Moses fled Egypt because he
   a) stole from the treasury
   b) was found to be a Hebrew
   c) killed an Egyptian for smiting a Hebrew
   d) killed a Hebrew for smiting a member of the royal court

. . .

7. Moses gained favor in Midian by
   a) helping sisters draw water
   b) telling the secrets of Pharaoh's court
   c) giving the citizens riches from Egypt
   d) teaching the Midianites how to build treasure cities

. . .

8. At the burning bush, what did God tell Moses to take off?

. . .

9. When God spoke to Moses, what name did the Lord use for Himself?

. . .

10. When the Lord commissioned Moses to speak to Pharaoh about releasing His people, Moses said he was
   a) not an eloquent speaker
   b) honored to be chosen
   c) not qualified since he wasn't a priest
   d) going to wait until after Passover

. . .

11. What sea was parted as the people exited?

. . .

12. To divide the sea, Moses lifted
   a) the belt of his robe
   b) both hands
   c) the name of the Lord
   d) his hand and his rod

Moses Answers

1. The Pentateuch—Genesis,
Exodus, Leviticus, Numbers,
Deuteronomy

2. false; his story begins in
Exodus, beginning with his
birth (Exodus 2).

3. because he was afraid
they would multiply and
eventually join Egypt's
enemies in war (Exodus 1:10)

4. b) Pharaoh's daughter
(Exodus 2:5)

5. false (Exodus 2:11)

6. c) killed an Egyptian for
smiting a Hebrew
(Exodus 2:11–12, 15)

7. a) helping sisters draw
water (Exodus 2:19–20)

8. his sandals (Exodus 3:5)

9. I AM or I AM THAT I
AM (Exodus 3:14)

10. a) not an eloquent
speaker (Exodus 4:10)

11. the Red Sea
(Exodus 13:18; 14:21–31)

12. d) his hand and his rod
(Exodus 14:16)

MOTHERS

1. Who was Solomon's
mother?

•••

2. Who was Timothy's
mother?

•••

3. Who was Moses'
biological mother?

•••

4. Which of Jesus' disciples
got their mother to ask
Jesus to let them sit on His
right and left hand in His
kingdom?

•••

5. Whose name means "the
mother of all living"?

•••

6. In Revelation 17:5, who is
referred to as "the mother of
harlots"?

•••

7. Who was Boaz's mother?

8. Who was called "a mother of nations"?

• • •

9. Who was the mother of John the Baptist?

10. Seth was born to a woman whose child had been murdered. Who was Seth's mother?

• • •

11. Besides Samuel, how many other children did Hannah have?

Mothers Answers

9. Elisabeth (Luke 1:13)

10. Eve (Genesis 4:25)

11. three sons, two daughters (1 Samuel 2:21)

1. Bathsheba (2 Samuel 12:24)

2. Eunice (2 Timothy 1:5)

3. Jochebed (Exodus 6:20)

4. James and John (Matthew 20:20–22)

5. Eve (Genesis 3:20)

6. Babylon the Great

7. Rahab (Matthew 1:5)

8. Sarah (Genesis 17:16–17)

MOUNTAINS

1. God gave Moses the Ten Commandments on Mount
   a) Sinai
   b) Pisgah
   c) Moriah
   d) Zion

• • •

2. Elijah called down fire from heaven to defeat the prophets of Baal on what mountain?
   a) Horeb
   b) Carmel
   c) Hor
   d) Moriah

• • •

3. When God showed Moses all of the Promised Land, He took Moses up on Mount
   a) Sinai
   b) Horeb
   c) Pisgah
   d) Moriah

4. When God tested Abraham, He told Abraham to take Isaac up on Mount
   a) Zion
   b) Moriah
   c) Horeb
   d) Sinai

• • •

5. The Garden of Gethsemane was on
   a) the Mount of Olives
   b) Mount Hermon
   c) Mount Calvary
   d) Mount Zion

• • •

6. Which of the following mountains was called the "mountain of God" or the "mount [or mountain] of the Lord"?
   a) Zion
   b) Sinai
   c) Horeb
   d) all of the above

• • •

7. Mount Calvary is also called Golgotha, which means
   a) "death"
   b) "burning"
   c) "shame"
   d) "skull"

8. Jesus was transfigured on
   a) Mount Calvary
   b) a high mountain
   c) the Mount of Olives
   d) Mount Zion

• • •

9. Upon what mountain was Moses when he saw the burning bush?
   a) Sinai
   b) Horeb
   c) Tabor
   d) Midian

• • •

10. Which of the following tribes of Israel had a mountain named for it?
   a) Reuben
   b) Gad
   c) Ephraim
   d) Dan

Mountains Answers

1. a) Sinai
(Exodus 19:18–20:17)

2. b) Carmel
(1 Kings 18:19, 30–38)

3. c) Pisgah
(Deuteronomy 34:1–4)

4. b) Moriah
(Genesis 22:1–2)

5. a) the Mount of Olives
(Matthew 26:36;
Luke 22:39)

6. d) all of the above (Isaiah
2:3; Numbers 10:12, 33;
Exodus 3:1)

7. d) "skull" (Matthew 27:33)

8. b) a high mountain
(Matthew 17:1)

9. b) Horeb (Exodus 3:1–4)

10. c) Ephraim
(1 Samuel 1:1)

MOURNING/
MOURNERS

*Lamentations is
a book of mourning.*

1. Fill in the blank: Blessed
are they that mourn: for they
shall be _____.

• • •

2. Whose death caused Jesus
to weep?

3. The exiles in Babylon
mourned the loss of what
city?

• • •

4. Which of the following is
not mourned in the book of
Lamentations?
    a) slavery
    b) famine
    c) drought
    d) personal loss

• • •

5. On what occasion
did Jesus have mourners
removed so that He could
perform a miracle?

• • •

6. Fill in the blank:
Ecclesiastes 3:4 says there is
a time to mourn and a time
to _____.

• • •

7. Who said, "The LORD will
be your everlasting light, and
the days of your mourning
shall be ended"?

Mourning/Mourners Answers

1. comforted (Matthew 5:4)

2. Lazarus (John 11:35)

3. Jerusalem (Lamentations 1:1–9)

4. c) drought (Lamentations 5:8; 1:11; 3:1–21)

5. the raising of Jairus's daughter (Matthew 9:18–25)

6. dance (Ecclesiastes 3:4)

7. Isaiah (Isaiah 60:20 NKJV)

MUSICAL INSTRUMENTS

1. Who was called "the father of all who play the harp and flute"?
   a) Jubal
   b) Jabal
   c) Tubal-Cain
   d) Lamech

• • •

2. How many different musical instruments are mentioned in Psalm 150?

3. True or False: The very first instrument mentioned in the Bible is a harp.

• • •

4. True or False: Bells are not mentioned in the Bible.

• • •

5. Which of the following instruments is not mentioned in the Bible?
   a) tambourine
   b) lute
   c) trumpet
   d) trombone

Musical Instruments Answers

1. a) Jubal (Genesis 4:21)

2. seven (Psalm 150)

3. true (Genesis 4:21)

4. false (Exodus 28:33)

5. d) trombone (1 Samuel 18:6; Psalm 92:3; Joshua 6:4)

N

NAMES

1. Fill in the blank: "Wherefore God also hath highly exalted him, and given him a name which is above _____."

• • •

2. What title for the Messiah, from Isaiah, foretells Christ's role as a peacemaker?

• • •

3. What was Jesus' favorite title for Himself that emphasized His humanity?

• • •

4. In what New Testament book do we find this title for Christ: "author and finisher of our faith"?

• • •

5. What title was used by the voice from heaven to describe Jesus following His baptism?

6. What phrase did Jesus use to describe Himself after feeding the five thousand men?

• • •

7. How did Jesus describe Himself after this statement: "I must work the works of him that sent me, while it is day: the night cometh, when no man can work"?

• • •

8. What expression did Paul use to describe Christ's sacrifice for us?
   a) sacrificial lamb
   b) our Passover
   c) burnt offering

• • •

9. How did Christ describe Himself to Martha prior to raising Lazarus from the dead?

• • •

10. Fill in the blank: "I am Alpha and Omega, the _____."

11. Where does God say He has inscribed our names?

• • •

12. Jesus told the disciples to rejoice because their names are written where?

• • •

13. Who named Moses?

• • •

14. Who named Ruth and Boaz's son?

• • •

15. What did they name him?

Names Answers

1. every name (Philippians 2:9)

2. Prince of Peace (Isaiah 9:6; Ephesians 2:14)

3. Son of man (Matthew 8:20)

4. Hebrews (Hebrews 12:2)

5. My beloved Son (Matthew 3:17)

6. bread of life (John 6:10, 35)

7. light of the world (John 9:4–5)

8. b) our Passover (1 Corinthians 5:7)

9. the resurrection and the life (John 11:25)

10. beginning and the end (Revelation 21:6)

11. on the palms of His hands (Isaiah 49:15–16)

12. in heaven (Luke 10:20)

13. Pharaoh's daughter (Exodus 2:10)

14. the neighbor women (Ruth 4:17 NKJV)

15. Obed (Ruth 4:17)

NAMES OF THE LORD

After God helped them win the battle against the Amalekites, Moses built an altar and named it Jehovah Nissi, which means "The Lord is my banner" (Exodus 17:15).

1. To whom was God speaking when He said, "Say unto the children of Israel, I AM hath sent me unto you"?
   a) Aaron
   b) Moses
   c) Joshua
   d) Elijah

• • •

2. Who called the Lord "Thou God seest me"?
   a) Sarai
   b) Abram
   c) Hagar
   d) Ishmael

• • •

3. To whom was God speaking when He said, "I am the Almighty God"?
   a) Moses
   b) Aaron
   c) Abram
   d) Pharaoh

4. When Moses told the children of Israel to remember the days of old, he referred to the Lord as
   a) the Most High
   b) the Ancient of Days
   c) the Lord of Lords
   d) the Lord above all

• • •

5. Which of the Ten Commandments tells us not to take our Lord's name in vain?
   a) 1
   b) 2
   c) 3
   d) 4

• • •

6. Which of the following names is not in the list found in Isaiah 9:6?
   a) Bright and Morning Star
   b) Prince of Peace
   c) Mighty God
   d) Counselor

• • •

7. "KING OF KINGS, AND LORD OF LORDS" was written on Jesus'
   a) vesture and thigh
   b) shield
   c) sword
   d) breastplate

8. Which of the following names means "God with us"?
   a) Jesus
   b) Elohim
   c) Emmanuel
   d) Elyon

• • •

9. Philippians 2:9 says that God gave Jesus
   a) the name Jesus
   b) the name above every name
   c) a secret name
   d) b & c

• • •

10. Who said, "I know that my Redeemer lives"?
   a) David
   b) Job
   c) Moses
   d) Isaiah

• • •

11. Fill in the blank: Whosoever shall call upon the name of the Lord shall be
   _____.

Names of the Lord Answers

1. b) Moses (Exodus 3:14)

2. c) Hagar (Genesis 16:8, 13)

3. c) Abram (Genesis 17:1)

4. a) the Most High (Deuteronomy 31:30; 32:8)

5. c) 3 (Exodus 20:7)

6. a) Bright and Morning Star (Isaiah 9:6)

7. a) vesture and thigh (Revelation 19:16)

8. c) Emmanuel (Matthew 1:23)

9. b) the name above every name (Philippians 2:9)

10. b) Job (Job 19:1, 25 NKJV)

11. saved (Romans 10:13)

NATIVITY

1. Fill in the blank: At the time the angels announced that Mary would have the child to be named Jesus, she and Joseph were living in the town of _____.

• • •

2. Fill in the blank: Mary accepted what the angel said to her by saying, "I am the Lord's _____"

• • •

3. What verse in the Old Testament foretold that Jesus would be born in Bethlehem?
   a) Isaiah 7:14
   b) Micah 5:2
   c) Isaiah 9:6–7
   d) Joel 2:5

• • •

4. Who was Caesar at the time Jesus was born?
   a) Julius
   b) Nero
   c) Dominican
   d) Augustus

5. How old was Jesus when He was taken to the temple to be presented?
   a) 1 day
   b) 5 days
   c) 7 days
   d) 8 days

• • •

6. What sacrifice was given for Jesus' presentation at the temple?
   a) a lamb
   b) a bullock
   c) two turtledoves
   d) a goat

• • •

7. Whom did the wise men ask, "Where is he that is born King of the Jews?"

• • •

8. Whom did King Herod consult to learn where the king of the Jews would be born?
   a) chief priests and teachers of the law
   b) John the Baptist
   c) soothsayers
   d) the magi (wise men)

9. Where did God tell Joseph to take Mary and Jesus to keep them safe?
   a) Nazareth
   b) Egypt
   c) Jerusalem
   d) Caesarea

• • •

10. Herod ordered all the children in Bethlehem from the age of _____ and younger to be killed.
   a) 2 years
   b) 3 years
   c) 4 years
   d) 5 years

• • •

11. Mary and Joseph went to Bethlehem to be registered because of
   a) Herod
   b) a census
   c) a Roman law
   d) a desire to have their baby there

• • •

12. What was the first thing the angel said to the shepherds?
   a) "A light has been born for the Gentiles"
   b) "A Savior has been born"
   c) "Do not be afraid"
   d) "I bring you good news"

• • •

13. The angels told the shepherds that the sign unto them would be
   a) the star
   b) an angel
   c) the babe lying in a manger
   d) sheep grazing nearby

• • •

14. What reason did the angel give to Joseph that it was safe to return home?

Nativity Answers

1. Nazareth (Luke 1:26–27)

2. servant (Luke 1:38 niv)

3. b) Micah 5:2

4. d) Augustus (Luke 2:1)

5. d) 8 days (Luke 2:21–24)

6. c) two turtledoves (Luke 2:24)

NAZARITES

The difference between a Nazarite and a Nazarene was that a Nazarene came from the town of Nazareth (Matthew 2:23).

1. True or False: *Nazarite* means "one separated."

• • •

2. True or False: A Nazarite couldn't drink wine.

• • •

3. Which Nazarite vow did Samson break and caused his death?

• • •

4. True or False: A Nazarite could only touch a dead body if he was burying his mother or father.

• • •

5. True or False: A Nazarite could drink vinegar.

• • •

6. True or False: John the Baptist was a Nazarite.

7. Herod (Matthew 2:1–3)

8. a) chief priests and teachers of the law" (Matthew 2:4 NIV)

9. b) Egypt (Matthew 2:13)

10. a) 2 years (Matthew 2:16)

11. b) a census (Luke 2:1–5)

12. c) "Do not be afraid" (Luke 2:10)

13. c) the babe lying in a manger (Luke 2:8–12)

14. those trying to kill the child were dead (Matthew 2:19–20)

Nazarites Answers

1. true (Numbers 6:2)

2. true (Numbers 6:3)

3. he allowed his hair to be cut (Numbers 6:5)

4. false (Numbers 6:6)

5. false (Numbers 6:3)

6. false; the Bible doesn't specifically say he was

NEBUCHADNEZZAR'S DREAM IMAGE

(see also Daniel)

1. When Nebuchadnezzar had his dream, whom did he call to tell him what it was?
   a) magicians
   b) astrologers
   c) sorcerers
   d) all of the above

• • •

2. Why were Nebuchadnezzar's astrologers unable to give an interpretation of his dream?
   a) Daniel told them to remain silent
   b) Nebuchadnezzar would not tell them the contents of the dream
   c) They feared telling Nebuchadnezzar that his kingdom would crumble
   d) Nebuchadnezzar's rivals threatened them

• • •

3. Fill in the blanks: "Thou, O king, art a _____ of _____."

• • •

4. True or False: Daniel told Nebuchadnezzar the interpretation right away.

• • •

5. True or False: Daniel told Nebuchadnezzar that he (Daniel) interpreted the dream.

• • •

6. Who prayed with Daniel concerning the interpretation?

• • •

7. Choose A or B: God revealed the secret to Daniel a) by an angel or b) in a night vision.

8. Daniel said the statue in Nebuchadnezzar's dream represented how many kingdoms?

• • •

9. Fill in the blank: The image's head was made of _____.

• • •

10. Fill in the blank: The image's chest and arms were made of _____.

• • •

11. Fill in the blank: The image's belly and thighs were made of _____.

• • •

12. Fill in the blank: The image's legs were made of _____.

• • •

13. Fill in the blanks: The image's feet were made of _____ mixed with _____.

14. When Nebuchadnezzar made his own image, how did it differ from the one in his dream?

Nebuchadnezzar's Dream Image Answers

1. d) all of the above (Daniel 2:2)

2. b) Nebuchadnezzar would not tell them the contents of the dream (Daniel 2:1–9)

3. king, kings (Daniel 2:37)

4. false (Daniel 2:16)

5. false (Daniel 2:28)

6. Hananiah, Mishael, Azariah (Daniel 2:17–18)

7. b) in a night vision (Daniel 2:19)

8. four (Daniel 2:30–31, 40)

9. gold (Daniel 2:32)

10. silver (Daniel 2:32)

11. bronze (Daniel 2:32)

12. iron (Daniel 2:33)

13. iron, clay (Daniel 2:33)

14. it was all gold (Daniel 3:1)

NEIGHBORS

Withhold not good from them to whom it is due, when it is in the power of thine hand to do it. Say not unto thy neighbour, Go, and come again, and to morrow I will give; when thou hast it by thee. Devise not evil against thy neighbour, seeing he dwelleth securely by thee.

PROVERBS 3:27–29

1. What parable did Jesus tell to answer the question, "Who is my neighbor?"

• • •

2. Who asked the question in question 1?

• • •

3. At the end of the parable, what did Jesus tell the person to do?

• • •

4. Better is a neighbor nearby than what?

5. Fill in the blanks: You shall not bear _____ _____ against your neighbor.

• • •

6. True or False: You shall not covet your neighbor's house, wife, male servant, female servant, ox, donkey, or anything.

• • •

7. Fill in the blank: Cursed is the one who moves his neighbor's _____.

• • •

8. True or False: You should not take your neighbor hastily to court.

• • •

9. True or False: You shouldn't visit your neighbor frequently.

Neighbors Answers

1. the good Samaritan (Luke 10:25–37)

2. a lawyer (Luke 10:25–37)

3. "Go and do likewise."
(Luke 10:37)

4. a brother far away
(Proverbs 27:10 NKJV)

5. false witness
(Exodus 20:16)

6. true (Exodus 20:17)

7. landmark
(Deuteronomy 27:17 NKJV)

8. true (Proverbs 25:8 NKJV)

9. true (Proverbs 25:17)

NEW HEAVEN AND NEW EARTH

1. Who described the Christian's "lively [living] hope" this way: "To an inheritance incorruptible, and undefiled, and that fadeth not away, reserved in heaven for you"?

• • •

2. Who said if our earthly house is destroyed, "we have a building from God, a house not made with hands, eternal in the heavens"?

3. Fill in the blank: "Beloved, now are we the sons of God, and it doth not yet appear what we shall be: but we know that, when he shall appear, we shall be like him; for we shall see _____."

• • •

4. Who were those seen in white robes around the throne of heaven who serve God "day and night in his temple"?

• • •

5. Why did a voice from heaven say, "Blessed are the dead which die in the Lord from henceforth"?

• • •

6. To what did John liken his first glimpse of the "holy city, new Jerusalem"?

• • •

7. Fill in the blank: "Behold, the tabernacle of God is with men, and he will dwell with them. . .and _____."

8. Why did John say there would be no more death, sorrow, or pain in heaven?

• • •

9. Why did John not see a temple in heaven?

• • •

10. Name the Lamb's record of all who are saved, mentioned in Revelation.

New Heaven and New Earth Answers

1. Peter (1 Peter 1:3–4)

2. Paul (2 Corinthians 5:1 NKJV)

3. him as he is (1 John 3:2)

4. those who "came out of great tribulation" (Revelation 7:14–15)

5. they rest from their labors and their works follow them (Revelation 14:13)

6. "as a bride adorned for her husband" (Revelation 21:2)

7. be their God (Revelation 21:3)

8. because "the former things are passed away" (Revelation 21:4)

9. "The Lord God Almighty and the Lamb are its temple." (Revelation 21:22 NKJV)

10. The Lamb's Book of Life (Revelation 21:27)

O

OATHS

(see also Vows)

For when God made promise to Abraham, because he could swear by no greater, he sware by himself.
HEBREWS 6:13

1. What did Joseph make the children of Israel swear an oath to do?

• • •

2. Numbers 30:2 says that a man who made an oath was to do all according to what?

• • •

3. Who made an oath to give someone up to half his kingdom?

• • •

4. Who swore an oath that he didn't know Jesus?

• • •

5. Who swore an oath that they would neither eat nor drink until they had killed Paul?

6. James tells us not to swear by any oath but rather what?

Oath Answers

1. carry his bones out of Egypt (Genesis 50:25)

2. all that proceeded out of his mouth (Numbers 30:2)

3. Herod (Mark 6:21, 23)

4. Peter (Matthew 26:72)

5. a band of Jews (Acts 23:14, 21)

6. let your yea be yea, your nay, nay (James 5:12)

OBEDIENCE

1. Fill in the blanks: James said we are to be _____ of the word; not _____ only.

• • •

2. Fill in the blank: The psalmist says that in keeping God's law there is great _____.

243

3. Fill in the blank: Daniel _____ in his heart that he would not defile himself.

• • •

4. Who said, "We ought to obey God rather than men"?

• • •

5. Which of the following is not listed in Micah 6:8?
   a) do justly
   b) love mercy
   c) walk humbly with God
   d) live by faith

• • •

6. Which two of Paul's epistles tell children to obey their parents?

• • •

7. Who said, "To obey is better than sacrifice," and to whom did he say it?

Obedience Answers

1. doers, hearers (James 1:22)

2. reward (Psalm 19:11)

3. purposed (Daniel 1:8)

4. Peter and the other apostles (Acts 5:29)

5. d) live by faith (Micah 6:8)

6. Ephesians 6:1; Colossians 3:20

7. Samuel, Saul (1 Samuel 15:22)

OCCUPATIONS

1. What job was Moses doing when God spoke to him from the burning bush?

• • •

2. With whom were James and John partners?

• • •

3. What did Priscilla and Aquila do when they weren't teaching the gospel?

• • •

4. Who did Delilah work for?

• • •

5. What was the occupation of the Ethiopian eunuch in Acts 8?

6. For which two servants of Pharaoh did Joseph interpret dreams?

• • •

7. What was Pontius Pilate's job?

• • •

8. Who were two tax collectors associated with Jesus?

• • •

9. Who is the only witch mentioned in the Bible?

• • •

10. Before which two governors, whose names both begin with F, did Paul appear?

• • •

11. Who was King Artaxerxes' cupbearer?

• • •

12. What position did Joseph hold in Egypt?

13. Who told Naaman to go see the prophet and be healed?

• • •

14. What job did Abel, Rachel, and Zipporah have in common?

• • •

15. What metals did Tubal-cain work with?

• • •

16. What did Amos do before he was a prophet?

• • •

17. What was Luke's occupation?

• • •

18. What was Potiphar's job?

• • •

19. What occupation did Paul say the law held in regard to us?

20. What is the occupation of the man other than the Pharisee in the parable of the two men who go to the temple to pray?

• • •

21. Who was appointed governor of Judah by Nebuchadnezzar?

• • •

22. What did Nebuchadnezzar appoint Shadrach, Meshach, and Abednego to do?

• • •

23. What did Zimri do before he became king of Israel?

• • •

24. Who was the priest of Midian?

• • •

25. What did Huldah and Anna have in common?

26. The people Jesus drove out of the temple were
   a) money lenders
   b) money changers
   c) both

• • •

27. What were Peter and Andrew doing when Jesus called them to follow Him?

• • •

28. What were James and John doing when Jesus called them to follow Him?

• • •

29. True or False: The Bible never actually says that Luke was a physician.

Occupations Answers

1. herding sheep (Exodus 3:1)

2. Simon Peter (Luke 5:1–10; John 21:2–4)

3. they were tentmakers (Acts 18:3)

4. the lords of the Philistines (Judges 16:4–5)

5. treasurer (Acts 8:27)

19. schoolmaster (tutor) (Galatians 3:24)

18. captain of the guard (Genesis 39:1)

17. physician (Colossians 4:14)

16. shepherd (Amos 1:1)

15. brass and iron (Genesis 4:22)

14. shepherds (Genesis 4:2; 29:9; Exodus 2:16, 21)

13. his wife's slave girl (2 Kings 5:2–4)

12. second only to Pharaoh (Genesis 41:40)

11. Nehemiah (Nehemiah 1:11–2:1)

10. Felix and Festus (Acts 24:27)

9. the witch of Endor (1 Samuel 28:7–8)

8. Matthew (Matthew 9:9–13) and Zacchaeus (Luke 19:1–10)

7. governor of Judea (Luke 3:1)

6. baker and butler (cupbearer) (Genesis 40)

29. false (Colossians 4:14 NKJV)

28. mending their nets (Matthew 4:21)

27. casting a net into the sea (Matthew 4:18)

26. b) money changers (Mark 11:15)

25. they were both prophetesses (2 Chronicles 34:22; Luke 2:36)

24. Reuel (Jethro) (Exodus 2:16–18)

23. he was servant to Elah who was king of Israel before him (1 Kings 16:8–9)

22. he set them over the affairs of the province of Babylon (Daniel 3:12)

21. Gedaliah (Jeremiah 40:5)

20. publican (tax collector) (Luke 18:10)

OFFERINGS

(see also Sacrifices)

1. Which of the following was not an offering?
   a) trespass offering
   b) grain offering
   c) peace offering
   d) wine offering

•••

2. True or False: Sin offerings and trespass offerings were the same thing.

•••

3. True or False: There was a continual burnt offering.

•••

4. In a wave offering, what was waved?

•••

5. True or False: The offerings were offered in a particular order.

•••

6. Fill in the blank: In order to build the tabernacle, the Israelites brought a _____ offering.

Offerings Answers

1. d) wine offering (Leviticus 5:1–6; 2:1–16; 3:1–17)

2. false (Leviticus 4:1–35; 5:1–6)

3. true (Exodus 29:38)

4. sheaves, loaves (Leviticus 23:15–17)

5. true (Numbers 28–29)

6. freewill (Exodus 35:29 nkjv)

OLD AGE

Now Joshua was old and stricken in years; and the LORD said unto him, Thou art old and stricken in years.
JOSHUA 13:1

1. Fill in the blanks: In Isaiah 46:4, God says, "Even to _____ _____ I will carry you."

•••

2. How old was Caleb when he volunteered to drive out the giants on the mountain in Hebron?

3. The eighty-four-year-old widow who saw Mary and Joseph bring Jesus into the temple was named
   a) Miriam
   b) Joanna
   c) Anna
   d) Deborah

•••

4. What was the name of the oldest living man, and how long did he live?

•••

5. How old was Noah when he begat Shem, Ham, and Japheth?

•••

6. How old was Abraham when Ishmael was born?

•••

7. How many years does Psalm 90:10 say are "the days of our lives"?

•••

8. When they first spoke to Pharaoh, how old were Moses and Aaron?

9. How old was Sarah when Isaac was born?

•••

10. How old was Abraham when Isaac was born?

•••

11. How old was Noah when he died?
   a) 650
   b) 750
   c) 850
   d) 950

•••

12. How old was Adam when he died?
   a) 900
   b) 910
   c) 920
   d) 930

•••

13. How old was Noah when the flood came?

•••

14. How old was Abraham when he died?

•••

15. How old was Sarah when she died?

Old Age Answers

1. gray hairs (Isaiah 46:4 NKJV)

2. 85 (Joshua 14:7, 10–12)

3. c) Anna (Luke 2:36–37)

4. Methuselah, 969 years (Genesis 5:27)

5. 500 (Genesis 5:32)

6. 86 (Genesis 16:16)

7. 70 years (Psalm 90:10)

8. Moses, 80; Aaron, 83 (Exodus 7:7)

9. 90 (Genesis 17:17)

10. 100 (Genesis 21:5)

11. d) 950 (Genesis 9:29)

12. d) 930 (Genesis 5:5)

13. 600 (Genesis 7:11)

14. 175 (Genesis 25:7)

15. 127 (Genesis 23:1)

OVERCOME

1. In Revelation 2:7, the church at Ephesus was told that if they overcame, they would be given to eat from what?

2. In Revelation 2:11, the church at Smyrna was told that if they overcame, they would not be hurt by what?

•••

3. In Revelation 2:17, the church at Pergamos was told that if they overcame, they would be given what to eat?

•••

4. Fill in the blank: In Revelation 2:26, the church at Thyatira was told that if they overcame, they would be given power over _____.

•••

5. In Revelation 3:5, the church at Sardis was told that if they overcame, they would be clothed in what?

•••

6. In Revelation 3:12, the church at Philadelphia was told that if they overcame, they would become what?

7. In Revelation 3:21, the church at Laodicea was told that if they overcame, they would be granted what?

•••

8. Jesus told us to be of good cheer because He has overcome what?

•••

9. John said that what can overcome the world?

•••

10. When Jacob was blessing his sons, which son did he say would overcome at last?
   a) Reuben
   b) Simeon
   c) Gad
   d) Asher

1. the tree of life (Revelation 2:7)

2. the second death (Revelation 2:11)

3. hidden manna (Revelation 2:17)

4. the nations (Revelation 2:26)

5. white garments (Revelation 3:5)

6. pillars in the temple of God (Revelation 3:12)

7. to sit with Him on His throne (Revelation 3:21)

8. the world (John 16:33)

9. our faith (1 John 5:4)

10. c) Gad (Genesis 49:19 NKJV)

P

PARABLES OF JESUS

1. What question was Jesus answering when He told the parable of the good Samaritan?

•••

2. Whom did the five foolish virgins ask for oil for their lamps?

•••

3. What did the parable of the vineyard owner and the parable of the wicked husbandmen teach about Jesus?

•••

4. What parable taught that God will avenge His elect?

•••

5. What parable did Jesus give following the parables of the lost sheep and the lost coin?

•••

6. To whom does Jesus compare someone who does not give up everything to be His disciple?

7. Which parable includes "God be merciful to me a sinner"?

•••

8. What did the merchant do when he found the pearl of great price?

•••

9. What parable illustrates how God feels about those who don't forgive others?

•••

10. How does the parable of the talents differ numerically from the parable of the pennies (denarii)?

•••

11. What prophet told an adulterous king the parable of a man with one ewe lamb?

•••

12. What did Isaiah's parable of the vineyard say about Israel?

13. What parable included the concept of "eat, drink, and be merry"?

•••

14. Under what two places did Jesus say that a lamp should not be put?

•••

15. How many soils are described in the parable of the sower?

•••

16. What three hazards befell the seeds in Jesus' parable of the sower?

•••

17. What parable illustrates the principle that no man can serve two masters?

•••

18. Where was the man who was robbed going in the parable of the good Samaritan, and from where had he come?

19. What parable teaches that being rich doesn't automatically get you into heaven?

•••

20. What parable ends with "wailing and gnashing of teeth"?

•••

21. Why didn't Jesus speak to His disciples in parables?

•••

22. In Jesus' illustration of how God wants to give us good things, what did the Lord say a father would not give his son if he asked for bread?

•••

23. To what did Jesus compare the mustard seed?

•••

24. In what parable did Jesus tell the chief priests and elders that publicans and harlots would enter the kingdom of God before they did?

25. What parable ends with "So the last shall be first and the first last"?

Parables of Jesus Answers

1. "And who is my neighbour?" (Luke 10:29)
2. the five wise virgins (Matthew 25:8)
3. the last would be first and the first would be last; Jesus would be killed (Matthew 20:1–16; Luke 20)
4. the unjust judge (Luke 18:1–8)
5. the prodigal son (Luke 15)
6. a man building a tower or a king going into battle, neither of whom had "counted the cost" (Luke 14:26–33)
7. two men praying at the temple (Luke 18:9–14)
8. sold all he had and bought it (Matthew 13:46)
9. the unforgiving servant (Matthew 18:22–35)
10. In the talents, the men were given respectively five, two, and one talent; in the pennies/denarii, each man received only one penny/denarius (Matthew 25:15; 20:1–16)
11. Nathan (2 Samuel 12)
12. that they didn't deal justly with each other (Isaiah 5:1–7)
13. the rich fool (Luke 12:16–21)
14. basket, bed (Mark 4:21)
15. four (Matthew 13:3–8)
16. birds, the sun, thorns (Matthew 13:4–7)
17. the unjust steward (Luke 16:1–13)
18. to Jericho from Jerusalem (Luke 10:30)
19. the rich man and Lazarus (Luke 16:19–31)
20. the fishing net (Matthew 13:47–50)
21. it had been given to the disciples to know the mysteries of the kingdom but not to the general population (Matthew 13:10–11)

22. a stone (Luke 11:11)

23. the kingdom of heaven (Matthew 13:31)

24. the parable of the two sons (Matthew 21:31)

25. the parable of the laborers (Matthew 20:1–16)

PASSOVER

(see also Leaving Egypt)

1. Choose A or B: The lamb of the first Passover was to be **a)** male or **b)** female.

•••

2. Fill in the blank: The lamb of question 1 was to be without ____.

•••

3. The lamb was to be killed on what day of the month?
   a) first
   b) tenth
   c) fourteenth
   d) thirtieth

4. True or False: The blood of the lamb was to be put on the two side posts and the upper doorpost of each house.

•••

5. Fill in the blanks: The Israelites were to eat the roasted lamb with _____ bread and ____ herbs.

•••

6. True or False: The Israelites were to eat with shoes on their feet and their staffs in their hands.

•••

7. Why was this event called Passover?

•••

8. Choose A or B: "And this day shall be unto you for **a)** a memorial or **b)** sacrifice."

•••

9. True or False: The feast was to last nine days.

10. What type of plant was to be dipped in the blood to put the blood on the doorposts?
 a) hazel
 b) hyssop
 c) hickory
 d) grass

Passover Answers

1. a) male (Exodus 12:5)

2. blemish (Exodus 12:5)

3. c) fourteenth (Exodus 12:6)

4. true (Exodus 12:7)

5. unleavened, bitter (Exodus 12:8)

6. true (Exodus 12:11)

7. God said, "When I see the blood, I will pass over you, and the plague shall not be upon you to destroy you" (Exodus 12:13)

8. a) a memorial (Exodus 12:14)

9. false; it was to last seven days (Exodus 12:15)

10. b) hyssop (Exodus 12:22)

PAUL

1. Paul, in Jerusalem. . .
 a) was transferred directly from there to Rome
 b) was told by his nephew of a plot to kill him
 c) preached at the site of an idol to an unknown god

•••

2. True or False: Because he was taken to Felix, Paul was rescued from certain death at the hands of more than forty Jews who opposed his teachings.

•••

3. Who did Paul say tried to keep him from making progress?

•••

4. After Paul's arrest in Jerusalem, why did the centurion hesitate to flog Paul?

•••

5. Fill in the blank: After being struck while before the Sanhedrin, Paul said, "God will strike you, you _____ wall!"

6. Fill in the blank: The Roman commander called for soldiers, horsemen, and spearmen to safely take Paul to Governor Felix in the city of _____.

•••

7. Fill in the blank: As Paul spoke of the judgment to come, Felix became fearful and said, "You may leave. When I find it _____, I will send for you."

•••

8. Fill in the blanks: Festus told Paul, "You have appealed to _____. To _____ you will go!"

•••

9. Which of Paul's inquisitors said, "Do you think that in such a short time you can persuade me to be a Christian?"
   a) Ananias, the high priest
   b) Felix
   c) Festus
   d) King Agrippa

10. How did the centurion named Julius treat Paul during the voyage to Rome?
   a) kept him in chains below deck
   b) showed Paul kindness

•••

11. Fill in the blank: After landing at Fair Havens, Paul predicted a disastrous voyage if they continued, but the centurion followed the advice of the pilot and the _____ of the ship.

•••

12. True or False: The Jewish leaders in Rome told Paul, "We are convinced we should not listen to you."

•••

13. For how many years had Paul been in Rome when Acts ends?

Paul Answers

1. b) was told by his nephew of a plot to kill him (Acts 23:14, 16)

2. true (Acts 23:12–24)

257

PAUL'S MISSIONARY JOURNEYS

1. How did the believers react to Paul when he returned to Jerusalem after his conversion?

•••

2. Fill in the blank: "The disciples were called Christians first in _____."

•••

3. How did the church at Antioch set Barnabas and Paul apart for missionary service?

•••

4. Who was the sorcerer at Paphos who was struck blind by Paul for his heresy?

•••

5. At Lystra, what motivated the crowd to proclaim Paul and Barnabas as gods?

---

3. Satan (1 Thessalonians 2:18)

4. because Paul was a Roman citizen (Acts 22:25)

5. whitewashed (Acts 23:3 NKJV)

6. Caesarea (Acts 23:23–24)

7. convenient (Acts 24:25 NIV)

8. Caesar, Caesar (Acts 25:12 NIV)

9. d) King Agrippa (Acts 26:28)

10. b) showed Paul kindness (Acts 27:1–3)

11. owner (Acts 27:8–11)

12. false; they said, "We want to hear what your views are" (Acts 28:17–22 NIV)

13. two (Acts 28:30)

6. In Paul's vision at Troas, what appeal did the man from Macedonia make?

•••

7. When an earthquake rocked the prison at Philippi, what did the jailer cry out to Paul and Silas?

•••

8. Why did Paul and Timothy decide not to minister in Asia and Bithynia?

•••

9. What was Paul accused of saying in Ephesus that offended Demetrius, the silversmith?

•••

10. Fill in the blank: While praying in the temple, Paul had a vision in which the Lord said, "Depart: for I will send thee far hence _____."

•••

11. Who interceded for Paul when the believers at Jerusalem were reluctant to accept him as a convert?

12. What missionary associate did Paul and Barnabas have a disagreement over?

•••

13. Which missionary companion had a godly Jewish mother and a Greek father?

•••

14. Who was Paul's companion in the jail at Philippi?

•••

15. Name the tentmaking couple who offered hospitality to Paul in Corinth.

•••

16. Who was the companion who chronicled much of Paul's missionary activities in Acts?

•••

17. Which companion is described: "A certain Jew... born at Alexandria, an eloquent man, and mighty in the scriptures"?

18. Who brought gifts from the Philippians to Paul while he was imprisoned in Rome?

•••

19. When Paul was near death in prison, whom did he urge to "come before winter"?

•••

20. What traveling companion was sent by Paul to correct problems in the church at Corinth?

Paul's Missionary Journeys Answers

1. they were afraid of him (Acts 9:26)

2. Antioch (Acts 11:26 NIV)

3. they fasted, prayed, and laid their hands on them (Acts 13:1–3)

4. Bar-jesus/Elymas (Acts 13:6, 8–11)

5. the healing of a crippled man (Acts 14:8–12)

6. "Come over into Macedonia, and help us" (Acts 16:9)

7. "Sirs, what must I do to be saved?" (Acts 16:29–30)

8. they were forbidden by the Holy Spirit (Acts 16:1–3, 6–7)

9. there are no gods made with hands (Acts 19:26)

10. unto the Gentiles (Acts 22:17, 21)

11. Barnabas (Acts 9:27–28)

12. John Mark (Acts 15:37–39)

13. Timothy (Acts 16:1)

14. Silas (Acts 16:19, 23)

15. Aquila and Priscilla (Acts 18:2–3)

16. Luke (Acts 1:1; 16:10; Luke 1:3)

17. Apollos (Acts 18:24)

18. Epaphroditus (Philippians 4:18)

19. Timothy (2 Timothy 4:21)

20. Titus (2 Corinthians 8:23)

PHARISEES

1. How did Jesus reply when the Pharisees asked why He was eating with publicans and sinners?

•••

2. How did Jesus reply when asked why His disciples did not fast, but the Pharisees often fasted?

•••

3. When the chief priests and elders asked about His authority for doing the things He did, how did Jesus respond?
   a) by asking a question about the baptism of John the Baptist
   b) by ignoring the question
   c) by quoting from the Law and the Prophets
   d) by talking about bread from heaven

•••

4. True or False: When Jesus talked about the stone that the builders rejected, the Pharisees were not aware He was speaking of them.

5. When Jesus preached, "Woe unto you, scribes and Pharisees, hypocrites!" how did He use a gnat and a camel to illustrate His point?

•••

6. Why did the scribes and Pharisees watch Jesus?
   a) to find an accusation against Him
   b) to identify His disciples and bring them before Pilate
   c) to learn how He performed miracles
   d) to see if He was paying the temple tax

•••

7. True or False: Jesus refused to eat with the Pharisees.

•••

8. What was "the leaven of the Pharisees"?
   a) hypocrisy
   b) manna from heaven
   c) marriage questions
   d) the old law

9. True or False: Nicodemus, the ruler of the Jews, who came to see Jesus by night, was a Pharisee.

• • •

10. Why did some Pharisees object when Jesus healed the blind man by making clay, putting it in his eyes, and having him wash in the pool of Siloam?

Pharisees Answers

1. "They that be whole need not a physician, but they that are sick" (Matthew 9:12).

2. "The bridegroom is with them" (Matthew 9:15).

3. a) by asking a question about the baptism of John the Baptist (Matthew 21:23, 25).

4. False; they perceived He was talking about them (Matthew 21:42, 45).

5. "Ye blind guides, which strain at a gnat, and swallow a camel" (Matthew 23:23–24).

6. a) to find an accusation against Him (Luke 6:7).

7. False; he ate in their houses (Luke 7:36).

8. a) hypocrisy (Luke 12:1)

9. true (John 3:1–2)

10. because He healed him on the Sabbath day (John 9:14–16)

PLACES OF WORSHIP

1. What sacrifice were Mary and Joseph to make when they brought Jesus to the temple to present Him to the Lord?

• • •

2. How many loaves of the Bread of the Presence, or shewbread, were to be on the table in the tabernacle Sabbath after Sabbath?

• • •

3. How many pieces of gold were used to make the candlestick?

4. Who alone could enter the Holy of Holies and on what occasion?

•••

5. Why wasn't David allowed to build the temple?

•••

6. How long did it take Solomon to build the temple?

•••

7. Why is there no temple in the New Jerusalem?

•••

8. How often did the high priest burn incense on the golden altar?

•••

9. Who was famous for making a detailed organization of temple personnel?

•••

10. Who supplied the materials to build the tabernacle?

11. What were the holders on the lampstand in the tabernacle designed to look like?

•••

12. What material was used to make the altar of incense in the tabernacle?

•••

13. What separated the Holy Place from the Most Holy Place?

•••

14. What material was to be used to make the tent pegs of the tabernacle?

•••

15. What son of Shealtiel is credited with helping to rebuild the temple after the Babylonian captivity?

•••

16. Who destroyed Solomon's temple?

•••

17. By what act could someone claim sanctuary in the temple?

18. When the Israelites moved into the Promised Land, what city became the permanent home of the tabernacle?

•••

19. On what site did Solomon build the temple?

•••

20. What two types of materials were used to make the curtains in the tabernacle?

•••

21. Where will the ark of the covenant ultimately be found?

•••

22. On what article of the high priest's clothing were the Urim and Thummim placed?

•••

23. How did God show His presence at the dedication of Solomon's temple?

24. How many days did the people celebrate following the completion of Solomon's temple?

•••

25. What writer of psalms was a supervisor of the music at Solomon's temple?

Places of Worship Answers

1. a pair of turtledoves or two young pigeons (Luke 2:24)

2. twelve (Leviticus 24:5)

3. one (Exodus 25:31)

4. the high priest on the Day of Atonement (Leviticus 16:3, 30–34)

5. he had shed too much blood (1 Chronicles 22:7–8)

6. seven years (1 Kings 6:38)

7. the Lord Himself is the temple (Revelation 21:22)

8. every day (Exodus 30:7–9)

9. David (1 Chronicles 23–24)

24. fourteen (1 Kings 8:65)

25. Asaph (Psalm 50 nkjv; 1 Chronicles 16:4–6)

PLAGUES ON EGYPT

God visited the plagues on Egypt so that the Egyptians would know that He is Lord.

1. Put the plagues in the order in which they occurred:
   - boils
   - darkness
   - water to blood
   - locusts
   - death of firstborn
   - frogs
   - diseased livestock
   - flies
   - hail and fire
   - lice

•••

2. When the water turned to blood, what happened to the fish in the river?

•••

3. How many days passed between the first and second plagues?

10. the people of Israel, through freewill offerings (Exodus 35:29 nkjv)

11. almond blossoms (Exodus 37:20)

12. shittim wood (Exodus 37:25)

13. a veil or curtain (Exodus 26:33)

14. brass (Exodus 27:19)

15. Zerubbabel (Ezra 3:2)

16. Nebuchadnezzar (2 Kings 24:11–14; Jeremiah 52:12–23)

17. by grasping the horns of the altar (1 Kings 1:50)

18. Shiloh (Joshua 18:1)

19. Mount Moriah (2 Chronicles 3:1)

20. linen (Exodus 26:1) and goats' hair (Exodus 26:7)

21. in heaven (Revelation 11:19)

22. in the breastplate (Leviticus 8:8)

23. fire came down from heaven and consumed the sacrifices; God's glory filled the place (2 Chronicles 7:1)

4. How many of the plagues did Pharaoh's magicians duplicate?

•••

5. Which of the following plagues is not paralleled in the plagues of the tribulation in the book of Revelation?
  a) locusts
  b) darkness
  c) hail and fire
  d) boils

•••

6. Fill in the blank: God told Aaron to stretch out his rod so that the dust of the land would become _____.

•••

7. How long did darkness cover the land?

•••

8. True or False: When darkness covered the land, the children of Israel had light.

•••

9. About which plague did Pharaoh's magicians say, "This is the finger of God"?

10. Which part of Egypt was set apart so that the swarms of flies didn't go there?

•••

11. What did God tell Moses to scatter to cause boils on the Egyptians?

•••

12. Why does the Bible say that Pharaoh's magicians could not stand before Moses?
  a) they couldn't see in the darkness
  b) they were ashamed
  c) they were covered in boils
  d) they couldn't get through the swarms of flies

•••

13. Which wind brought the locusts?
  a) north
  b) south
  c) east
  d) west

14. What wind took the locusts away?
   a) north
   b) south
   c) east
   d) west

•••

15. Where did the wind blow the locusts?

•••

16. After the death of the firstborn, why did the Egyptians make the Israelites depart in haste?

Plagues on Egypt Answers

1. water to blood, frogs, lice, flies, diseased livestock, boils, hail and fire, locusts, darkness, death of firstborn
2. they died (Exodus 7:21)
3. seven days (Exodus 7:25)
4. three; rod to snake (Exodus 7:12); water to blood (Exodus 7:21–22); frogs (Exodus 8:7)
5. d) boils (Revelation 8:7; 9:2–3)
6. lice (Exodus 8:16)
7. three days (Exodus 10:22)
8. true (Exodus 10:23)
9. lice (Exodus 8:18–19)
10. the land of Goshen where God's people lived (Exodus 8:22)
11. handfuls of ashes from a furnace (Exodus 9:8–9)
12. c) they were covered in boils (Exodus 9:11 NKJV)
13. c) east (Exodus 10:13)
14. d) west (Exodus 10:19)
15. into the Red Sea (Exodus 10:19)
16. they said, "We shall all be dead" (Exodus 12:33 NKJV)

PRAYER

1. Fill in the blank: According to James, the effective prayers of a _____ man "availeth much."

•••

2. Who was the godly son born to Hannah and Elkanah in answer to prayer?

•••

3. What did Solomon request of the Lord as he began his reign?

•••

4. Whom did Elijah defeat on Mount Carmel when fire from heaven fell?

•••

5. Who cried to the Lord in the wilderness when there was no water fit to drink?

•••

6. Name the elderly priest whose wife bore a son who was a kinsman of Jesus.

7. Fill in the blank: After praying to the Father, Jesus raised Lazarus from the dead with the command: "Lazarus, _____."

•••

8. What historic outpouring of God's Spirit in Jerusalem followed an upper room prayer meeting?

•••

9. Fill in the blank: As Jesus was dying on the cross, He prayed for His enemies:"Father, forgive them; for _____ _____."

•••

10. In Jesus' parable of two men at prayer, who prayed, "God be merciful to me a sinner"?

•••

11. Fill in the blank: The psalmist said, "If I regard iniquity in my heart, the Lord _____."

12. What blessing did Christ promise believers who prayed to the Father in secret?

•••

13. Why did Jesus discourage long prayers and "vain repetitions"?

•••

14. Fill in the blank: Jesus said, "Ask, and it shall be given you; seek, and ye shall find; knock, _____.

•••

15. How did Jesus spend the night before choosing the apostles?

•••

16. What were Peter, James, and John doing while Jesus was praying and agonizing in Gethsemane?

•••

17. What was Paul's "heart's desire and prayer to God" for Israel?

18. Fill in the blank: Paul charged the Philippians: "Be careful for nothing; but in every thing by prayer and supplication with thanksgiving let your _____ unto God."

•••

19. What did James advise those who were lacking in wisdom to do?

•••

20. Fill in the blank: John declared, "This is the confidence that we have in him, that, if we ask any thing _____, he heareth us."

Prayer Answers

1. righteous (James 5:16)

2. Samuel
(1 Samuel 1:19–20, 27)

3. wisdom/an understanding heart (1 Kings 3:9, 12)

4. prophets of Baal
(1 Kings 18:19, 36–40)

5. Moses (Exodus 15:23–25)

6. Zacharias (Luke 1:13, 36)

PREPARED

But as it is written,
Eye hath not seen, nor ear
heard, neither have entered
into the heart of man, the things
which God hath prepared for
them that love him.
1 CORINTHIANS 2:9

1. True or False: The parable about the ten virgins is about being prepared.

•••

2. What did Samuel tell the Israelites to prepare for the Lord?

•••

3. What does the Lord prepare for us in the presence of our enemies?

•••

4. The voice of one crying in the wilderness, "Prepare ye…" what?

•••

5. Where is Jesus preparing a place for us?

7. come forth (John 11:41–44)

8. Pentecost (Acts 1:13–14; 2:1, 4)

9. they know not what they do (Luke 23:34)

10. the publican/tax collector (Luke 18:13–14)

11. will not hear me (Psalm 66:18)

12. the Father will reward them openly (Matthew 6:6)

13. the Father knows what we need before we ask (Matthew 6:7–8)

14. and it shall be opened unto you (Matthew 7:7)

15. He prayed all night on a mountain (Luke 6:12–13)

16. sleeping (Matthew 26:36–40)

17. that they might be saved (Romans 10:1)

18. requests be made known (Philippians 4:6)

19. ask God in faith (James 1:5–6)

20. according to his will (1 John 5:14)

Prepared Answers

1. true (Matthew 25:1–13)

2. their hearts (1 Samuel 7:3)

3. a table (Psalm 23:5)

4. "the way of the LORD" (Isaiah 40:3)

5. in His Father's house (John 14:2)

PRIDE

1. True or False: Pride goeth before a fall.

•••

2. Paul said we are not to think of ourselves what?

•••

3. Which of David's sons was overly proud of his physical beauty?

•••

4. Who said, "I will say to my soul, Soul, you have many goods laid up for many years"?

5. Fill in the blank: By pride comes nothing but _____.

Pride Answers

1. false; pride goeth before destruction (Proverbs 16:18)

2. more highly than we ought (Romans 12:3)

3. Absalom (2 Samuel 14:25–27)

4. the rich fool in Jesus' parable (Luke 12:16–20 NKJV)

5. strife (Proverbs 13:10 NKJV)

PRIESTS

1. What was the short outer garment priests wore over their robes?

•••

2. What high priest anointed Solomon as king?

•••

3. What was the three-step process of appointing a high priest?

4. What priest also served as a scribe, documenting the return of the Babylonian captives to Jerusalem?

•••

5. What priest was also a king?

•••

6. What kind of tree supplied the wood for Aaron's rod that budded?

•••

7. What annual occasion witnessed the priest using the scapegoat?

•••

8. What noisemakers hung off the hem of the priest's garment?

•••

9. Which New Testament writer says we are a holy priesthood and a royal priesthood?

•••

10. What king made priests from every class of people, an act that destroyed his house?

•••

11. What priest kept Joash safe when all Joash's siblings were killed?

•••

12. What priest had sons named Hophni and Phinehas?

•••

13. What was engraved on the front of the high priest's turban?

•••

14. Who killed all of Ahab's household, including his priests?

•••

15. What high priest in King Josiah's reign discovered the Book of the Law while repairing the temple?

•••

16. What high priest said it was expedient that one man should die for the people?

17. Whose wife was the daughter of an Egyptian priest?

•••

18. How many cities were allotted to the priests in the Promised Land?

•••

19. What high priest did Paul call a whitewashed wall?

•••

20. What king was condemned for acting as a priest?

•••

21. To what priestly division did Zechariah belong?

•••

22. What priest allowed David to eat the shewbread?

•••

23. What were the seven sons of the priest Sceva trying to do?

•••

24. What priest during the reign of King Ahaz built an altar based on the design of an altar in Damascus?

•••

25. What part of Jerusalem during Nehemiah's time did the high priest Eliashib build?

Priests Answers

1. an ephod (Exodus 28:6–14)

2. Zadok (1 Kings 1:39)

3. anointing, consecrating, and sanctifying (Exodus 28:41)

4. Ezra (Ezra 7:11)

5. Melchizedek (Genesis 14:18)

6. almond (Numbers 17:8)

7. Day of Atonement (Leviticus 16; 23:26–32)

8. bells (Exodus 28:33–34)

9. Peter (1 Peter 2:5, 9)

10. Jeroboam (1 Kings 13:33)

11. Jehoiada (2 Kings 11:1–4)

12. Eli (1 Samuel 4:11)

13. a gold plate was engraved with "Holiness to the Lord" (Exodus 28:36)

14. Jehu (2 Kings 10:11)

15. Hilkiah (2 Kings 22:8)

16. Caiaphas (John 11:49–50)

17. Joseph's wife (Genesis 41:45)

18. thirteen (Joshua 21:19)

19. Ananias (Acts 23:2–3)

20. Saul (1 Samuel 13:8–14)

21. Abijah (Luke 1:5 NIV)

22. Ahimelech (1 Samuel 21:1, 6)

23. trying to cast out evil spirits (Acts 19:13–16)

24. Urijah (2 Kings 16:11)

25. the Sheep Gate (Nehemiah 3:1)

PROMISED LAND

1. True or False: The Israelites were told to stay close enough to touch the ark of the covenant as they crossed the Jordan.

•••

2. Fill in the blank: The ark of the covenant was carried by priests from the tribe of

_____.

•••

3. Fill in the blank: God told Joshua that Israel would know that God was with him as He was with

_____.

•••

4. What was the condition of the Jordan River?

•••

5. When did the Jordan River begin to go dry?
   a) as a strong east wind began blowing
   b) when Caleb said, "God will give us the land if we set our feet on it"

274

c) when the ark of the covenant was a great distance away

d) when the priests' feet touched the water's edge

•••

6. Where did the priests carrying the ark stand while all Israel crossed over Jordan?

   a) on the spot where they first entered the river

   b) in the middle of the Jordan River

   c) on a cairn of stones taken from the dry riverbed

   d) on the plains of Jericho

•••

7. How many stones were used to make the memorial to the river crossing?

•••

8. True or False: God stopped supplying the manna from heaven for the Israelites the day that Moses died.

9. In all, how many times did Joshua's army march around the walls of Jericho?

•••

10. In all, how many times did the men of Joshua's army give a great shout?

•••

11. What kind of trumpets did the priest sound?

   a) the horns of bulls, coated with blood

   b) the horns of wild oxen

   c) trumpets of bronze

   d) the horns of rams

•••

12. True or False: Rahab alone was saved when Jericho was taken.

•••

13. Fill in the blank: After Jericho's success, the Israelites failed at first to take the small city of

_____.

•••

14. Where was Achan's plunder secretly hidden?

15. What military tactic did Joshua use to finally take the small city?
   a) attacked at night while the city slept
   b) laid siege
   c) made his army appear larger than it really was
   d) set up an ambush

Promised Land Answers

1. false; follow, but not go near it (Joshua 3:4)

2. Levi (Joshua 3:3)

3. Moses (Joshua 3:7)

4. at flood stage (Joshua 3:15)

5. d) when the priests' feet touched the water's edge (Joshua 3:15–16)

6. b) in the middle of the Jordan River (Joshua 3:17)

7. twelve (Joshua 4:3)

8. false; the day after they ate food from the land of Canaan (Joshua 5:12)

9. thirteen; once each day for six days, seven times on the seventh day (Joshua 6:3–4)

10. once, at the end of the final march (Joshua 6:10, 16)

11. d) the horns of rams (Joshua 6:4)

12. false; she and her family were saved (Joshua 6:23)

13. Ai (Joshua 7:4–5)

14. under the ground inside his tent (Joshua 7:21)

15. d) set up an ambush (Joshua 8:3–4, 21–22)

PROPHETS

1. What prophet brought a Shunammite's son back to life?

•••

2. How many kings did Isaiah serve as a prophet?

•••

3. When Daniel first arrived in Babylon, what did he immediately refuse to do?

•••

4. Who was the first prophet?

5. What prophet had a live coal put on his mouth?

•••

6. What two minor prophets prophesied at the same time as Isaiah?

•••

7. What was the name of Jeremiah's scribe?

•••

8. What prophet told a king that he would be as an ox and eat grass in the field?

•••

9. What prophet said, "Can two walk together, except they be agreed?"

•••

10. Who was the prophet who literally ate the Word of the Lord?

•••

11. What king burned the scroll of Jeremiah's prophecies?

12. Who had four daughters who prophesied?

•••

13. What Old Testament prophet describes a city similar to the one in Revelation 21?

•••

14. What prophet's bones revived a dead man?

•••

15. What prophet had two children whose names meant "not loved" and "not my people"?

•••

16. What king did the prophet Nathan help anoint?

•••

17. What happened to the prophet who ate and drank when God told him not to?

•••

18. Who did Samuel say would prophesy and be "turned into another man"?

19. What prophet got so angry at God that he told God to just go ahead and kill him?

•••

20. When the disciples asked Jesus to tell them the signs of His coming and the end of the age, what prophet did Jesus quote?

•••

21. Besides Elijah, what prophet did Ahab complain always prophesied against him?

•••

22. For how long was Ezekiel commanded to lie on his left side?

•••

23. What prophet was commanded to marry an unfaithful wife?

•••

24. Of what country did Obadiah prophesy?

25. What false prophet prophesied against Jeremiah and died?

•••

26. How many books of prophecy are in the Old Testament?

•••

27. What Old Testament prophet mentioned Daniel and Job?

•••

28. True or False: Jonah is mentioned in 2 Kings.

Prophets Answers

1. Elisha (2 Kings 4:18–37)

2. four (Isaiah 1:1)

3. eat unclean food (Daniel 1:8)

4. Moses (Numbers 12:6–8)

5. Isaiah (Isaiah 6:6–7)

6. Amos (Amos 1:1) and Micah (Micah 1:1) [Isaiah 1:1]

7. Baruch (Jeremiah 36:4, 17–18)

PROPHETS, LESSER KNOWN

1. What book of the Bible comes right before Habakkuk?

•••

2. Besides Elijah, which prophet did Ahab hate?

•••

3. True or False: The group called "the sons of the prophets" was associated with Isaiah.

•••

4. True or False: The prophet in 1 Kings 13 is not named in the Bible.

•••

5. In addition to being a prophet, Iddo the Seer also
   a) kept the king's treasury
   b) was captain of the king's army
   c) kept genealogies
   d) rode a donkey

8. Daniel (Daniel 4:25)

9. Amos (Amos 3:3)

10. Ezekiel (Ezekiel 2:9–3:3)

11. Jehoiakim (Jeremiah 36:9–26)

12. Philip the evangelist (Acts 21:8–9)

13. Ezekiel (Ezekiel 48:30–35)

14. Elisha (2 Kings 13:20–21)

15. Hosea (Hosea 1:6, 9 NIV)

16. Solomon (1 Kings 1:34)

17. a lion killed him (1 Kings 13:20–24)

18. Saul (1 Samuel 9:27; 10:6)

19. Jonah (Jonah 4:3)

20. Daniel (Matthew 24:15)

21. Micaiah (1 Kings 22:15–18)

22. 390 days (Ezekiel 4:4–5)

23. Hosea (Hosea 1:2)

24. Edom (Obadiah 1:1)

25. Hananiah (Jeremiah 28)

26. seventeen; Isaiah through Malachi

27. Ezekiel (14:14)

28. true; (2 Kings 14:25)

279

Prophets, Lesser Known Answers

1. Nahum

2. Micaiah (1 Kings 22:8–28)

3. false; Elisha (2 Kings 6:1)

4. true (1 Kings 13)

5. c) kept genealogies (2 Chronicles 12:15)

PROVERBS

In addition to the book of Proverbs, there are proverbs scattered throughout the Bible.

1. Who said, "Come to Heshbon, let it be built"?

•••

2. Fill in the blank: A proverb about King Saul said, "Is Saul also among the _____?"

•••

3. Fill in the blank: Wickedness proceeds from the _____.

4. How many proverbs does 1 Kings 4:32 say Solomon spoke?

•••

5. True or False: God told Isaiah to take up a proverb against the king of Babylon.

•••

6. True or False: The proverb "Like mother, like daughter" is in the Bible.

•••

7. Fill in the blank: The days are prolonged, and every vision _____.

•••

8. Fill in the blank: The fathers have eaten sour grapes, and the children's _____ are set on edge.

•••

9. True or False: "A dog returns to his own vomit" is in the Bible.

Proverbs Answers

1. those who speak in proverbs (Numbers 21:27 nkjv)
2. prophets (1 Samuel 10:12)
3. wicked (1 Samuel 24:13)
4. three thousand (1 Kings 4:32)
5. true (Isaiah 14:4)
6. true (Ezekiel 16:44)
7. fails (Ezekiel 12:22 nkjv)
8. teeth (Ezekiel 18:2 nkjv)
9. true (2 Peter 2:22 nkjv)

PUNISHMENTS

1. What was Adam's punishment for disobeying God in the Garden of Eden?

•••

2. Who responded, "My punishment is greater than I can bear" when the Lord told him he was "cursed from the earth" for killing his brother?

3. Which two sons of Jacob slew all the males of Shechem's city in retaliation against a prince of the city who raped their sister Dinah?

•••

4. Whose wife was turned into a pillar of salt for looking back at the destruction of a wicked city?

•••

5. Who was swallowed up by the earth, along with his fellow conspirators, because they had formed a rebellion against Moses and Aaron?

•••

6. Whose sons were consumed by fire for offering an unholy sacrifice in the tabernacle?

•••

7. Who was denied entrance into the Promised Land for an act of impatience and faithlessness at Meribah?

8. What was Achan's sin that resulted in his being stoned to death?

•••

9. Fill in the blank: Uzzah died after accidentally touching the

_____

as it was being transported to Jerusalem.

•••

10. According to Mosaic law, what was the punishment for one who blasphemed God's name?

•••

11. True or False: Haman was punished, but his ten sons were spared.

•••

12. Who punished Judas Iscariot for what he did to Jesus?

•••

13. What happened to two sets of fifty men each that the king sent to capture Elijah?

14. What punishment did Pharaoh give the Israelites after his first encounter with Moses and Aaron?

Punishments Answers

1. banishment to till the ground (Genesis 3:23–24)

2. Cain (Genesis 4:11, 13)

3. Simeon and Levi (Genesis 34:4–5, 25–27)

4. Lot's wife (Genesis 19:23, 26)

5. Korah (Numbers 16:1–2, 32–33)

6. Aaron's (Leviticus 10:1–2)

7. Moses and Aaron (Numbers 20:12–13)

8. he withheld spoils of war (Joshua 6:26; 7:1, 25)

9. ark of the covenant (2 Samuel 6:6–7)

10. being stoned to death (Leviticus 24:16)

11. false; his ten sons were hanged as well (Esther 9:13–14)

12. he punished himself (Matthew 27:5)

13. fire came down from heaven and consumed them (2 Kings 1:9–12)

14. he made the people gather their own straw to make bricks and still meet their quota (Exodus 5:7–8)

Q

QUEENS

1. Esther's husband, Ahasuerus (also known as Xerxes), ruled 127 provinces from
   a) India to Ethiopia
   b) Egypt to Israel
   c) Canaan to Egypt
   d) Egypt to Ethiopia

•••

2. True or False: Queen Vashti willingly joined the king's feast so he could show her beauty to everyone present.

•••

3. After Esther became queen, Mordecai found favor by:
   a) doubling the grapes produced by the king's vineyards
   b) foiling an assassination attempt on a provincial governor
   c) foiling an assassination attempt on the king
   d) storing enough grain to take the provinces through a seven-year famine

4. True or False: Queen Esther discovered something was wrong when her maids told her that Mordecai was grieving.

•••

5. After Esther agreed to speak to the king, she told Mordecai to tell her people to
   a) tear their clothes
   b) spread sheep's blood on their doors
   c) fast for three days
   d) not worry

•••

6. Why was Esther's act of speaking to the king so courageous?

•••

7. True or False: Haman was worried about attending Esther's banquets.

•••

8. Why did Queen Vashti lose favor with King Xerxes?

9. True or False: In deciding what to do about Queen Vashti, King Xerxes consulted priests of Baal.

•••

10. When Queen Esther came unannounced to see King Xerxes, she would be killed unless the king did what?

•••

11. Fill in the blank: Esther said, "I will go to the king, even though it is against the law. And if I _____, I _____."

•••

12. After Queen Esther identified Haman as her enemy to King Xerxes, what did Haman do that enraged King Xerxes still further?
   a) tried to escape by entering the women's court
   b) appealed to Esther and fell on her couch
   c) asked palace guards to hide him
   d) used the king's signet ring to forge a document refuting Esther's claim

13. How many queens of Israel are mentioned by name?

•••

14. How many queens of Judah are mentioned by name?

•••

15. How are those two queens related?

•••

16. What horrible thing did Athaliah do?

•••

17. How many queens are mentioned in Esther?

•••

18. How did Jezebel die?

QUESTIONS JESUS ASKED

To whom was Jesus speaking when He asked:

1. Whosoever liveth and believeth in me shall never die. Believest thou this?

•••

2. Woman, why weepest thou?

18. she was thrown out a window and dogs devoured her in the street (2 Kings 9:32–36)

17. two

16. killed all her grandchildren so she could be queen (2 Kings 11:1)

15. they are mother and daughter

14. one (Athaliah) (2 Kings 11:1)

13. one (Jezebel) (1 Kings 16:31)

Queens Answers

1. a) India to Ethiopia (Esther 1:1)

2. false (Esther 1:12)

3. c) foiling an assassination attempt on the king (Esther 2:21–23)

4. true (Esther 4:1–7)

5. c) fast for three days (Esther 4:16)

6. asking to speak to the king could have resulted in her death (Esther 4:11)

7. false; he was very proud that he was the only one invited other than the king (Esther 5:12)

8. she refused to come when Xerxes sent for her (Esther 1:12)

9. false; he consulted his wise men (Esther 1:13–15)

10. extended his gold scepter to her (Esther 4:11)

11. perish, perish (Esther 4:16 NIV)

12. b) appealed to Esther and fell on her couch (Esther 7:8)

3. Do you love Me more than these?

•••

4. What is that to you?

•••

5. Why are you persecuting Me?

•••

6. Why are ye fearful, O ye of little faith?

•••

7. Why do you think evil in your hearts?

•••

8. Can the friends of the bridegroom mourn as long as the bridegroom is with them?

•••

9. Do you believe that I am able to do this?

•••

10. Who do men say that I am?

•••

11. Why do you call Me good?

•••

12. The baptism of John—where was it from?

•••

13. Could you not watch with Me one hour?

•••

14. Are you not therefore mistaken, because you do not know the Scriptures?

•••

15. Did you not know that I must be about My Father's business?

•••

16. What is your name?

Questions Jesus Asked Answers

1. Martha (John 11:24–26)
2. Mary Magdalene (John 20:15)
3. Peter (John 21:15 NKJV)
4. Peter (John 21:22 NKJV)

QUESTIONS GOD ASKED

To whom was God speaking when He asked:

1. Where were you when I laid the foundations of the earth?

•••

2. Where are you?

•••

3. Why are you angry?

•••

4. What is that in your hand?

•••

5. Ask! What shall I give you?

•••

6. From where do you come?

•••

7. Is it right for you to be angry?

•••

8. How have I wearied you?

5. Paul (Acts 9:4 nkjv)

6. disciples (Matthew 8:25–26)

7. scribes (Matthew 9:3–4 nkjv)

8. disciples of John (Matthew 9:14–15 nkjv)

9. blind men (Matthew 9:28 nkjv)

10. disciples (Matthew 16:13 nkjv)

11. the Bible doesn't name him (Matthew 19:17 nkjv)

12. chief priests and elders (Matthew 21:23–25 nkjv)

13. Peter (Matthew 26:40 nkjv)

14. Sadducees (Mark 12:18, 24 nkjv)

15. Mary and Joseph (Luke 2:49 nkjv)

16. Legion (man with devils) (Luke 8:27–30 nkjv)

9. Whom shall I send, and who will go for Us?

•••

10. Is anything too hard for the LORD?

Questions God Asked Answers

1. Job (Job 38:4)
2. Adam (Genesis 3:9 NKJV)
3. Cain (Genesis 4:6 NKJV)
4. Moses (Exodus 4:2 NKJV)
5. Solomon (1 Kings 3:5 NKJV)
6. Satan (Job 1:7 NKJV)
7. Jonah (Jonah 4:1, 4 NKJV)
8. Israel (Micah 6:3 NKJV)
9. Isaiah (Isaiah 6:8 NKJV)
10. Abraham (Genesis 18:14 NKJV)

QUOTATIONS

Who said:

1. Am I my brother's keeper?

2. If thou be the Son of God, command that these stones be made bread.

•••

3. Lord, if it is You, command me to come to You.

•••

4. Thou art the Christ.

•••

5. Where is He who has been born King of the Jews?

•••

6. Whatever you ask me, I will give you, up to half my kingdom.

•••

7. Speak, for Your servant hears.

•••

8. Behold the maidservant of the Lord!

•••

9. Your people shall be my people.

10. Thou art the man.

•••

11. Vanity of vanities; all is vanity.

•••

12. I cast it into the fire, and this calf came out.

•••

13. The son of this bond-woman shall not be heir with my son.

•••

14. As for me and my house, we will serve the LORD.

•••

15. We ought to obey God rather than men.

•••

16. Silver and gold have I none.

•••

17. What is truth?

•••

18. The LORD gave, and the LORD hath taken away; blessed be the name of the LORD.

Quotations Answers

1. Cain (Genesis 4:9 NKJV)
2. Satan (Matthew 4:3)
3. Peter (Matthew 14:28 NKJV)
4. Peter (Matthew 16:16)
5. wise men (Matthew 2:2 NKJV)
6. Herod (Mark 6:22–23 NKJV)
7. Samuel (1 Samuel 3:10 NKJV)
8. Mary (Luke 1:38 NKJV)
9. Ruth (Ruth 1:16 NKJV)
10. Nathan (2 Samuel 12:7)
11. Solomon (Ecclesiastes 1:1–2)
12. Aaron (Exodus 32:24 NKJV)
13. Sarah (Genesis 21:10)
14. Joshua (Joshua 24:15 NKJV)
15. Peter and the apostles (Acts 5:29 NKJV)
16. Peter (Acts 3:6)
17. Pilate (John 18:38)
18. Job (Job 1:21)

R

RAISING THE DEAD

The Holy Spirit raised Jesus from the dead (Romans 8:11).

1. What two Old Testament prophets raised a boy from the dead?

•••

2. A dead man came back to life because his body fell on the bones of what prophet?

•••

3. True or False: Besides Jesus, no one in the New Testament raised someone from the dead.

•••

4. Fill in the blank: After seeing the son of the widow of Nain raised from the dead, the people said, "A great _____ is risen up among us."

•••

5. Fill in the blank: The names of Lazarus's two sisters were Mary and _____.

6. When Jesus heard that Lazarus was sick, when did Jesus leave to be with him?
   a) after hearing that Lazarus was dead
   b) after two days
   c) immediately
   d) the next morning

•••

7. Fill in the blank: When Thomas learned Jesus was going to the home of Lazarus, he said, "Let us also go, that we may _____ with him."

•••

8. What city was Bethany near?

•••

9. When Jesus arrived at the tomb, how long had Lazarus been dead?

•••

10. How many people did Jesus raise from the dead?

•••

11. Who were they?

Raising the Dead Answers

1. Elijah, Elisha (1 Kings 17:17–24; 2 Kings 4:32–37)

2. Elisha (2 Kings 13:21)

3. false; Peter raised Dorcas from the dead (Acts 9:36–41)

4. prophet (Luke 7:16)

5. Martha (John 11:1)

6. b) after two days (John 11:6)

7. die (John 11:16)

8. Jerusalem (John 11:18)

9. four days (John 11:39)

10. three people

11. Jairus's daughter, Lazarus, the widow of Nain's son

REBUILDING JERUSALEM

1. Choose A or B: Eliashib the high priest and his priests built the **a)** Sheep Gate or **b)** East Gate.

2. Choose A or B: The sons of Hassenaah built the **a)** North Gate or **b)** Fish Gate.

•••

3. True or False: The nobles of the Tekoites did not do the Lord's work.

•••

4. Choose A or B: Hanun and the inhabitants of Zanoah repaired the **a)** South Gate or **b)** Valley Gate.

•••

5. Fill in the blanks: Nehemiah set people in the ____ and on the ____ places behind the wall with swords, spears, and bows.

•••

6. Who said, "Ye exact usury, every one of his brother"?

•••

7. True or False: The nobles and rulers agreed to restore to the people their lands.

8. True or False: When Sanballat and Geshem asked Nehemiah to leave his work and come meet with them, Nehemiah agreed.

•••

9. The wall was finished in
   a) fifty-two days
   b) seventy-five days
   c) ninety days
   d) a year

•••

10. Who did Nehemiah put in charge of opening and shutting the gates of Jerusalem and guarding the city?
   a) Hanani and Hananiah
   b) Shadrach and Meshach
   c) Daniel and Joel
   d) Matthew and Mark

•••

11. The king of Persia who made the proclamation to allow God's people to go back to Jerusalem was
   a) Belteshazzar
   b) Hazael
   c) Cyrus
   d) Darius

•••

12. True or False: The three tribes of Israel that went back to Jerusalem were Judah, Benjamin, and Levi.

•••

13. Fill in the blank: The king of Persia "brought forth the ____ of the house of the LORD, which Nebuchadnezzar had brought forth out of Jerusalem."

•••

14. Choose A or B: The first thing the Israelites built after returning to Jerusalem was **a)** an altar or **b)** the wall of the city.

•••

15. Fill in the blanks: "The people of the land ____ the hands of the people of Judah, and ____ them in building."

•••

16. True or False: Some people wrote a letter to King Artaxerxes of Persia, accusing the inhabitants

of Jerusalem of building a rebellious and bad city.

•••

17. Fill in the blank: The Jews were made to ____ building "by force and power."

•••

18. The two prophets prophesying in Jerusalem at this time were
   a) Isaiah and Jeremiah
   b) Habakkuk and Zephaniah
   c) Hosea and Joel
   d) Haggai and Zechariah

•••

19. Who began to build the house of God again?
   a) Zerbubbabel
   b) Iddo
   c) Jeshua
   d) a & c

•••

20. True or False: King Darius issued a decree forbidding the rebuilding of the house of God.

Rebuilding Jerusalem Answers

1. a) Sheep Gate (Nehemiah 3:1)

2. b) Fish Gate (Nehemiah 3:3)

3. true (Nehemiah 3:5)

4. b) Valley Gate (Nehemiah 3:13)

5. lower, higher (Nehemiah 4:13)

6. Nehemiah (Nehemiah 5:7)

7. true (Nehemiah 5:12)

8. false; he refused to meet with them (Nehemiah 6:2–3)

9. a) fifty-two days (Nehemiah 6:15)

10. a) Hanani and Hananiah (Nehemiah 7:2–3)

11. c) Cyrus (Ezra 1:1)

12. true (Ezra 1:5)

13. vessels (Ezra 1:7)

14. a) an altar (Ezra 3:3)

15. weakened, troubled (Ezra 4:4)

16. true (Ezra 4:11–12)

17. cease (Ezra 4:23)

18. d) Haggai and Zechariah (Ezra 5:1)

19. d) a & c (Ezra 5:2)

20. false (Ezra 6:1, 7)

RELATIVES PART 1

1. Whose wife told him to curse God and die?

•••

2. Who was Abram's father?

•••

3. Which two of Aaron's sons were devoured by fire?

•••

4. Who was Noah's great-grandfather?

•••

5. How were Esther and Mordecai related?

•••

6. What famous spy was the uncle of Othniel?

7. Who was Jethro's son-in-law?

•••

8. What king was Mephibosheth's grandfather?

•••

9. What wicked pair took issue with the prophecies of Elijah?

•••

10. Who were the sons of Zebedee?

•••

11. Who was Laban's brother-in-law?

•••

12. What king claimed Ruth and Boaz as his great-grandparents?

•••

13. What two men told foreign rulers that their wives were their sisters?

•••

14. What good advice did Moses' father-in-law give him?

15. How was Joab, the commander of David's army, related to David?

•••

16. Whose son was Mahershalalhashbaz?

•••

17. Who was married to Elimelech and had sons named Mahlon and Chilion?

•••

18. What same man did Michal, Abigail, and Ahinoam marry?

•••

19. What were the complaints against Samuel's sons?

•••

20. Who was King David's great-great-grandmother?

•••

21. Who were the four mothers of Jacob's twelve sons and one daughter?

22. Match the mothers from question 1 for Jacob's children: Reuben, Simeon, Levi, Judah, Dan, Naphtali, Gad, Asher, Issachar, Zebulon, Dinah, Joseph, and Benjamin.

•••

23. How many siblings did Abram have, and what were their names?

•••

24. What judge of Israel had seventy sons?

•••

25. Who unknowingly offered to sacrifice his daughter to God?

Relatives Part 1 Answers

1. Job (Job 2:9)

2. Terah (Genesis 11:31)

3. Nadab and Abihu (Leviticus 10:1–2)

4. Enoch (Genesis 5:22–29)

RELATIVES PART 2

1. What happened to the only son of the widow of Nain?

•••

2. What son was given to Adam and Eve to replace Abel?

25. Jephthah (Judges 11:30–31, 34)

24. Gideon (Judges 8:29–32)

23. three—Nahor, Haran (Genesis 11:27); Sarai (Genesis 20:12)

22. Leah: Reuben, Simeon, Levi, Judah, Issachar, Zebulun, Dinah; Rachel: Joseph, Benjamin; Bilhah: Dan, Naphtali; Zilpah: Gad, Asher (Genesis 29:31–30:24; 35:18)

21. Leah, Rachel, Bilhah, Zilpah (Genesis 29:23–30:24; 35:18)

20. Rahab (Matthew 1:5 NIV)

19. they took bribes and perverted justice (1 Samuel 8:3)

18. David (1 Samuel 18:27; 30:5)

17. Naomi (Ruth 1:2)

16. Isaiah (Isaiah 8:3)

15. Joab was David's nephew, his sister's son (1 Chronicles 2:12–16; 1 Samuel 26:6)

14. appoint seventy men to help him hear all the complaints of the people (Exodus 18:13–24)

13. Abraham, Isaac (Genesis 12:11–13; 20:1–3; 26:7–11)

12. David (Ruth 4:17)

11. Isaac (Genesis 24:29)

10. James and John (Matthew 4:21–22)

9. Ahab and Jezebel (1 Kings 19:1–2)

8. Saul (2 Samuel 9:6)

7. Moses (Exodus 18:1–2)

6. Caleb (Judges 3:9)

5. they were cousins (Esther 2:7)

3. Who was Samuel's mother?

•••

4. Who was Leah's firstborn?

•••

5. What father and son both wrote psalms?

•••

6. Who was Orpah's sister-in-law?

•••

7. What was the name of King Saul's cousin who was the commander of his army?

•••

8. Who was King Manasseh's father?

•••

9. Which of Solomon's children became king?

•••

10. Who was Methuselah's grandson?

11. In the Old Testament, what evil person had a wife who was as actively evil as he?

•••

12. Who was David's oldest brother?

•••

13. Which of his brothers did Absalom kill to avenge Tamar's honor?

•••

14. What king of Israel started out good and then let his wives lead him into worship of Ashtoreth and other false gods?

•••

15. What famous leader of Israel married an Ethopian woman?

•••

16. Who killed a whole city of men to avenge their sister's honor?

•••

17. Of what significance was Publius's father to Paul?

18. Whose daughters were said to be the most beautiful in the land?

•••

19. Who was stricken with leprosy because she spoke against her brother's wife?

•••

20. Who was King Saul's father?

•••

21. The ancestors of what two warring nations fought together before they were born?

•••

22. What woman, besides Hannah, was Elkanah's wife?

•••

23. In Mark 6:3, what are the names of Jesus' brothers?

•••

24. What Old Testament man unknowingly slept with his own daughter-in-law—then accused her of being a harlot?

25. When Jacob died, where did his sons bury him?

Relatives Part 2 Answers

1. he was raised from the dead by Jesus (Luke 7:11–15)

2. Seth (Genesis 4:25)

3. Hannah (1 Samuel 1:9–11)

4. Reuben (Genesis 29:32)

5. David and Solomon (Psalms 62, 72 NKJV)

6. Ruth (Ruth 1:14–15)

7. Abner (1 Samuel 14:50)

8. Hezekiah (2 Kings 21:1–3)

9. Rehoboam (1 Kings 11:43)

10. Noah (Genesis 5:25–29)

11. Ahab (1 Kings 19:1–2)

12. Eliab (1 Samuel 17:28)

13. Amnon (2 Samuel 13:28–29)

14. Solomon (1 Kings 11:4–5)

15. Moses (Numbers 12:1)

2. Fill in the blank: He who speaks _____ declares righteousness.

•••

3. What did Abram do that was counted to him for righteousness?

•••

4. Fill in the blank: James said, "The effective, fervent prayer of a righteous man _____ much."

•••

5. Fill in the blank: David said he had never seen the righteous _____.

•••

6. Fill in the blank: The psalmist said the Lord surrounds the righteous with _____.

•••

7. Fill in the blank: The Lord _____ the righteous.

•••

8. True or False: The Bible says that the righteous man regards the life of his animal.

16. Simeon and Levi (Genesis 34:25)

17. Paul healed him of a fever (Acts 28:7–8)

18. Job (Job 42:15)

19. Miriam (Numbers 12:1, 10)

20. Kish (1 Samuel 9:1)

21. Israelites (Jacob) and Edomites (Esau) (Genesis 25:21–26)

22. Peninnah (1 Samuel 1:2)

23. James, Joses, Juda, and Simon (Mark 6:3)

24. Judah (Genesis 38)

25. in the cave Abraham bought for a burial place (Genesis 50:13)

RIGHTEOUS PEOPLE

(see also God's Faithful, God's Hall of Fame)

1. Proverbs 28:1 says that the righteous are as bold as what?

9. Who does Peter call "a preacher of righteousness"?
   a) Moses
   b) Noah
   c) Jonah
   d) Jeremiah

Righteous People Answers

1. a lion
2. truth (Proverbs 12:17)
3. he believed in the Lord (Genesis 15:6)
4. avails (James 5:16 NKJV)
5. forsaken (Psalm 37:25)
6. favor (Psalm 5:12 NKJV)
7. loves (Psalm 146:8)
8. true (Proverbs 12:10 NKJV)
9. b) Noah (2 Peter 2:5)

RIVERS

(see also Geography)

1. How many rivers came out of the Garden of Eden?

2. How many times was the Jordan River parted?

•••

3. True or False: One of the rivers that came out of the Garden of Eden was the Euphrates.

•••

4. Which of the following is not the name of a river in the Bible?
   a) Jabbok
   b) Ulai
   c) Ebal
   d) Kishon

•••

5. Fill in the blank: The psalmist said God gives His people drink from the river of His _____.

•••

6. The River Chebar was in
   a) Jerusalem
   b) Babylon
   c) Assyria
   d) Samaria

7. True or False: The phrase "peace like a river" was said by Isaiah.

8. True or False: John the Baptist baptized people in the Jordan River.

•••

9. What river did John see in the new heaven?

•••

10. True or False: Jesus said if we believe in Him, out of our hearts will flow rivers of living water.

Rivers Answers

1. four (Genesis 2:10)

2. three (Joshua 3:16; 2 Kings 2:8, 14)

3. true (Genesis 2:14)

4. c) Ebal (Deuteronomy 3:16; Daniel 8:2; Judges 5:21)

5. delights (Psalm 36:8 NIV)

6. b) Babylon (Ezekiel 1:1)

7. false; the Lord said it (Isaiah 66:12)

8. true (Mark 1:5)

9. the river of the water of life (Revelation 22:1 NKJV)

10. true (John 7:38)

S

SABBATH

1. Why did God bless and sanctify the seventh day?

•••

2. What provision did God make for the Israelites in the wilderness to have manna on the Sabbath?

•••

3. Fill in the blank: God spoke from Mount Sinai: "Remember the sabbath day, to _____."

•••

4. What punishment was given to a man in the wilderness for picking up sticks on the Sabbath?

•••

5. According to Mark, what did Jesus often do in Nazareth on the Sabbath?

•••

6. Fill in the blank: After His disciples plucked corn on the Sabbath, Jesus declared: "The sabbath was made for man, and not man for the sabbath: therefore the Son of man is _____."

•••

7. Fill in the blanks: Jesus healed the sick on the Sabbath, indicating that it is _____ to do good on the _____.

•••

8. Why did Jesus call a synagogue official a hypocrite for objecting to a crippled woman's being healed on the Sabbath?

•••

9. After what great event did Christians begin to observe the first day of the week as their Sabbath?

•••

10. What church worshipped on the first day of the week and brought offerings for the suffering saints in Judea?

11. True or False. The first mention of the Sabbath in the Bible is after the Israelites left Egypt.

•••

12. What was the only time God commanded His people to work on the Sabbath?

Sabbath Answers

1. creation was completed, and God rested on that day (Genesis 2:3)

2. they gathered twice as much the previous day (Exodus 16:22–23)

3. keep it holy (Exodus 20:8)

4. he was stoned to death (Numbers 15:32–36)

5. He taught in the synagogue (Mark 6:2)

6. Lord also of the sabbath (Mark 2:23, 27–28)

7. lawful, Sabbath days (Matthew 12:10–13)

8. because he watered work animals on the Sabbath but denied relief to a suffering woman (Luke 13:10–16)

9. the resurrection of Christ (John 20:1, 19)

10. Corinth (1 Corinthians 16:1–2)

11. true (Exodus 16:23)

12. when they marched around Jericho (Joshua 6:3–4)

SACRIFICES

1. To what mountain did Abraham take Isaac to sacrifice him?

•••

2. What did Jephthah vow to sacrifice to God?

•••

3. The psalmist offered God the sacrifice of _____.

•••

4. Who said, "To obey is better than sacrifice"?

•••

5. True or False: In Malachi, the Israelites were offering blind animals as sacrifices.

6. What are we to present to God as a living sacrifice?

•••

7. What are we to continually offer to God as a sacrifice?

Sacrifices Answers

1. Moriah (Genesis 22:2)

2. whatever came out of his doors to meet him (Judges 11:30–31)

3. thanksgiving (Psalm 116:17)

4. Samuel (1 Samuel 15:22)

5. true (Malachi 1:8)

6. our bodies (Romans 12:1)

7. the sacrifice of praise, the fruit of our lips (Hebrews 13:15 NKJV)

SALVATION

And Moses said unto the people, Fear ye not, stand still, and see the salvation of the LORD.
EXODUS 14:13

1. Salvation belongs to whom?

•••

2. Fill in the blank: The Lord is my _____ and my salvation.

•••

3. Who said, "My eyes have seen your salvation"?
   a) Simeon
   b) Anna
   c) Zacharias
   d) Elisabeth

•••

4. To whom did Jesus say, "Today salvation has come to this house"?

•••

5. Fill in the blank: Nor is there salvation in any other, for there is no other _____ under heaven given among men by which we must be saved.

Salvation Answers

1. the Lord (Psalm 3:8)

2. light (Psalm 27:1)

3. a) Simeon (Luke 2:25–30)

4. Zacchaeus
(Luke 19:8–9 nkjv)

5. name (Acts 4:12 nkjv)

SAMSON

1. Samson's story is found in what book of the Bible?

•••

2. True or False: Samson's parents were pleased by his marriage to a Philistine woman.

•••

3. Samson killed a lion with
a) his bare hands
b) a slingshot
c) a sword
d) the jawbone of a donkey

•••

4. After Samson killed the lion, he later found what edible substance inside its carcass?

5. To avenge himself over the loss of his wife, Samson
a) took one hundred Philistine foreskins to his king
b) burned the Philistines' corn
c) destroyed the statue of the Philistine god, Dagon
d) killed the Philistine king with a sword

•••

6. What happened when the Jews bound Samson as punishment, planning to turn him over to the Philistines?

•••

7. True or False: Samson killed one thousand Philistines with his bare hands.

•••

8. When enemies tried to kill Samson in Gaza, he:
a) blew a horn until the city walls fell
b) killed the enemies with the jaw of a jackass

c) took Delilah hostage
d) carried away the city gate

•••

9. What secret of Samson's were his enemies eager to discover?

•••

10. True or False: The enemies bribed Samson's girlfriend, Delilah, with eleven hundred pieces of silver each to tell them Samson's secret

•••

11. Fill in the blank: That he told her all his heart, and said unto her, There hath not come a razor upon mine head; for I have been a _____ unto God from my mother's womb: if I be shaven, then my strength will go from me, and I shall become weak, and be like any other man.

•••

12. True or False: Samson's capture caused the Philistines to praise Jehovah.

13. Fill in the blank: And _____ called unto the LORD, and said, O Lord GOD, remember me, I pray thee, and strengthen me, I pray thee, only this once, O God, that I may be at once avenged of the Philistines for my two eyes.

•••

14. In order to kill three thousand Philistines, Samson
   a) destroyed the pillars of a crowded house, causing its collapse
   b) enlisted the help of the Israelite army
   c) turned his staff into many poisonous serpents that bit them
   d) picked up the city gate and swung it at them

•••

15. True or False: Samson prayed to die along with the Philistines.

Samson Answers

1. Judges

2. false (Judges 14:3)

3. a) his bare hands (Judges 14:5–6)

4. honey (Judges 14:8)

5. b) burned the Philistines' corn (Judges 15:1–10)

6. the Spirit of the Lord loosed the bonds (Judges 15:14)

7. false; he killed them with a donkey's jawbone (Judges 15:15)

8. d) carried away the city gate (Judges 16:2–3)

9. the source of his strength (Judges 16:5)

10. true (Judges 16:5)

11. Nazarite (Judges 16:17)

12. false; the Philistines praised their own god (Judges 16:24)

13. Samson (Judges 16:28)

14. a) destroyed the pillars of a crowded house, causing its collapse (Judges 16:29–30)

15. true (Judges 16:30)

SATAN

1. When God asked Satan where he had come from, what did Satan answer?

•••

2. How many times did Satan tempt Jesus?

•••

3. To whom did Jesus say, "Get thee behind me, Satan"?

•••

4. Who saw Satan fall as lightning from heaven?

•••

5. What two books of the Bible describe Michael fighting with Satan?

•••

6. According to Peter, how are we to resist Satan?

•••

7. What example did Jesus give us for how to resist Satan?

8. According to James, what will Satan do if we resist him?

a) the works of the Lord
b) other ships
c) God's wonders in the deep
d) a & c

•••

Satan Answers

1. from going to and fro in the earth (Job 1:7)

2. three (Matthew 4:1–11)

3. Peter (Matthew 16:23)

4. Jesus (Luke 10:18)

5. Jude 9; Revelation 12:7

6. by standing steadfast in the faith (1 Peter 5:9)

7. Jesus quoted scripture (Matthew 4:1–11)

8. flee from us (James 4:7)

SEAS

1. Psalm 104:25 says the great and wide sea is full of
a) innumerable things
b) teeming things
c) living things great and small
d) all of the above

•••

2. Those who go down to the sea in ships see what?

3. True or False: God assigned the sea a limit.

•••

4. What group of people drowned in the Red Sea?

•••

5. What will fill the earth as waters cover the sea?

•••

6. When Jesus stilled the storm, the disciples said even the _____ and the sea obey Him.

•••

7. In John's vision of heaven, he saw a sea of _____ like _____ before the throne of God.

•••

8. True or False: When the first heaven and earth pass away, there will be no more sea.

9. Which of the following were also names for the sea of Galilee?
   a) the Great Sea
   b) Chinnereth
   c) Gennesaret
   d) b & c

•••

10. What we refer to today as the Dead Sea is called what in the Bible?

Seas Answers

1. d) all of the above (Psalm 104:25 NKJV)

2. d) a & c (Psalm 107:23–24 NKJV)

3. true (Proverbs 8:29)

4. the army of Pharaoh (Exodus 14:28)

5. the knowledge of the glory of God (Habakkuk 2:14 NKJV)

6. winds (Matthew 8:27)

7. glass, crystal (Revelation 4:6 NKJV)

8. true (Revelation 21:1)

9. d) b & c (Numbers 34:11; Luke 5:1)

10. the Salt Sea (Deuteronomy 3:17 NKJV)

SERMON ON THE MOUNT

1. Fill in the blank: The Sermon on the Mount starts with what we call the _____.

•••

2. The Sermon on the Mount is contained in what three chapters of Matthew?

•••

3. True or False: The Golden Rule is in the Sermon on the Mount.

•••

4. On what mountain does the Sermon on the Mount take place?

•••

5. Choose A or B: As for the Law and the Prophets, Jesus came to **a)** destroy them or **b)** fulfill them.

6. Fill in the blank: "But I say unto you, _____ your enemies."

•••

7. What should a person do when giving alms?
   a) also lay up treasures on earth
   b) do so in secret
   c) never give silver or gold
   d) sound a trumpet to glorify God

•••

8. Fill in the blank: "For where your treasure is, there will your _____ be also."

•••

9. What plant did Jesus say was arrayed with greater splendor than Solomon?

•••

10. Choose A or B: "Strait is the gate, and a) broad or b) narrow is the way, which leadeth unto life."

•••

11. According to Jesus' warning, how might false prophets come?

a) as a good tree with bad fruit
b) as dry clouds with a whirlwind
c) as fowls of the air
d) as wolves in sheep's clothing

Sermon on the Mount Answers

1. Beatitudes
2. Matthew 5, 6, and 7
3. true (Matthew 7:12)
4. the Bible doesn't specify (Matthew 5:1)
5. b) fulfill them (Matthew 5:17)
6. love (Matthew 5:44)
7. b) do so in secret (Matthew 6:4)
8. heart (Matthew 6:21)
9. lilies of the field (Matthew 6:28–29)
10. b) narrow (Matthew 7:14)
11. d) as wolves in sheep's clothing (Matthew 7:15)

SERVANTS

Serve the LORD with gladness.
PSALM 100:2

1. The passage on the Ethiopian eunuch is found in what book of the Bible?

•••

2. The eunuch was
   a) head of the king's harem
   b) the treasurer
   c) the king's cupbearer
   d) the court jester

•••

3. Gehazi was the servant of what prophet?

•••

4. How many eunuchs did King Ahasuerus have waiting on him?

•••

5. Who was Leah's maidservant?

•••

6. Who was Rachel's maidservant?

7. How many deacons were selected in Acts 6?

•••

8. What was the name of the servant whom Abraham was going to make his heir before Isaac was born?

•••

9. What was the name of the servant Ahab commanded to go find Elijah?
   a) Micah
   b) Nahum
   c) Obadiah
   d) Hosea

•••

10. What was the name of Herod's steward?
   a) Chemoth
   b) Chuza
   c) Zacharias
   d) Zebedee

•••

11. Baruch was the servant of
   a) Jeremiah
   b) Isaiah
   c) Elijah
   d) Daniel

Servants Answers

1. Acts 8:26–40

2. b) the treasurer (Acts 8:27)

3. Elisha (2 Kings 5:29)

4. seven (Esther 1:10)

5. Zilpah (Genesis 29:24)

6. Bilhah (Genesis 30:2–3)

7. seven (Acts 6:3)

8. Eliezer of Damascus (Genesis 15:2)

9. c) Obadiah (1 Kings 18:5–16)

10. b) Chuza (Luke 8:3)

11. a) Jeremiah (Jeremiah 32:12)

SHEEP

1. Fill in the blank: When he worked for Laban, Jacob agreed to take all the _____ sheep as his pay.

•••

2. Isaiah said, "All we like sheep have" what?

3. True or False: The story of the lost sheep can be found in Matthew and Luke.

•••

4. Fill in the blank: What man of you, having an hundred sheep, if he lose one of them, doth not leave the ninety and nine in the wilderness, and go after that which is lost, until he _____ it?

•••

5. When the sheep is found, the shepherd rejoices and lays it
   a) in the manger
   b) upon the hay
   c) by its mother
   d) on his shoulders

•••

6. Who said, "I am the good shepherd: the good shepherd giveth his life for the sheep"?

•••

7. How did Jesus describe one who enters the sheepfold other than by the door?

8. Fill in the blank: "But he that entereth in by the door is the _____."

•••

9. Fill in the blank: Jesus said, "My sheep hear my voice, and I know them, and _____."

•••

10. Fill in the blank: For one judgment, Jesus said that all the nations will be gathered before Him, and the people will be separated like sheep are separated from _____.

•••

11. Fill in the blank: Peter said we were like sheep gone astray but now we are returned to the Shepherd and Overseer of our _____.

Sheep Answers

1. speckled (Genesis 30:32)

2. gone astray (Isaiah 53:6)

3. true (Matthew 18:12–14; Luke 15:4–7)

4. find (Luke 15:4)

5. d) on his shoulders (Luke 15:5)

6. Jesus (John 10:11)

7. as a thief and a robber (John 10:1)

8. shepherd of the sheep (John 10:2)

9. they follow me (John 10:27)

10. goats (Matthew 25:33)

11. souls (1 Peter 2:25 NKJV)

SHEPHERDS

1. Fill in the blank: "The LORD is my shepherd; I shall _____."

•••

2. Why did the psalmist say he would "fear no evil" in spite of walking in the "shadow of death"?

•••

3. Fill in the blank: "Thou preparest a table before me in the _____."

4. What did the psalmist say would follow him "all the days of my life"?

•••

5. The Shepherd Psalm ends with what comforting assurance for the future of all believers?

•••

6. Who wrote, "And when the chief Shepherd shall appear, ye shall receive a crown of glory that fadeth not away"?

•••

7. How did the Egyptians feel about shepherds?
   a) they didn't care one way or another
   b) they tolerated them
   c) they thought they were an abomination
   d) there were no shepherds in Egypt

•••

8. Fill in the blanks: Jesus is called the _____ Shepherd, the _____ Shepherd, and the _____ Shepherd.

9. Fill in the blank: He will gather the _____ with his arms.

•••

10. How did Zechariah describe the worthless shepherd?

•••

11. To whom was Jesus speaking when he said, "I will strike the Shepherd, and the sheep of the flock will be scattered"?

Shepherds Answers

1. not want (Psalm 23:1)

2. "For thou art with me; thy rod and thy staff they comfort me" (Psalm 23:4)

3. presence of mine enemies (Psalm 23:5)

4. goodness and mercy (Psalm 23:6)

5. "I will dwell in the house of the LORD for ever" (Psalm 23:6)

6. Peter (1 Peter 5:4)

7. c) they thought they were
an abomination
(Genesis 46:34)

8. Chief, Great, Good
(1 Peter 5:4; Hebrews 13:20;
John 10:11)

9. lambs (Isaiah 40:11)

10. as one who leaves the
flock (Zechariah 11:17 NKJV)

11. his disciples
(Matthew 26:30–31 NKJV)

SIGNS

*And many other signs truly
did Jesus in the presence of
his disciples, which are not
written in this book: but these
are written, that ye might
believe that Jesus is the Christ,
the Son of God; and that
believing ye might have life
through his name.*
JOHN 20:30–31

1. Circumcision was a sign of
the covenant between God and:
   a) Moses
   b) Abraham
   c) Joshua
   d) the Israelites

2. The sign Gideon asked of
God involved a what?

•••

3. To whom was Isaiah
speaking when he gave the
sign of the virgin birth?

•••

4. What book of the Bible
says in its first verse that it
was signified by an angel?

•••

5. When the scribes and
Pharisees demanded a sign
from Jesus, what sign did He
give them?

•••

6. What did God create that
He said would be for signs
and seasons and days and
years?

•••

7. True or False: The apostles
did many signs and wonders.

Signs Answers

1. b) Abraham
(Genesis 17:9–11)

2. fleece (Judges 6:37)

3. King Ahaz
(Isaiah 7:10–14)

4. Revelation 1:1 NKJV

5. Jonah (Matthew 12:39–41)

6. the sun, moon, and stars
(Genesis 1:14–16)

7. true (Acts 2:43)

SIN

*I will forgive their iniquity,
and I will remember
their sin no more.*
JEREMIAH 31:34

1. According to Psalm 103:12, how far has God removed our sin from us?
   a) as far as north is from south
   b) as far as east is from west
   c) as far as heaven is from hell
   d) as far as the earth is from the sun

2. When does God forgive us our sins and cleanse us from all unrighteousness?

•••

3. Fill in the blank: Romans 6:23 says the wages of sin are _____.

•••

4. Who said, "Through one man sin entered the world?"

•••

5. What colors did Isaiah use to describe sin?

•••

6. God said He would make our sin as white as
   a) snow
   b) wool
   c) clouds
   d) a & b

•••

7. How does James define sin?

•••

8. What psalmist spoke of secret sins and presumptuous sins?

9. True or False: The Bible says your sin will find you out.

•••

10. Whom did God say was blameless and upright and didn't sin with his lips?

•••

11. True or False: The Bible says we can be angry and not sin.

•••

12. Who said, "My sin is always before me"?

•••

13. Sin is a _____ to any people.
   a) disaster
   b) abomination
   c) reproach
   d) comfort

•••

14. Whom do we make a liar if we say we have not sinned?

Sin Answers

1. b) as far as east is from west (1 John 1:9)
2. when we confess our sins (1 John 1:9)
3. death (Romans 6:23)
4. Paul (Romans 5:12 NKJV)
5. crimson, scarlet (Isaiah 1:18)
6. d) a & b (Isaiah 1:18)
7. knowing to do good but not doing it (James 4:17)
8. David (Psalm 19:12–13)
9. true (Numbers 32:23)
10. Job (Job 1:8; 2:10)
11. true (Psalm 4:4 NKJV)
12. David (Psalm 51:3)
13. c) reproach (Proverbs 14:34)
14. God (1 John 1:10)

SISTERS

(see also Brothers, Fathers, Mothers)

1. How many sisters did the sons of Jacob have?

•••

2. Who were the sisters of the man Jesus raised from the dead?

•••

3. Zeruiah and Abigail were the sisters of what famous king?

•••

4. Who was Abram's sister?

•••

5. Who killed a whole city of men to avenge their sister's honor?

•••

6. Who was Laban's sister?

•••

7. Of what two sisters was it said that one was tender eyed and the other was beautiful and well favored?

Sisters Answers

1. one—Dinah (Genesis 34:1)

2. Mary and Martha (John 11:1)

3. David (1 Chronicles 2:13–16)

4. Sarai (Genesis 20:11–12)

5. Simeon and Levi (Genesis 34:25)

6. Rebekah (Genesis 24:29)

7. Leah and Rachel (Genesis 29:17)

SLAVES

1. Which epistle did Paul write that dealt with the return of a runaway slave?

•••

2. What was the name of the slave in question 1?

•••

3. True or False: Paul was writing to say he was sending the slave back home.

4. How was the slave helping Paul?

•••

5. If the slave owes Philemon money, Paul says the debt will be repaid by
   a) the slave
   b) Paul
   c) Jesus
   d) Timothy

•••

6. Whose slave convinced her master to seek out a prophet of Israel concerning his disease?

•••

7. True or False: Every seventh year the Israelites were to set free any Hebrew slave they had.

•••

8. What did Jesus say we are slaves to?

•••

9. Fill in the blank: Paul said we can become slaves of
_____.

10. True or False: Paul said that if a slave was called to be a Christian, he should stay a slave.

•••

11. Fill in the blank: Paul told the Galatians that we are no longer slaves but
_____.

Slaves Answers

1. Philemon
2. Onesimus (Philemon10)
3. true (Philemon 1:12)
4. he was ministering to Paul (Philemon13)
5. b) Paul (Philemon 18–19)
6. Naaman's (2 Kings 5:2–3)
7. true (Deuteronomy 15:12)
8. sin (John 8:34)
9. righteousness (Romans 6:19 NKJV)
10. true, but Paul also said, "If you can gain your freedom, do so" (1 Corinthians 7:20–22 NIV)
11. sons (Galatians 4:7)

SNAKES/SERPENTS

1. The Bible says that the serpent in the Garden of Eden was more _____ than any beast of the field.

•••

2. What apostle was bitten by a poisonous snake but had no harm come to him?

•••

3. What did the people of Malta say about the apostle when the snakebite didn't kill him?
    a) that he was lucky
    b) that he was a demon
    c) that he was a god
    d) that he was really tough

•••

4. To whom was Jesus speaking when He said, "I give you the authority to trample on serpents"?

5. When Jacob was blessing his sons, which son did he say was like a serpent and a viper?
    a) Reuben
    b) Asher
    c) Dan
    d) Levi

•••

6. In the Great Commission, Jesus says that those who believe in Him will do what to serpents?

•••

7. True or False: The Israelites were bitten by snakes when they wandered in the wilderness.

•••

8. Whom did John the Baptist call a generation of vipers?

•••

9. When Pharaoh's magicians turned their rods into serpents, what happened?

Snakes/Serpents Answers

1. subtil/cunning (Genesis 3:1 kjv, nkjv)

2. **Paul** (Acts 28:3–5)

3. c) that he was god (Acts 28:1–6)

4. the seventy whom He sent out (Luke 10:17–19 nkjv)

5. c) Dan (Genesis 49:17)

6. take up (Mark 16:18)

7. true (Numbers 21:6)

8. Pharisees and Sadducees (Matthew 3:7)

9. Aaron's rod that was a serpent swallowed their serpents (Exodus 7:12)

SONGS

God rejoices over us with singing (Zephaniah 3:17).

1. The first song in the Bible and the last song in the Bible are written by the same person. Who?
   a) Jesus
   b) an angel
   c) Moses
   d) Adam

   •••

2. Who sang, "The horse and its rider He has thrown into the sea"?

   •••

3. What did the Israelites sing a song to in the wilderness?
   a) a rock
   b) the pillar of cloud
   c) the moon
   d) a well

   •••

4. Who sang a song with Barak after the Canaanite king was defeated?

5. When did Hannah sing her song of praise to the Lord?
   a) when she gave birth to Samuel
   b) when she found out she was going to have Samuel
   c) when she dedicated Samuel to the Lord
   d) when she had more children after Samuel

•••

6. What song did the women sing that make King Saul even more jealous of David?

•••

7. Where has God put a new song?

•••

8. Like vinegar on soda is one who sings songs to whom?

•••

9. What type of songs does Ephesians 5:19 say we are to sing?

Songs Answers

1. c) Moses (Exodus 15:1; Revelation 15:3)

2. Miriam (Exodus 15:21 NKJV)

3. d) a well (Numbers 21:17)

4. Deborah (Judges 5:1)

5. c) when she dedicated Samuel to the Lord (1 Samuel 1:28; 2:1–10)

6. "Saul has slain his thousands, and David his ten thousands" (1 Samuel 18:7 NKJV)

7. in my mouth (Psalm 40:3)

8. someone with a heavy heart (Proverbs 25:20 NKJV)

9. spiritual

SONS

(see also Daughters, Fathers, Mothers, Sons of Jacob)

1. How many sons did David have?
   a) 11
   b) 13
   c) 15
   d) 19

2. Who was the son of Nun?

•••

3. Who were the sons of Zebedee?

•••

4. How many sons did Abraham have with Keturah?
   a) 2
   b) 4
   c) 6
   d) 8

•••

5. What prophet did God call "son of man"?

•••

6. How many sons did Ishmael have?

•••

7. Fill in the blank: A wise son maketh a glad father: but a foolish son is the _____ of his mother.

•••

8. How many sons did the father have in the parable of the prodigal son?

9. Which of Jacob's sons had twin sons born to him?

•••

10. What priest's sons were called "sons of Belial"?
   a) Aaron
   b) Eli
   c) Samuel
   d) Phinehas

•••

11. Absalom, David's son, led a rebellion against his father and was finally captured and killed because
   a) his hair got caught in a tree
   b) his servants turned on him
   c) the Lord struck him down
   d) his own soldiers captured him

•••

12. Who circumcised Moses' son?
   a) Moses
   b) Aaron
   c) Zipporah
   d) Jethro

SONS OF JACOB PART 1

13. How many sons did
Esau have?

•••

14. After Job's children were
all killed, how many sons did
God give Job again?

SONS OF JACOB
PART 1

Match the son to his
mother:

1. Dan
2. Reuben
3. Joseph
4. Levi
5. Gad
6. Benjamin
7. Zebulun
8. Naphtali
9. Simeon
10. Issachar
11. Judah
12. Asher

•••

a. Leah
b. Rachel
c. Bilhah
d. Zilpah

Sons Answers

1. d) 19 (1 Chronicles 3:19)
2. Joshua (Exodus 33:11)
3. James and John
(Matthew 4:21)
4. c) 6 (Genesis 25:1–2)
5. Ezekiel (Ezekiel 33:2)
6. twelve (Genesis 17:20)
7. heaviness (Proverbs 10:1)
8. two (Luke 15:11–32)
9. Judah (Genesis 38:26–30)
10. b) Eli (1 Samuel 2:12)
11. a) his hair got caught in
a tree
(2 Samuel 14:25–26; 18:9)
12. c) Zipporah (Exodus 4:25)
13. five (Genesis 36:4–5)
14. seven (Job 42:13)

325

Sons of Jacob– Part 1 Answers

All answers are found in
Genesis 35:22–26

1. c
2. a
3. b
4. a
5. d
6. b
7. a
8. c
9. a
10. a
11. a
12. d

SONS OF JACOB PART 2

1. Which son kept his brothers from killing Joseph and instead threw Joseph into a pit?
   a) Reuben
   b) Issachar
   c) Levi
   d) Gad

•••

2. Which son convinced his brothers to sell Joseph into slavery?
   a) Dan
   b) Asher
   c) Judah
   d) Zebulun

•••

3. How many shekels of silver did Joseph's brothers sell him for?
   a) 10
   b) 20
   c) 30
   d) 40

•••

4. When the sons of Jacob went to Egypt for the first time, which one was left as hostage?

a) Benjamin
b) Naphtali
c) Reuben
d) Simeon

•••

5. When Joseph made himself known to his brothers, which brother did he embrace first?
    a) Reuben
    b) Benjamin
    c) Judah
    d) Gad

•••

6. One of Jacob's sons was originally named Ben-Oni. What does Ben-Oni mean?

Sons of Jacob Part 2 Answers

1. a) Reuben (Genesis 37:21–22)

2. c) Judah (Genesis 37:26–27)

3. b) 20 (Genesis 37:28)

4. d) Simeon (Genesis 42:24)

5. b) Benjamin (Genesis 45:14)

6. son of my trouble (Genesis 35:18 NIV)

SPIES

1. From what location did Moses send the twelve spies into the Promised Land?

•••

2. Fill in the blanks: "Send thou men, that they may _____the _____ of Canaan."

•••

3. How many men were sent to explore the land?

•••

4. Choose A or B: Moses sent the men a) to the river Jordan or b) up into a mountain to see the land.

•••

5. Moses told the spies to see
    a) whether the land was good or bad
    b) whether the people were strong or weak
    c) whether the people lived in tents or strongholds
    d) all of the above

6. Choose A or B: The spies went into the land of Canaan from **a)** the north or **b)** south.

•••

7. True or False: They found coconuts so large that it took two men to carry three or four in a basket.

•••

8. How many days were the spies gone?
   a) 10
   b) 20
   c) 30
   d) 40

•••

9. Fill in the blanks: The spies said the land flowed with ____ and _____.

•••

10. Who quieted the people before Moses and challenged them to take the land immediately?

•••

11. How did the people respond to this challenge?

12. What book of the Bible records Rahab's story?

•••

13. According to the Bible, Rahab was a
   a) prostitute
   b) widow
   c) virgin
   d) priestess

•••

14. The spies were sent out of
   a) Canaan
   b) Egypt
   c) Shittim
   d) Bethlehem

•••

15. Who sent the spies?

•••

16. True or False: The king of Jericho soon discovered that Rahab was hiding spies.

•••

17. The king decided to
   a) kill Rahab as a traitor
   b) kill Rahab and the spies
   c) ask Rahab to turn in the spies

d) bribe Rahab with thirty talents to turn in the spies

•••

18. True or False: Rahab lied to the king about the spies' whereabouts.

•••

19. Rahab hid the spies
   a) on the roof of her house
   b) at the house of a friend
   c) in the cellar of her house
   d) with a priest at the temple

•••

20. Why did Rahab help the spies?

•••

21. In return for her help, what did the spies promise Rahab?

•••

22. Fill in the blank: Rahab was to mark her house with a _____ thread.

23. True or False: The spies broke their word to Rahab because Joshua opposed the deal they made with her.

Spies Answers

1. wilderness of Paran (Numbers 13:3)

2. search, land (Numbers 13:1–2)

3. twelve, one from each tribe (Numbers 13:4–15)

4. b) up into a mountain (Numbers 13:17)

5. d) all of the above (Numbers 13:18–19)

6. b) the south (Numbers 13:22)

7. false; they found huge clusters of grapes that two men had to carry on a pole between them (Numbers 13:23)

8. d) 40 (Numbers 13:25)

9. milk, honey (Numbers 13:27)

10. Caleb (Numbers 13:30)

SPIRITUAL WARFARE

(see also Armor of God)

Elisha prayed for the Lord to open his servant's eyes and show him the army of the Lord surrounding him (2 Kings 6:17).

1. Whose body did Michael fight with Satan over?
   a) Moses
   b) Elisha
   c) Adam
   d) David

•••

2. What does Paul say we do not "wrestle against"? What are we really "wrestling against"?

•••

3. Besides Elisha, who else saw the army of the Lord?

•••

4. Fill in the blank: Paul says we are more than _____ through Him who loved us.

11. they refused to move out and take the land (Numbers 13:31)

12. Joshua (Joshua 2:1)

13. a) prostitute (Joshua 2:1)

14. c) Shittim (Joshua 2:1)

15. Joshua (Joshua 2:1)

16. true (Joshua 2:2–3)

17. c) ask Rahab to turn in the spies (Joshua 2:3)

18. true (Joshua 2:5)

19. a) on the roof of her house (Joshua 2:6)

20. because she believed in the Lord; she had heard stories of the Lord's greatness and knew the Lord had given the Israelites the land (Joshua 2:9)

21. they promised to spare her family when the city was attacked (Joshua 2:12–14)

22. scarlet (Joshua 2:18, 21)

23. false (Joshua 6:17, 22–23)

5. True or False: Gabriel was hindered in getting to Daniel and Michael had to help him.

Spiritual Warfare Answers

1. a) Moses (Jude 9)

2. flesh and blood; we wrestle against principalities, powers, the rulers of darkness in this world, spiritual wickedness in high places (Ephesians 6:12)

3. John (Revelation 19:14)

4. conquerors (Romans 8:37)

5. true (Daniel 9:21; 10:12–13)

STARS

Who laid the corner stone thereof; when the morning stars sang together, and all the sons of God shouted for joy?
JOB 38:6–7

1. Fill in the blank: According to Numbers 24:17, a Star (meaning the Messiah) shall come out of _____.

2. Who saw the star in the east?

•••

3. True or False: The Bible says one star differs from another in glory.

•••

4. What was the name of the great star that fell in Revelation 8:10–11?
   a) Ashtar
   b) Ariel
   c) Wormwood
   d) Marah

•••

5. What book of the Bible contains the verse where Jesus says He is the Bright and Morning Star?

•••

6. On what day of creation did God make the stars?

•••

7. In addition to the stars, what other heavenly bodies are commanded to praise the Lord in Psalm 148:3?

8. God told Abraham that He would multiply Abraham's descendants as the stars of the heavens and as what?

• • •

9. True or False: The Bible speaks of wandering stars.

• • •

10. On whose head was a garland of twelve stars?

• • •

11. What did the seven stars in Revelation 1:20 represent?

Stars Answers

1. Jacob

2. wise men (Matthew 2:1–2)

3. true (1 Corinthians 15:41 NKJV)

4. c) Wormwood (Revelation 22:16)

5. Revelation

6. fourth (Genesis 1:16–19)

7. sun and moon (Psalm 148:3)

8. the sand which is on the seashore (Genesis 22:17)

9. true (Jude 13)

10. a woman (Revelation 12:1)

11. the angels of the seven churches (Revelation 1:20)

STONES

Brimstone was an inflammable mineral substance found on the shores of the Dead Sea. The cities of the plain were destroyed by a rain of fire and brimstone (Genesis 19:24–25). In Isaiah 34:9, an allusion is made to the destruction of these cities. This word figuratively denotes destruction or punishment (Job 18:15; Psalm 11:6; Isaiah 30:33, 34:9; Ezekiel 38:22). It is used to express the idea of excruciating torment in Revelation 14:10; 19:20; and 20:10.

• • •

1. True or False: The Lord said the Messiah would be a stone of stumbling and a rock of offense to the Israelites.

2. Fill in the blank: Paul said Jesus is the chief _____.

•••

3. Who set the ark of the covenant on the great stone of Abel?
   a) Samuel
   b) David
   c) Levites
   d) Philistines

•••

4. When he went to fight Goliath, how many stones did David take out of the brook?

•••

5. What patriarch used a stone for a pillow?

•••

6. When Jacob was blessing his sons, which son's blessing contained a reference to the Stone of Israel?
   a) Naphtali
   b) Asher
   c) Joseph
   d) Benjamin

•••

7. What would be written on the white stone promised to those who overcame?

8. True or False: Paul was stoned.

•••

9. After the angel rolled the stone away from Jesus' tomb, what did he do with it?

Stones Answers

1. true (Isaiah 8:14)
2. cornerstone (Ephesians 2:20)
3. c) Levites (1 Samuel 6:15–18)
4. five (1 Samuel 17:40)
5. Jacob (Genesis 28:11)
6. c) Joseph (Genesis 49:24)
7. a new name (Revelation 2:17)
8. true (Acts 14:19)
9. he sat on it (Matthew 28:2 nkjv)

T

TABERNACLE

(see also Offerings, Places of Worship, Sacrifices, Temple)

1. How many curtains did the tabernacle have?

•••

2. The curtains contained which of the following colors?
   a) blue
   b) purple
   c) scarlet
   d) all of the above

•••

3. Fill in the blank: "And the ___ shall divide unto you between the holy place and the most holy."

•••

4. What was put in the most holy place?

•••

5. Choose A or B: The four corners of the altar had a) rings or b) horns.

6. Fill in the blank: The altar was overlaid with ____.

•••

7. True or False: The oil for the lamp was to be pure whale oil.

•••

8. Whom did God choose as the master craftsman who would build the tabernacle?
   a) Hiram
   b) Bezaleel
   c) Aaron
   d) Joab

•••

9. In what city did the tabernacle stay once the Israelites entered the Promised Land?

•••

10. True or False: God gave the Israelites a recipe for the shewbread.

•••

11. How many loaves of the shewbread were to be on the table Sabbath after Sabbath?

12. How many pieces of gold were used to make the lampstand?

•••

13. Who alone could enter the Holy of Holies and on what occasion?

•••

14. Who supplied the materials to build the tabernacle?

•••

15. What were the holders on the lampstand designed to look like?

•••

16. What material was used to make the tent pegs of the tabernacle?

•••

17. What two types of materials were used to make the curtains in the tabernacle?

•••

18. True or False: Badger skins and rams' skins were used for the outside covering of the tabernacle.

Tabernacle Answers

1. ten (Exodus 26:1)

2. d) all of the above (Exodus 26:1)

3. vail, or veil (Exodus 26:33)

4. the ark of the testimony or covenant (Exodus 26:34)

5. b) horns (Exodus 27:2)

6. brass (Exodus 27:2)

7. False; it was to be pure olive oil (Exodus 27:20)

8. b) Bezaleel (Exodus 31:1–7)

9. Shiloh (Joshua 18:1)

10. true (Leviticus 24:5–6)

11. twelve (Leviticus 24:5)

12. one (Exodus 25:31)

13. the high priest on the Day of Atonement (Leviticus 16:3, 30–34)

14. the people of Israel through freewill offerings (Exodus 35:29 NKJV)

15. almond blossoms (Exodus 37:20)

16. brass (Exodus 27:19)

17. linen and goat's hair (Exodus 26:1, 7)

18. true (Exodus 26:14)

TEMPLE

(see also Offerings, Places of Worship, Rebuilding Jerusalem, Sacrifices, Tabernacle)

1. True or False: David was given permission by the Lord to build the temple.

•••

2. Fill in the blank: Solomon got the cedars of Lebanon to use in building the temple from King _____ of Tyre.

•••

3. How were the trees sent from Lebanon to Solomon?

•••

4. Fill in the blank: The Lord gave Solomon _____ as he had promised him.

5. Choose A or B: The temple windows were **a)** narrow or **b)** wide.

•••

6. Fill in the blanks: God promised Solomon, "I will _____ among the children of Israel, and will not _____ my people Israel."

•••

7. Fill in the blank: The inside of the house of the Lord was overlaid with _____.

•••

8. Choose A or B: The figures inside the oracle where the ark of the covenant was placed were **a)** seraphim or **b)** cherubim.

•••

9. Which of the following was not carved on the doors of the temple?
    a) lions
    b) cherubim
    c) flowers
    d) palm trees

10. Who brought the ark of the covenant into the temple after it was completed?
    a) Solomon's army
    b) Solomon himself
    c) the priests
    d) the scribes

•••

11. How long did it take Solomon to build the temple?

•••

12. What king made a detailed organization of temple personnel?

•••

13. By what act could someone claim sanctuary in the temple?

•••

14. Who destroyed Solomon's temple?

•••

15. Who rebuilt the temple when the Israelites returned from Babylon?

16. On what site did Solomon build the temple?

•••

17. How did God show His presence at the dedication of Solomon's temple?

•••

18. How many days did the people celebrate following the completion of Solomon's temple?

•••

19. True or False: The temple in Jesus' day was the same design Solomon's temple.

Temple Answers

1. false; he was forbidden to build the temple (1 Kings 5:3)
2. Hiram (1 Kings 5:1–6)
3. they were floated on the sea (1 Kings 5:8–9)
4. wisdom (1 Kings 5:12)
5. a) narrow (1 Kings 6:4)
6. dwell, forsake (1 Kings 6:13)

TEN COMMANDMENTS

1. Fill in the blanks: "Thou shalt have ___ ____ ____ before me."

•••

2. "Thou shalt not make unto thee any _____ _____."
   a) false weights
   b) stone tablets
   c) graven image
   d) strong wine

•••

3. Choose A or B: Thou shalt not bow down or serve other gods because **a)** the Lord is a jealous God or **b)** a plague will come upon you.

•••

4. Fill in the blanks: "The LORD will not hold him guiltless that taketh his name ___ ____."

•••

5. Fill in the blank: "_____ the sabbath day, to keep it holy."

---

7. gold (1 Kings 6:21)

8. b) cherubim (1 Kings 6:23)

9. c) flowers (1 Kings 7:32–36)

10. c) the priests (1 Kings 8:6)

11. seven years (1 Kings 6:38)

12. David (1 Chronicles 23–24)

13. by grasping the horns of the altar (1 Kings 1:50)

14. Nebuchadnezzar (2 Kings 24:11–14)

15. Zerubbabel (Ezra 5:2)

16. Mount Moriah (2 Chronicles 3:1)

17. fire came down from heaven and God's glory filled the place (2 Chronicles 7:1)

18. fourteen (1 Kings 8:65)

19. false; it had been destroyed and rebuilt since Solomon's time.

6. True or False: the fifth commandment is "Honour thy father and thy mother: that thy days may be long upon the land."

•••

7. Fill in the blank: The next commandment after "Honour thy father and mother" is "Thou shalt not ____."

•••

8. Fill in the blank: "Thou shalt not commit _____."

9. Fill in the blanks: "Thou shalt not bear _____ _____ against thy neighbour."

•••

10. "Thou shalt not covet thy neighbour's..."
   a) house
   b) wife
   c) manservant
   d) all of the above

Ten Commandments Answers

1. no other gods (Exodus 20:3)

2. c) graven image (Exodus 20:4)

3. a) the Lord is a jealous God (Exodus 20:5)

4. in vain (Exodus 20:7)

5. Remember (Exodus 20:8)

6. true (Exodus 20:12)

7. kill (Exodus 20:13)

8. adultery (Exodus 20:14)

9. false witness (Exodus 20:16)

10. d) all of the above (Exodus 20:17)

THIEVES

But know this, that if the goodman of the house had known in what watch the thief would come, he would have watched, and would not have suffered his house to be broken up.
MATTHEW 24:43

1. True or False: If a thief broke in and he was struck so that he died, the one who struck him would be guilty of his blood.

•••

2. When is a thief not to be despised?

•••

3. What did Paul say would come as a thief in the night?

•••

4. True or False: In the Sermon on the Mount, Jesus spoke about laying up our treasures in heaven because they would be safe from thieves.

5. To whom was Jesus speaking when He said, "My house shall be called the house of prayer; but ye have made it a den of thieves"?

•••

6. Fill in the blank: Proverbs 29:24 says that whoever is a partner with a thief hates his own _____.

•••

7. When is a thief ashamed?

•••

8. What minor prophet said the Israelites "enter at the windows like a thief"?

•••

9. Whom did Jesus describe as a thief and a robber?

•••

10. To which church in Revelation does Jesus say He will come upon them as a thief?

•••

11. Fill in the blank: "Your princes are rebellious, and _____ of thieves."

12. True or False: Barabbas, whom the people chose instead of Jesus, was a robber.

Thieves Answers

1. false; there would be no guilt for his bloodshed (Exodus 22:2)

2. if he steals food when he is starving (Proverbs 6:30)

3. the day of the Lord (1 Thessalonians 5:2)

4. true (Matthew 6:19–20)

5. the money changers (Matthew 21:12–13)

6. life (Proverbs 29:24 NKJV)

7. when he is found out (Jeremiah 2:26)

8. Joel (Joel 2:9 NKJV)

9. the one who does not enter the sheepfold by the door (John 10:1)

10. Sardis (Revelation 3:1, 3)

11. companions (Isaiah 1:23 NKJV)

12. true (John 18:40)

THIEVES CRUCIFIED WITH JESUS

1. True or False: Scriptures mentioning the criminal crucified with Christ are found in all four Gospels.

•••

2. Matthew says that the criminals crucified with Christ were
   a) murderers
   b) tax collectors
   c) thieves
   d) all of the above

•••

3. Mark tells us the criminals
   a) were both saved
   b) reviled Jesus
   c) were Gentiles
   d) witnessed the stoning of Stephen

•••

4. The unrepentant criminal asked Jesus to
   a) turn stones into bread
   b) ask a centurion for a cup of water
   c) bless him and his family
   d) save himself and them

5. In asking for this, the unrepentant criminal was asking Jesus to prove what?

•••

6. Fill in the blank: But the other answering rebuked him, saying, Dost not thou fear _____, seeing thou art in the same condemnation?

•••

7. True or False: The repentant criminal could see he was being justly punished.

•••

8. The criminals are identified only as "others" in which Gospel?

•••

9. True or False: Both criminals thought Jesus was guilty of the crimes with which He was charged.

•••

10. The repentant criminal asked Jesus to
   a) remember him
   b) reward him for defending Him against the other criminal
   c) save him
   d) be buried with him

•••

11. Fill in the blank: And Jesus said unto him, Verily I say unto thee, _____ shalt thou be with me in paradise.

•••

12. Why didn't Jesus save both of the criminals?

Thieves Crucified with Jesus Answers

1. true (Matthew 27:38–44; Mark 15:27–32; Luke 23:32–43; John 19:18)

2. c) thieves (Matthew 27:44)

3. b) reviled Jesus (Mark 15:32)

4. d) save himself and them (Luke 23:39)

5. that he was the Christ (Luke 23:39)

6. God (Luke 23:40)

7. true (Luke 23:41)

8. John (John 19:18)

9. false (Luke 23:41)

10. a) remember him (Luke 23:42)

11. today (Luke 23:43)

12. The first criminal didn't ask. We must accept Jesus Christ as our personal Lord and Savior if we are to make the leap from lost sinner to a servant who is found.

TRANSFIGURATION

1. Whom did Jesus take to a high mountain with Him?

•••

2. Fill in the blank: When Jesus was transfigured, His face shone like the _____.

•••

3. Who appeared and talked to Jesus?

•••

4. Who said, "Let us make three tabernacles here"?

5. What overshadowed them?

•••

6. God said He was well pleased with His beloved Son and then commanded the disciples to do what?

•••

7. When the disciples heard God's voice, what did they do?

•••

8. What did Jesus do then?

Transfiguration Answers

All answers are found in Matthew 17:1–7 NKJV.

1. Peter, James, and John

2. sun

3. Moses, Elijah

4. Peter

5. a bright cloud

6. "Hear Him!"

7. fell on their faces

8. touched them and told them not to be afraid

343

TREES

(see also Flowers and Plants)

1. What tree is mentioned in Genesis and Revelation?

•••

2. What three trees are specifically mentioned in the Garden of Eden?

•••

3. What kind of tree did Deborah sit under?

•••

4. True or False: The Bible mentions apple trees.

•••

5. Isaiah 55:12 says all the trees of the field will what?

•••

6. What kind of tree did Zacchaeus climb in order to see Jesus?

Trees Answers

1. Tree of Life (Genesis 2:9; Revelation 2:7)

2. the Tree of Life, the Tree of Knowledge of Good and Evil, fig tree (Genesis 2:9; 3:7)

3. palm (Judges 4:4–5)

4. true (Song of Solomon 2:3 nkjv)

5. clap their hands

6. sycamore (Luke 19:4)

TRIBES OF ISRAEL

God designated two mountains—Ebal for cursing and Gerizim for blessing. The tribes of Israel were to stand on the mountains facing each other and yell the blessings and curses. The tribes of Simeon, Levi, Judah, Issachar, Benjamin, and Joseph stood on Mount Gerizim. The tribes of Reuben, Gad, Asher, Zebulun, Dan, and Naphtali stood on Mount Ebal (Deuteronomy 27:12–13).

1. From what tribe did Jesus descend?

•••

2. What tribe had a book of the Bible named for them?

•••

3. What tribe was Moses from?

•••

4. What disciple of Jesus had the same name as one of the tribes?

•••

5. What two tribes gathered, planning to make war against Israel to regain the kingdom for Rehoboam?

•••

6. Who received the allotment for the tribe of Joseph?

•••

7. What tribe must John the Baptist have come from?

•••

8. In the city described in Revelation 21, are the twelve gates or the twelve foundations named for the tribes?

•••

9. What word, which was difficult to pronounce, was used to trap the Ephraimites?

•••

10. What king caused Israel to split into ten tribes and two tribes?

•••

11. What was the first tribe to set foot in the Promised Land?

•••

12. Which of the tribes established its own idolatrous cult?

•••

13. When the Israelites camped in the wilderness, on what side of the tabernacle did the tribes of Judah, Zebulun, and Issachar camp together?

14. What was the function of the Levites who were not priests?

•••

15. In Matthew 10:5–6, how did Jesus refer to the twelve tribes of Israel?

•••

16. What New Testament book is specifically addressed to the twelve tribes?

•••

17. Against which tribe did the children of Israel wage war for evil done to the concubine of a Levite?

•••

18. For what was the tribe of Benjamin famous?

•••

19. Which tribe was often identified as a "half tribe"?

•••

20. After the tribes were split into the kingdoms of Israel and Judah, by what tribal name was the kingdom of Israel referred?

21. What tribe, which could not occupy its allotted place in the Promised Land, took over somewhere else?

•••

22. How many from the tribes of Israel are "sealed" in the book of Revelation?

•••

23. Which tribe, according to Jacob's blessing, was "a hind let loose"?

•••

24. What tribes settled east of the Jordan River?

•••

25. What tribe settled north and northwest of the Sea of Galilee?

Tribes of Israel Answers

1. Judah (Matthew 1:3)
2. Levi (Leviticus)
3. Levi (Exodus 2) (Mark 2:14)
4. Matthew—Levi
5. Judah and Benjamin (1 Kings 12:21)
6. the tribes of Ephraim and Manasseh (Joshua 16:1–4 NIV)
7. Levi, since his father was a priest (Luke 1:5)
8. gates (Revelation 21:12)
9. Shibboleth (Judges 12:4–6)
10. Rehoboam (1 Kings 12)
11. Levi (Joshua 3:6)
12. Dan (Judges 18:30)
13. east (Numbers 2:3–9)
14. the physical maintenance of the tabernacle and later the temple (Numbers 3:7)
15. as the lost sheep of the house of Israel (Matthew 10:5–6)
16. James (James 1:1)
17. Benjamin (Judges 20:4–20)
18. having left-handed men who could sling a stone at a hair's breadth and not miss (Judges 20:15–16)
19. Manasseh (Deuteronomy 3:13)
20. Ephraim (Isaiah 7:2)
21. Dan (Judges 18)
22. 144,000 (Revelation 7:4)
23. Naphtali (Genesis 49:21)
24. Reuben, Gad, and Manasseh (Joshua 18:7)
25. Naphtali (Deuteronomy 33:23)

U

UNBELIEVING

1. What didn't Jesus do because of people's unbelief?

•••

2. Who were the unbelieving people in question 1?

•••

3. Who said, "Lord, I believe, help my unbelief"?

•••

4. Who said he obtained mercy because he acted ignorantly in unbelief?

•••

5. Fill in the blanks: 2 Corinthians 6:14 says Christians are not to be _____ _____ with unbelievers.

Unbelieving Answers

UNDERSTANDING

1. Psalm 119:34 says, "Give me understanding, and I shall" what?

•••

2. Fill in the blank: According to Psalm 147:5, God's understanding is _____.

•••

3. Fill in the blank: In Proverbs 2:2, Solomon tells his son to apply his _____ to understanding.

•••

4. Fill in the blank: A man of understanding has _____.

•••

5. Fill in the blank: Paul prayed that the Colossians would be filled with _____ understanding.

6. Fill in the blank: Proverbs 3:5–6 says we should not lean on our _____ understanding.

Understanding Answers

1. keep Your law (Psalm 119:34 nkjv)

2. infinite (Psalm 147:5)

3. heart (Proverbs 2:2)

4. wisdom (Proverbs 10:23)

5. spiritual (Colossians 1:9)

6. own (Proverbs 3:5–6)

UNFAMILIAR NAMES FOR FAMILIAR PEOPLE AND THINGS

In the days of King Hezekiah, people were worshipping the bronze serpent Moses made in the wilderness and calling it Nehushtan (2 Kings 18:4).

1. Who was known as "the son of perdition"?

2. What was Joshua's name before Moses called him Joshua?

•••

3. What does Solomon call himself in Ecclesiastes 1:1?

•••

4. What prophet was called "the Tishbite"?

•••

5. Who were the "sons of thunder"?

•••

6. By what other name is Passover known?

•••

7. Whose description included the fact that he ate locusts and honey?

•••

8. What was Esther's Hebrew name?

•••

9. What was the result of Jacob's wrestling with the angel?

10. What disciple was known also as Levi?

•••

11. Who was the "ambassador in bonds"?

•••

12. By what other names do we know Hananiah, Mishael, and Azariah?

•••

13. What was the potter's field also known as?

•••

14. What two descriptions of Satan appear in Revelation 12:9?

•••

15. What ruler in Egypt was called Zaphnath-paaneah?

•••

16. What was Daniel's Babylonian name?

•••

17. To what did Naomi want to change her name?

18. What judge's other name was Jerubbaal?

•••

19. Who was known as a mighty hunter before God?

•••

20. What early Bible figure was described as the father of those who dwell in tents?

•••

21. By what description do we know the following group of men: Shammua, Shaphat, Igal, Palti, Gaddiel, Gaddi, Ammiel, Sethur, Nahbi, Geuel?

•••

22. What more familiar name now applies to the ancient city of Jebus?

•••

23. What was Euroclydon?

Unfamiliar Names for Familiar People and Things Answers

1. Judas (John 17:12)
2. Hoshea (Numbers 13:16 nkjv)
3. the Preacher (Ecclesiastes 1:1)
4. Elijah (1 Kings 17:1)
5. James and John (Mark 3:17)
6. Feast of Unleavened Bread (Exodus 23:15)
7. John the Baptist (Matthew 3:4)
8. Hadassah (Esther 2:7)
9. his name was changed to Israel (Genesis 32:28)
10. Matthew (Matthew 10:3; Mark 2:14)
11. Paul (Ephesians 6:20)
12. Shadrach, Meshach, and Abednego (Daniel 1:7)
13. the field of blood (Matthew 27:7–8)
14. the great dragon, that old serpent (Revelation 12:9)
15. Joseph (Genesis 41:45)
16. Belteshazzar (Daniel 1:7)
17. Mara (Ruth 1:20)
18. Gideon (Judges 7:1)
19. Nimrod (Genesis 10:9)
20. Jabal (Genesis 4:20)
21. the ten spies who gave a bad report (Numbers 13)
22. Jerusalem (Judges 19:10)
23. the name of a storm (Acts 27:14)

V

VALLEYS

(see also Geography)

1. What psalm mentions the valley of the shadow of death?

•••

2. What did Jeremiah prophesy that the Valley of Hinnom would come to be called?
   a) the valley of slaughter
   b) the valley of death
   c) the valley of Gehenna
   d) the valley of peace

•••

3. What famous bad girl in the Old Testament lived in the Valley of Sorek?

•••

4. What famous fight took place in the Valley of Elah?

•••

5. Fill in the blank: According to Luke 3:5, every valley shall be _____.

Valleys Answers

1. Psalm 23
2. a) the valley of slaughter (Jeremiah 7:32)
3. Delilah (Judges 16:4)
4. David and Goliath (1 Samuel 17)
5. filled (Luke 3:5)

VESSELS

1. True or False: The vessel Jeremiah saw at the potter's was broken.

•••

2. The Lord told Ananias that what man was His chosen vessel?

•••

3. Fill in the blank: Paul said we have _____ in earthen vessels.

•••

4. What king in Daniel's time decided to drink wine from the vessels taken from the temple in Jerusalem?

5. Who said, "They shall be dashed to pieces like the potter's vessels"?

Vessels Answers

1. false; it was marred (Jeremiah 18:4)

2. Paul (Acts 9:11–12, 15)

3. treasure (2 Corinthians 4:7)

4. Belshazzar (Daniel 5:2)

5. Jesus (Revelation 2:27 NKJV)

VIALS (REVELATION 16)

(see also Seals, Trumpets)

1. What the vials contained was collectively called what?

•••

2. Put the following items describing what happened when the vials were poured out into their proper chronological order:
   - sea becomes blood
   - beast's kingdom becomes full of darkness
   - cities of the nations fall
   - loathsome sores
   - river Euphrates dries up
   - rivers and springs of water become blood
   - men scorched with great heat

Vials (Revelation 16) Answers

1. the wrath of God (Revelation 16:1)

2. loathsome sores, sea becomes blood, rivers and springs of water become blood, men scorched with great heat, beast's kingdom becomes full of darkness, river Euphrates dries up, cities of the nations fall

VISIONS

(see also Dreams)

1. How many living creatures did Ezekiel see in his vision?

2. Fill in the blank: Each of the living creatures had faces of a human being, a lion, an ox, and an _____.

•••

3. True or False: Each of the living creatures had wings.

•••

4. Fill in the blank: Throughout the book of Ezekiel, the prophet is addressed by the Lord as "_____ of man."

•••

5. What was Ezekiel told to do with the scroll filled with lament, mourning, and woe?
   a) burn it and scatter the ashes
   b) bury it for forty days
   c) eat it
   d) read it to the people of Israel

•••

6. How was Ezekiel to serve the people of Israel?
   a) as a bearer of light
   b) as a voice calling in the wilderness
   c) as a high priest
   d) as a watchman

7. While in exile, Ezekiel made a model of and laid siege works against what city?

•••

8. In the valley showed to him by the Lord, as Ezekiel prophesied, what happened to cause the rattling sound?

•••

9. How did the words "Mene, Mene, Tekel, Upharsin" come to appear on the plaster wall of King Belshazzar's palace?

•••

10. What was the meaning of the writing on the wall?

•••

11. Fill in the blank: In Revelation, the Lord God told John, "I am the Alpha and the _____."

•••

12. In Revelation, which of the four horses is the one whose rider represents death?

a) black horse
b) fiery red horse
c) pale horse
d) white horse

•••

13. True or False: The scroll that John was told to eat tasted as sweet as honey in his mouth.

•••

14. Fill in the blank: This city is described in Revelation as "Fallen! Fallen is _____ the Great!" and "The merchants of the earth grew rich from her excessive luxuries."

•••

15. What was the vision Peter saw?

•••

16. True or False: Isaiah saw a vision of a flying scroll.

Visions Answers

1. four (Ezekiel 1:5)

2. eagle (Ezekiel 1:10)

3. true (Ezekiel 1:6)

4. son (Ezekiel 2:3 and elsewhere)

5. c) eat it (Ezekiel 2:10–3:1)

6. d) as a watchman (Ezekiel 3:17)

7. Jerusalem (Ezekiel 4:1–2)

8. dry bones coming together (Ezekiel 37:4–7)

9. they were written by the fingers of a human hand that came out of nowhere (Daniel 5:5, 25)

10. Babylon was being taken over by the Medes and Persians (Daniel 5:26–28)

11. Omega (Revelation 1:8)

12. c) pale horse (Revelation 6:8)

13. true (Revelation 10:10)

14. Babylon (Revelation 18:2–3 NIV)

15. a sheet filled with unclean animals (Acts 10:9–17)

16. false; Zechariah saw the vision of a flying scroll (Zechariah 5:1)

VOWS

(see also Oaths)

When thou vowest a vow unto God, defer not to pay it; for he hath no pleasure in fools: pay that which thou hast vowed. Better is it that thou shouldest not vow, than that thou shouldest vow and not pay.

ECCLESIASTES 5:4–5

1. What judge made a vow to sacrifice the first thing he saw when he returned home?

•••

2. What did Hannah vow?

•••

3. Jacob's vow was that if God did what Jacob asked, then he would do what?

•••

4. Paul did what because he had taken a vow?

•••

5. True or False: Paul joined four men who had taken a vow.

Vows Answers

1. Jephthah (Judges 11:30–31)

2. to dedicate her child to the Lord (1 Samuel 1:11)

3. Jacob would make the Lord his God (Genesis 28:20–21)

4. cut off his hair (Acts 18:18)

5. true (Acts 21:23–26)

W

WAYS

1. Fill in the blanks: A man's _____ plans his way, but the LORD directs his _____.

• • •

2. When a man's ways please the Lord, what does the Lord make happen?

• • •

3. From where will we hear a voice say, "This is the way, walk ye in it"?

• • •

4. To whom was Jesus speaking when He said, "I am the way, the truth, and the life"?

• • •

5. On what occasion did Samuel tell the Israelites, "I will teach you the good and the right way"?

6. Fill in the blank: Job said, "He knows the way that I take; when He has tested me, I shall come forth as _____."

• • •

7. Of whom was the prophet speaking when he prophesied, "The voice of one crying in the wilderness, Prepare ye the way of the Lord"?

Ways Answers

1. heart, steps (Proverbs 16:9 NKJV)
2. make his enemies be at peace with him (Proverbs 16:7)
3. from behind (Isaiah 30:21)
4. His disciples (John 14:6)
5. when they wanted a king (1 Samuel 12:19, 23)
6. gold (Job 23:10 NKJV)
7. John the Baptist (Matthew 3:1–3)

WE DARE YOU TO ANSWER THESE

1. Why, according to the King James Version, can it be argued that Shem, Ham, and Japheth were triplets?

•••

2. What was Levirate marriage?

•••

3. What are the colors of the four horses mentioned in Revelation 6?

•••

4. Who were the seven men of honest report mentioned in Acts 6?

•••

5. What people were the Israelites battling on the day the sun stood still?

•••

6. What famous ancestor did the Moabites and Ammonites have in common?

7. Who was Keturah's husband?

•••

8. What was the name of Aaron's wife?

•••

9. What Old Testament man had daughters named Mahlah, Noah, Hoglah, Milcah, and Tirzah—who won the right to inherit his property when he died?

•••

10. From what land were the traders who bought Joseph from his brothers?

•••

11. Who were the fourteen judges of Israel?

•••

12. Who were Jacob's children?

•••

13. What power did the second horseman have in Revelation 6?

14. What grandson of Noah had a name that became symbolic for all those who would try to destroy God's people?

•••

15. Who was Anak?

•••

16. What Old Testament book says, "And the name of the city from that day shall be The LORD is there"?

•••

17. In what order did the following kings of Israel rule?
  - Baasha
  - Pekahiah
  - Hoshea
  - Omri
  - Saul
  - Joram
  - Jehu
  - David
  - Jeroboam I
  - Shallum
  - Jehoahaz
  - Menahem
  - Pekah
  - Ahab
  - Solomon
  - Nadab
  - Zimri
  - Elah
  - Ahaziah
  - Zechariah
  - Jeroboam II
  - Jehoash

•••

18. In what order did the following kings (and queen) of Judah rule?:
  - Josiah
  - Manasseh
  - Solomon
  - Asa
  - Ahaziah
  - Rehoboam
  - Amaziah
  - Joash
  - Ahaz
  - David
  - Jehoshaphat
  - Jehoram
  - Athaliah
  - Amon
  - Jehoahaz
  - Abijah
  - Azariah
  - Hezekiah
  - Zedekiah
  - Jotham
  - Jehoiakim
  - Jehoiachin

19. What group of kings took Lot captive until Abraham rescued him?

•••

20. What do the wives of Noah, Lot, and Job have in common?

•••

21. What twelve jewels were used in the foundation of the city described in Revelation 21:19–20?

•••

22. What was named Nehushtan?

•••

23. Who was the last person on earth to see the ark of the covenant?

•••

24. What two workmen did God appoint to make the things needed to build the tabernacle and clothe the priests?

•••

25. Who prophesied with a harp?

We Dare You to Answer These Answers

1. because it indicates they were born when "Noah was five hundred years old" (Genesis 5:32)

2. If a man died without children, his brother was required to have a child with the widow, and that child would be considered the child of the man who had died (Deuteronomy 25:5–10)

3. white, red, black, pale (Revelation 6)

4. Stephen, Philip, Prochorus, Nicanor, Timon, Parmenas, Nicolas (Acts 6:5)

5. Amorites (Joshua 10:12–14)

6. Lot (Genesis 19:35–38)

7. Abraham (Genesis 25:1)

8. Elisheba (Exodus 6:23)

9. Zelophehad (Numbers 27:1–11)

10. Midian (Genesis 37:28)

25. Jeduthun
(1 Chronicles 25:3)

24. Bezaleel and Aholiab
(Exodus 31:1–11)

23. the apostle John
(Revelation 11:19)

22. the bronze serpent
Moses made in the
wilderness (2 Kings 18:4)

21. jasper, sapphire,
chalcedony, emerald,
sardonyx, sardius, chrysolite,
beryl, topaz, chrysoprasus,
jacinth, amethyst
(Revelation 21:19–20)

20. none are mentioned by
name

19. Amraphel, king of
Shinar; Arioch, king of
Ellasar; Chedorlaomer, king
of Elam; and Tidal, king of
nations (Genesis 14:1)

18. David, Solomon,
Rehoboam, Abijah, Asa,
Jehoshaphat, Jehoram,
Ahaziah, Athaliah, Joash,
Amaziah, Azariah, Jotham,
Ahaz, Hezekiah, Manasseh,
Amon, Josiah, Jehoahaz,
Jehoiakim, Jehoiachin,
Zedekiah (1 and 2 Kings;
1 and 2 Chronicles)

17. Saul, David, Solomon,
Jeroboam I, Nadab, Baasha,
Elah, Zimri, Omri, Ahab,
Ahaziah, Joram, Jehu,
Jehoahaz, Jehoash, Jeroboam
II, Zechariah, Shallum,
Menahem, Pekahiah, Pekah,
Hoshea (1 and 2 Kings;
1 and 2 Chronicles)

16. Ezekiel (Ezekiel 48:35)

15. the ancestor of the
giants in the land of Canaan
(Numbers 13:33)

14. Magog (Genesis 10:2;
Ezekiel 38)

13. power to take peace from
the earth (Revelation 6:4)

12. Reuben, Asher, Simeon,
Issachar, Gad, Judah, Joseph,
Levi, Benjamin, Zebulun,
Naphtali, Dan, Dinah
(Genesis 35:23–26)

11. Othniel, Ehud, Shamgar,
Deborah, Gideon, Tola,
Jair, Jephthah, Ibzan, Elon,
Abdon, Samson, Eli, Samuel
(Judges and 1 Samuel)

WEAPONS

God can use anything as a weapon. He told Jehoshaphat to send a singing choir against the enemy, and while the enemy was distracted by the choir, God ambushed them (2 Chronicles 20:17–22).

1. Who killed two people with one spear?

•••

2. When he was a boy, what was David's weapon of choice?

•••

3. What brave woman used a tent stake to kill one of Israel's enemies?

•••

4. What judge of Israel used the jawbone of a donkey to kill his enemies?

•••

5. Whose army fought with pitchers and torches?

6. When Moses had to keep his arms raised in order for the Israelites to prevail in battle, who held his arms up for him?

•••

7. What judge of Israel used an ox goad to kill his enemies?

•••

8. What pair of famous friends used arrows as a signal between them?

•••

9. What tribe of Israel was famous for its left-handed sling users?

Weapons Answers

1. Phinehas (Numbers 25:7–8)
2. sling (1 Samuel 17:40, 49–50)
3. Jael (Judges 4:21)
4. Samson (Judges 15:15–16)
5. Gideon's (Judges 7:20)

6. Aaron and Hur
(Exodus 17:8–16)

7. Shamgar (Judges 3:31)

8. David and Jonathan
(1 Samuel 20:18–22)

9. Benjamin
(Judges 20:15–16)

WEIRD BIBLE WORDS

Match the word with its meaning:

1. Nabal
2. Mizpah
3. Selah
4. Shittim
5. Ebenezer
6. manna
7. Sheol
8. Golgotha
9. Moses
10. Immanuel
11. Maranatha
12. Anathema
13. Sabbath
14. Boanerges
15. Pur/Purim
16. Peniel
17. Bethel

18. Abaddon
19. Apollyon
20. Anakim
21. Cephas
22. Ecclesiastes
23. Beer Lahai Roi
24. Ichabod
25. mene
26. Beelzebub
27. upharsin
28. Zamzummims
29. tekel
30. teraphim

•••

a. a pause, the end
b. O Lord, come!
c. hell
d. stone of help
e. drawn out of the water
f. ceasing
g. churl
h. the lot
i. the Lord watch between you and me
j. house of God
k. the place of the skull
l. angel of the bottomless pit (Hebrew)
m. giants
n. thorns, wood
o. What is it?
p. God with us
q. accursed

r. sons of thunder
s. seen God's face
t. angel of the bottomless pit (Greek)
u. the prince of devils
v. Preacher
w. a stone
x. who reckons or is counted
y. giants
z. the well of Him who seeth
aa. weight
bb. idols
cc. divided
dd. the glory has departed

Weird Bible Words Answers

1. g (1 Samuel 25:3)
2. i (Genesis 31:49 nkjv)
3. a (Psalm 3:8)
4. n (Exodus 25:10)
5. d (1 Samuel 7:12)
6. o (Exodus 16:15 amp)
7. c (Psalm 16:10 kjv/nkjv)
8. k (Matthew 27:33)
9. e (Exodus 2:10)
10. p (Matthew 1:23)
11. b (1 Corinthians 16:22 nkjv)
12. q (1 Corinthians 16:22 nkjv)
13. f (Genesis 2:2)
14. r (Mark 3:17)
15. h (Esther 9:24–26)
16. s (Genesis 32:30)
17. j (Genesis 28:17, 19 nkjv)
18. l (Revelation 9:11)
19. t (Revelation 9:11)
20. m (Deuteronomy 2:11)
21. w (John 1:42)
22. v (Ecclesiastes 1:1)
23. z (Genesis 16:13–14)
24. dd (1 Samuel 4:21)
25. x (Daniel 5:26)
26. u (Matthew 12:24)
27. cc (Daniel 5:28)
28. y (Deuteronomy 2:20)
29. aa (Daniel 5:27)
30. bb (Judges 17:5)

WHAT DO THESE PEOPLE HAVE IN COMMON?

1. Paul, Esther
2. Matthew, Zacchaeus
3. Moses, Jacob
4. Ishmael, Jacob
5. Ammonites, Moabites
6. Shunammite woman, widow of Nain
7. sons of Jacob, Jesus' disciples
8. Mary, Daniel
9. Lot's wife, Noah's wife
10. Simon, Thaddeus
11. Nicanor, Timon
12. Elisha, John
13. Peter, boy with lunch
14. Eliphaz, Zophar

•••

a. Gabriel appeared to them
b. Jesus' disciples
c. tribe of Benjamin
d. twelve sons
e. saw the army of the Lord
f. chosen to serve widows
g. brought to Jesus by Andrew
h. tax collectors
i. twelve
j. Job's friends
k. saw the face of God
l. not named in the Bible
m. son raised from dead
n. common ancestor—Lot

What Do These People Have in Common? Answers

1. c (Philippians 3:5; Esther 2:5–7)
2. h (Matthew 10:3; Luke 19:2)
3. k (Exodus 33:11; Genesis 32:30)
4. d (Genesis 17:20; Genesis 49)
5. n (Genesis 19:36–37)
6. m (2 Kings 4:1–37; Luke 7:12–16)
7. i
8. a (Luke 1:26–27; Daniel 8:16)
9. l (Genesis 6; Genesis 19)
10. b (Matthew 10:2–3)
11. f (Acts 6:5)
12. Elisha, John, boy with lunch
13. Nicanor, Timon
14. Eliphaz, Zophar

WHERE IS THIS VERSE FOUND?

1. Vanity of vanities; all is vanity.

•••

2. They shall beat their swords into plowshares.

•••

3. Everyone who hears these sayings of Mine, and does not do them, will be like a foolish man who built his house on the sand.

•••

4. For God sent not his Son into the world to condemn the world; but that the world through him might be saved.

•••

5. Thou shalt have no other gods before me.

•••

6. Yea, though I walk through the valley of the shadow of death, I will fear no evil.

7. Make a joyful noise unto the LORD, all ye lands.

•••

8. God is love.

•••

9. We love him, because he first loved us.

•••

10. The wages of sin is death; but the gift of God is eternal life through Jesus Christ our Lord.

•••

11. All we like sheep have gone astray.

•••

12. All have sinned, and come short of the glory of God.

•••

13. The fruit of the Spirit is love, joy, peace, longsuffering, gentleness, goodness, faith, meekness, temperance: against such there is no law.

•••

14. Be anxious for nothing.

15. Trust in the LORD with all thine heart; and lean not unto thine own understanding.

•••

16. Train up a child in the way he should go: and when he is old, he will not depart from it.

•••

17. Thy word is a lamp unto my feet, and a light unto my path.

18. Thou shalt not kill.

•••

19. Hear, O Israel: the LORD our God is one LORD.

•••

20. Jesus wept.

•••

21. To everything there is a season, a time for every purpose under heaven.

•••

22. But my God shall supply all your need according to his riches in glory in Christ Jesus.

23. I can do all things through Christ which strengtheneth me.

•••

24. In the beginning God created the heaven and the earth.

•••

25. And I saw a new heaven and a new earth; for the first heaven and the first earth were passed away.

Where Is This Verse Found? Answers

1. Ecclesiastes 1:2
2. Isaiah 2:4
3. Matthew 7:26 NKJV
4. John 3:17
5. Exodus 20:3
6. Psalm 23:4
7. Psalm 100:1
8. 1 John 4:8
9. 1 John 4:19
10. Romans 6:23
11. Isaiah 53:6

12. Romans 3:23

13. Galatians 5:22–23

14. Philippians 4:6 NKJV

15. Proverbs 3:5

16. Proverbs 22:6

17. Psalm 119:105

18. Exodus 20:13

19. Deuteronomy 6:4

20. John 11:35

21. Ecclesiastes 3:1 NKJV

22. Philippians 4:19

23. Philippians 4:13

24. Genesis 1:1

25. Revelation 21:1

WHICH OF THESE PHRASES ARE ACTUALLY IN THE BIBLE?

1. God save the king.

•••

2. holier than thou

•••

3. wolf in sheep's clothing

4. The Lord helps those who help themselves.

•••

5. out of the mouth of babes

•••

6. The quality of mercy is not strained.

•••

7. Many are called, but few are chosen.

•••

8. Where there's a will, there's a way.

9. The spirit is willing, but the flesh is weak.

•••

10. the four horsemen of the Apocalypse

•••

11. How the mighty are fallen.

•••

12. Forgive and Forget.

13. give up the ghost

•••

14. scapegoat

•••

15. If you play with fire, you will get burned.

•••

16. A little bird told me.

•••

17. no peace for the wicked

•••

18. Eat, drink, and be merry.

•••

19. Live and let live.

•••

20. What hath God wrought?

•••

21. Physician, heal thyself.

•••

22. The wicked flourish like the green bay tree.

23. the ends of the earth

•••

24. four corners of the earth

•••

25. speak ill of the dead

•••

26. It rains on the just and the unjust.

•••

27. like mother, like daughter

Which of These Phrases Are Actually in the Bible? Answers

1. 2 Chronicles 23:11
2. Isaiah 65:5
3. Matthew 7:15
4. no
5. Psalm 8:2
6. no
7. Matthew 20:16
8. no
9. Matthew 26:41

WHO'S WHO?

1. Whose wife falsely accused Joseph, son of Jacob, of an improper sexual advance?

•••

2. What wife of King Herod engineered the execution of John the Baptist?

•••

3. Which disciple actually entered the empty tomb?

•••

4. Who rejected Jesus' offer of eternal life because he wouldn't give up what he had?

•••

5. Who was famous for saying, "As for me and my house, we will serve the LORD?"

6. Whose spirit was brought up from the dead by the witch of Endor?

•••

7. To what political party did Jesus' disciple Simon belong?

•••

10. no
11. 2 Samuel 1:19
12. no
13. Job 11:20
14. Leviticus 16:20–22
15. Proverbs 6:27
16. Ecclesiastes 10:20
17. Isaiah 57:21
18. Luke 12:19
19. no
20. Numbers 23:23
21. Luke 4:23
22. no
23. Deuteronomy 33:17
24. Revelation 7:1
25. no
26. Matthew 5:45
27. Ezekiel 16:44

8. What blind beggar in Jericho received sight from Jesus?

•••

9. Who was born looking red?

•••

10. Whom did Paul accuse of being a hypocrite?

•••

11. What New Testament preacher, like the Old Testament hero Samson, was never to drink wine or other fermented drink?

•••

12. What sleepy young man fell from an upper window and died during a sermon by the apostle Paul?

13. Who cursed the day he was born?

•••

14. Who was cursed with sorrow in conception and childbirth?

•••

15. What was the name of Timothy's mother?

•••

16. Who was the first recorded Christian martyr?

•••

17. What relative of the late King Saul cursed King David—even throwing dirt on him during Absalom's rebellion?

•••

18. Whom did the people of Lystra insist that Paul and Barnabas were?

•••

19. To whom were the elders referring when, to Boaz, they said Ruth should be as fertile as the two who built the house of Israel?

20. Who stole treasure from the devastated city of Jericho—and paid for his sin with his life?

•••

21. What tribal background did King Saul and the apostle Paul have in common?

22. Who used a fable about the king of trees to prove he was supposed to be in charge?

•••

23. Who had the second-longest recorded life span—962 years?

•••

24. Who was Korah, and what happened to him?

•••

25. To what goddess was Demetrius the silversmith famous for making shrines?

Who's Who? Answers

1. Potiphar (Genesis 39)
2. Herodias (Mark 6:14–29)
3. Peter (John 20:6)
4. the rich young ruler (Matthew 19:22)
5. Joshua (Joshua 24:2, 15)
6. Samuel (1 Samuel 28:7–25)
7. he was a Zealot (Luke 6:15; Acts 1:13)
8. Bartimaeus (Mark 10:46–52)
9. Esau (Genesis 25:25)
10. Peter (Galatians 2:11–14)
11. John the Baptist (Judges 13:4–5; Luke 1:13–15)
12. Eutychus (Acts 20:7–12)
13. Job (Job 3:1)
14. Eve (Genesis 3:16)
15. Eunice (2 Timothy 1:5)
16. Stephen (Acts 7:54–60)
17. Shimei (2 Samuel 16:5–14)
18. Jupiter and Mercurius (Zeus and Hermes NIV) (Acts 14:12)

19. Leah and Rachel
(Ruth 4:11)

20. Achan (Joshua 7)

21. Benjamin (1 Samuel
9:1–2; Philippians 3:5)

22. Abimelech (Judges 9)

23. Jared (Genesis 5:20)

24. He led a rebellion against
Moses and Aaron and was
swallowed by the earth
(Numbers 16:1–33)

25. Diana (Acts 19:24)

WHO'S WHO—
NEW TESTAMENT

1. Who held discarded coats
while Stephen was being
stoned?

•••

2. What were the Bereans
famous for?

•••

3. Who was the thirteenth
apostle?

4. What name did the
following people have in
common: son of Alphaeus,
brother of the apostle Judas
(not Iscariot), brother of
Jesus?

•••

5. Which two apostles raised
people from the dead?

•••

6. Who was Philemon's
runaway slave?

•••

7. Which disciple brought
the boy with the five loaves
and two fishes to Jesus?

•••

8. Who were Paul's three
primary coworkers on his
missionary journeys?

•••

9. In addition to Paul, what
other preacher did Priscilla
and Aquila work with, even
teaching him the Gospel?

10. Who was commanded to go lay hands on Saul (Paul) so that he would regain his sight?

•••

11. Who was elected to replace Judas Iscariot as an apostle?

•••

12. Whom did Paul circumcise and whom did he refuse to have circumcised?

•••

13. What were Barabbas's crimes?

•••

14. Who addressed the Sanhedrin with a face like an angel?

•••

15. How many descriptions are given of Judas Iscariot's death?

•••

16. What was the name of the girl who let Peter in after the angel had freed Peter from prison?

17. What apostle mentions Paul by name in his Bible book?

•••

18. In addition to betraying Jesus, what other crime did Judas Iscariot commit?

•••

19. What was the name of the evil spirit that possessed the man who lived in the tombs?

•••

20. Who had their mother ask Jesus for seats of honor for them in His kingdom?

•••

21. Name five Simons mentioned in the New Testament.

•••

22. Who were the only people Paul said he baptized in Corinth?

•••

23. What silversmith made shrines of the goddess Diana in Ephesus?

24. Why were the seven chosen in Acts 6?

•••

25. Who were the two women Paul urged to get along with each other in Philippians 4:2?

Who's Who—New Testament Answers

1. Saul, later known as Paul (Acts 7:58)
2. searching the scriptures (Acts 17:11)
3. Paul (Romans 1:1)
4. James (Matthew 10:3; 13:55; Luke 6:16)
5. Peter (Acts 9:36–43) and Paul (Acts 20:9–10)
6. Onesimus (Philemon 10)
7. Andrew (John 6:8–9)
8. Barnabas (Acts 13:2), Silas (Acts 15:40), and Timothy (Acts 16:1–3)
9. Apollos (Acts 18:24–28)
10. Ananias (Acts 9:10–18)
11. Matthias (Acts 1:26)
12. Timothy (Acts 16:3), Titus (Galatians 2:3)
13. robbery (John 18:40), insurrection/sedition, and murder (Mark 15:7; Luke 23:18–19)
14. Stephen (Acts 6:15)
15. two (Matthew 27:5; Acts 1:18)
16. Rhoda (Acts 12:13)
17. Peter (2 Peter 3:15)
18. he was a thief (John 12:4–6)
19. Legion (Mark 5:9)
20. James and John (Matthew 20:20; Mark 10:35–37)
21. Simon Peter (John 1:40); Simon, a brother of Jesus (Mark 6:3); Simon the Zealot, one of the disciples (Acts 1:13); Simon the leper (Matthew 26:6); Simon of Cyrene (Matthew 27:32); Simon the sorcerer (Acts 8:9); Simon the Pharisee (Luke 7:36, 40); Simon Iscariot, Judas's father (John 6:71); Simon the tanner (Acts 9:43)

22. Crispus and Gaius
(1 Corinthians 1:14)

23. Demetrius
(Acts 19:24)

24. to make sure the Greek
widows were provided for
(Acts 6:1–3)

25. Euodias and Syntyche
(Philippians 4:2)

WHO'S WHO—OLD
TESTAMENT

1. Which of Job's friends—
Zophar, Eliphaz, Elihu, or
Bildad—arrived last?

•••

2. How long did Job sit and
mourn silently?

•••

3. Why were the children of
Israel condemned to wander in
the wilderness for forty years?

•••

4. Who touched the ark of
the covenant and died?

5. When God asked Adam,
"Have you eaten from the
tree that I commanded you
not to eat from?" whom did
Adam blame for his sin?

•••

6. When Naaman was cured
of his leprosy, to what liar
was the leprosy given?

•••

7. Who led the victory song
after the Egyptians were
drowned in the Red Sea?

•••

8. Who, besides Moses,
had rods that turned into
serpents?

•••

9. Whose name means "day
star"?

•••

10. Who killed two people at
once with one spear?

•••

11. What two people had
time altered for them?

12. What three things did God command Moses to do at the burning bush?

•••

13. What happened to the Philistines who stole the ark of the covenant?

•••

14. What was the name of the servant Abraham was going to make his heir before Isaac was born?

•••

15. When told that his sons had been killed and the ark of the covenant had been taken, who fell over backward and died of a broken neck?

•••

16. Whom did Rahab marry, and whose mother was she?

•••

17. Who set up the Ebenezer?

•••

18. What bad man got his head nailed to the ground?

19. Who is described in the Bible as having weak eyes?

•••

20. What king's description says he came "delicately"?

•••

21. What man did God strike dead for refusing to help David?

•••

22. What was the name of the idol that kept falling on its face in front of the ark of the covenant?

•••

23. What did Heber's wife, Jael, do that made her famous?

•••

24. What two Old Testament figures didn't die?

•••

25. What law did Naomi invoke to convince Boaz to marry Ruth?

Who's Who—Old Testament Answers

1. Elihu (Job 2:11; 32:2–6)

2. seven days (Job 2:13)

3. because they refused to conquer the Promised Land when God told them (Numbers 14)

4. Uzzah (2 Samuel 6:6–7)

5. God and Eve (Genesis 3:11–12 NIV)

6. Gehazi (2 Kings 5:25–27)

7. Miriam (Exodus 15:20)

8. Aaron, the magicians of Egypt (Exodus 7:8–12)

9. Lucifer (Isaiah 14:12 NKJV)

10. Phinehas (Numbers 25:7–8)

11. Joshua, Hezekiah (Joshua 10:13; 2 Kings 20:9–11)

12. take off his sandals; pick up the rod turned into a serpent; put his hand into his bosom and take it out again (Exodus 3:5; 4:4–7)

13. they were smitten with tumors and died (1 Samuel 5:11–12 NIV)

14. Eliezer of Damascus (Genesis 15:2)

15. Eli (1 Samuel 4:16–18)

16. she married Salmon and became the mother of Boaz (Matthew 1:5 NIV)

17. Samuel (1 Samuel 7:12)

18. Sisera (Judges 4:17, 21)

19. Leah (Genesis 29:17 NIV)

20. Agag (1 Samuel 15:32)

21. Nabal (1 Samuel 25:38)

22. Dagon (1 Samuel 5:3)

23. she nailed a man's head to the ground with a tent peg (Judges 4:21)

24. Enoch—God took him (Genesis 5:24); Elijah—went in a whirlwind to heaven (2 Kings 2:1, 11)

25. The law of Levirate marriage (Deuteronomy 25:5–10; Ruth 4:10, 14)

WIDOWS

1. Fill in the blank: Exodus 22:22 says widows are not to be _____.

•••

2. When the widow gave her two mites, Jesus said she had given what?

•••

3. True or False: Anna, who saw the infant Jesus in the temple, was a widow.

•••

4. What king of Israel was referred to as "the widow's son"?

•••

5. True or False: Jesus told a parable about a widow and a landowner.

•••

6. In Acts 6:1, what two nationalities of widows were having a problem?

Widows Answers

1. afflicted (Exodus 22:22)

2. all she had (Mark 12:44)

3. true (Luke 2:37)

4. Jeroboam (1 Kings 11:26)

5. false; a widow and a judge (Luke 18:2–3)

6. Hebrew, Greek (Acts 6:1)

WILDERNESS WANDERINGS

1. When the people first questioned the leadership of Moses, they had been three days without
   a) water
   b) manna
   c) meat
   d) shelter

•••

2. Fill in the blank: And when they came to Marah, they could not drink of the waters of Marah, for they were _____: therefore the name of it was called Marah.

379

3. The Lord asked the Israelites for one thing. What was it?

•••

4. True or False: The people complained about having no meat.

•••

5. Fill in the blank: And all the people answered together, and said, All that the _____ hath spoken we will do.

•••

6. True or False: The people promised to obey all of God's laws.

•••

7. The people strayed when Moses
   a) questioned whether or not the Lord is true
   b) was unable to make the waters at Marah sweet
   c) murdered an Egyptian and fled
   d) delayed his return from the mountaintop

8. When Aaron discovered the Israelites were building an idol, he
   a) told them to stop
   b) said the Lord would surely punish them
   c) helped them build it
   d) suggested they build even more idols

•••

9. True or False: After the Israelites built the idol, the Lord sent them a plague.

•••

10. True or False: When the people repented, they donated their riches and talents to the Lord.

•••

11. What type of birds did the Lord send for the Israelites to eat?
   a) chickens
   b) doves
   c) quail
   d) geese

•••

12. Fill in the blank: "The people ____ on the seventh day."

13. What was the name of the wilderness where the Israelites were camping?
   a) Gaza
   b) Sinai
   c) Sin
   d) Tribulation

•••

14. Why did the Israelites complain against Moses?

•••

15. True or False: Moses got water from a rock by striking the rock.

•••

16. True or False: Moses called the name of the place Bethel and Berothah.

•••

17. Fill in the blank: "When the people complained, it _____ the LORD."

•••

18. Who said, "I am not able to bear all this people alone"?
   a) Moses
   b) Aaron

   c) God
   d) Miriam

•••

19. Miriam and Aaron spoke against Moses because
   a) they were jealous of his authority
   b) he was a weak leader
   c) he married an Ethiopian woman
   d) he had sinned against the Lord

•••

20. When the Israelites threatened to return to Egypt, who said, "If the LORD delight in us, then he will bring us into this land"?

•••

21. Because of their complaining, what punishment did the Lord pronounce on Israel?

•••

22. How many years was their punishment to last?

•••

23. What two men were the exception to the

Lord's pronouncement of punishment?

•••

24. True or False: When Moses told the people about the Lord's pronouncement of punishment, they mourned greatly.

•••

25. What did the Lord tell Moses to have the Israelites put on their clothes to help them remember His commandments?
    a) precious stones
    b) stripes
    c) fringes
    d) belts

•••

26. True or False: The Lord told Moses to speak to the rock and water would come forth.

•••

27. Why did the Lord tell Moses that Moses wouldn't bring the Israelites into the Promised Land?

28. When Aaron died, he was buried on Mount
    a) Sinai
    b) Moriah
    c) Horeb
    d) Hor

•••

29. What did the Lord send to punish the people when they complained against Moses and the Lord?
    a) stinging scorpions
    b) fierce lions
    c) biting insects
    d) fiery serpents

•••

30. Fill in the blank: Moses placed a brass _____ on a pole and held it up for the people to see and be saved.

Wilderness Wanderings Answers

1. a) water (Exodus 15:22, 24)

2. bitter (Exodus 15:23)

30. serpent (Numbers 21:9)

29. d) fiery serpents
(Numbers 21:5–6)

28. d) Hor
(Numbers 20:23, 28)

27. because Moses didn't
believe the Lord
(Numbers 20:12)26. true
(Numbers 20:8)

26. true (Numbers 20:8)

25. c) fringes
(Numbers 15:38–39)

24. true (Numbers 14:39)

23. Joshua and Caleb
(Numbers 14:38)

22. forty years
(Numbers 14:33)

21. "Surely they shall not see
the land which I sware unto
their fathers"
(Numbers 14:23)

20. Joshua and Caleb
(Numbers 14:6–8)

19. c) he married an Ethiopian
woman (Numbers 12:1)

18. a) Moses
(Numbers 11:11, 14)

17. displeased (Numbers 11:1)

16. false; he named it
Massah and Meribah
(Exodus 17:7)

15. true (Exodus 17:6)

14. because they had no
water to drink (Exodus 17:2)

13. c) Sin (Exodus 17:1)

12. rested (Exodus 16:30)11.
c) quail (Exodus 16:13)

11. c) quail (Exodus 16:13)

10. true (Exodus 35)

9. true (Exodus 32:35)

8. c) helped them build it
(Exodus 32:3–5)

7. d) delayed his return from
the mountaintop
(Exodus 32:1)

6. true (Exodus 24:3)

5. LORD (Exodus 19:8)

4. true (Exodus 16:3)

3. obedience: "If thou
wilt diligently hearken
to the voice of the LORD
thy God, and wilt do that
which is right in his sight,
and wilt give ear to his
commandments, and keep
all his statutes, I will put
none of these diseases upon
thee, which I have brought
upon the Egyptians: for I am

WISDOM

1. What chapter of Proverbs is devoted to a description of wisdom?

•••

2. What king asked God for wisdom rather than wealth?

•••

3. James said that if we lack wisdom, we can get it how?

•••

4. Where does Matthew 2 say the wise men had come from?

•••

5. What does the Bible say is the beginning of wisdom?

•••

6. Who increased in wisdom and stature, and in favor with God and man?

•••

7. Fill in the blank: Ecclesiastes 9:16 says wisdom is better than _____.

8. Whose wisdom is despised?

Wisdom Answers

1. 8 (Proverbs 8)
2. Solomon (1 Kings 4:29)
3. ask God for it (James 1:5)
4. the east (Matthew 2:1)
5. the fear of the Lord (Proverbs 9:10)
6. Jesus (Luke 2:52)
7. strength (Ecclesiastes 9:16)
8. the poor man's (Ecclesiastes 9:16)